MW01075271

What Is Hinduism?

A Guide for the Global Mind

David Frawley (Pandit Vamadeva Shastri)

BLOOMSBURY

NEW DELHI • LONDON • OXFORD • NEW YORK • SYDNEY

BLOOMSBURY INDIA
Bloomsbury Publishing India Pvt. Ltd
Second Floor, LSC Building No. 4, DDA Complex, Pocket C – 6 & 7,
Vasant Kunj New Delhi 110070

BLOOMSBURY, BLOOMSBURY INDIA and the Diana logo are trademarks of
Bloomsbury Publishing Plc

First published in India 2018
This edition published 2018

Bloomsbury Publishing Plc does not have any control over, or responsibility for, any third-party
websites referred to or in this book. All internet addresses given in this book were correct at the
time of going to press. The author and publisher regret any inconvenience caused if addresses
have changed or sites have ceased to exist, but can accept no responsibility for any such changes

ISBN: TPB: 978-9-3880-3863-8; eBook: 978-9-3880-3865-2

2 4 6 8 10 9 7 5 3 1

Typeset by Manipal Digital
Printed and bound in India by Replika Press

Bloomsbury Publishing Plc makes every effort to ensure that the papers used in the manufacture
of our books are natural, recyclable products made from wood grown in well-managed forests.
Our manufacturing processes conform to the environmental regulations of the country of origin.

To find out more about our authors and books visit www.bloomsbury.com and sign up for
our newsletters

Contents

Foreword

I still remember the occasion when I first came across Dr Frawley's book on Hinduism, now expanded in a new edition called *What Is Hinduism: A Guide for the Global Mind*.

It was 2004. I had just met my guru. Being a young seeker, my mind was full of queries related to culture, religion and spirituality.

Like the majority of middle-class Hindus, my schooling was conducted in English. In India, this means looking at the world through the Western intellectual paradigm. Though it did broaden my understanding of the world through science, there was nothing in my education which encouraged me to explore the issues pertaining to my own culture and civilization.

One area of enquiry where my education left me with more questions than answers was religion. Sometimes, religion was portrayed as a harbinger of peace, love and freedom; as a force of harmony and cooperation. But more often, it was depicted as a force of violence and pure evil, which led to the greatest, bloodiest and cruelest wars that humanity has ever known.

If the portrayal of religion left me confused, the depiction of Hinduism left me even more perplexed. Where does it stand on this spectrum of good and evil? Does it have any place in the modern world of science and technology? Or, is it just like any other religion?

In Western intellectual discourse, Hinduism is often associated with a belief in something unseen, miraculous and supernatural; that it demands faith and scorns reason and rational logic. Hinduism is portrayed as steeped in stultifying ritualism and abstruse metaphysics. It is depicted as the most primitive form of religion. Hindus are often depicted as worshippers of ghosts, goblins and a whole array of supernatural creatures. Most commonly, Hinduism is identified with the caste system which is alleged to have institutionalised the worst form of slavery.

Paradigm Shift

This was my frame of mind when my guru gifted me David Frawley's monumental work on Hinduism. It was a life-changing experience for me. It threw my confused worldview into a tailspin, ultimately organizing it, sifting the wheat from the chaff. It cleansed me of many misconceptions and helped me gain a deeper and truer understanding of Hinduism.

It was only later on that I realised that I was not alone in my quest. Millions of young Hindus had similarly been trying to understand Hinduism. For such seekers, Frawley's grand exposition on Hinduism has become a standard guide.

In Frawley's writings, Hinduism no longer remains a random collection of cults, ridden with primitive rituals and superstitions. It becomes an organic religion, unfolding and evolving in various branches on its own, without any external imposition or commandment.

Hinduism turns out not as a religion propagating a set of beliefs. Nor is it a matter of faith, demanding absolute surrender to an unquestioned dogma. Hinduism is a system of inquiry leading to the universal tradition of inner knowing. It is a quest for understanding the nature of things and how they really work. In fact, it seems to be closer to science than religion.

It became quite clear to me that the very term 'Hinduism' is a misnomer. It is no 'ism' or ideology. It is not a creation of the human mind. It is a complete way of life, rooted in cosmic intelligence, leading us all to live in harmony with nature and one's own Self. It is a search for the eternal and immutable truth which is beyond all thoughts, opinions and beliefs.

More importantly, I realised that Hinduism can be better understood only from the perspective of Santana Dharma or dharma. The word 'dharma' unfolded many layers of meaning and took me to the essence of Hinduism. The quest for understanding dharma is a quest to explore the most sublime aspect of our existence and life.

Unfortunately, this deeper understanding of Hinduism is not common, even among Hindus. It might look strange to outsiders, but a majority of Hindus find it hard to answer simple questions such as: What is Hinduism? What does it actually stand for? What is its core principles?

This, as Frawley states, brings us to a paradox.

On one hand, Hinduism is one of the oldest religions in the world with a literature larger than any other religion's. It has a glorious heritage of the most continuous, comprehensive and cumulative knowledge system in the world. It is the largest of the non-Abrahamic religions and the third largest religion after Christianity and Islam, with over a billion followers.

On the other hand, a majority of Hindus have lost the art of decoding their own spiritual tradition. They can explain a few aspects of Hinduism like Yoga or Ayurveda, but are unable to clearly articulate what Hinduism stands for.

Frawley resolves this paradox by tracing it back to its proper historical context. Prior to the advent of British rule, India had one of the finest education systems in the world. There was a decentralised network of institutions, consisting of schools in every nook and corner of the country. However, colonial education destroyed this traditional order and undermined the rights of Hindus to define themselves and their tradition.

Moreover, in the name of secular education, India's great gurus were delegitimised in the newly institutionalised education system. Similarly, *ashramas* (traditional schools), which had been successfully transmitting traditional knowledge from one generation to another, were either ignored or marginalised. This led to a complete disconnect of the saints from mainstream academic scholarship. As a result, the original practitioners and inheritors of Hinduism, who could provide an insider's perspective, were completely replaced in mainstream academia in the name of modernity, objectivity and rationality.

Even after India gained political independence, these distortions continued under different guises in the name of Marxism, Modernism, Post-Modernism or other such ideologies. Hinduism continues to be depicted as a culture of darkness and oppression—a religion of heathens mired in idolatry, practising absurd rituals and traditions. These ideologies have never bothered to study the underlying unity beneath the multiplicity of traditions. There is practically no place left for practitioners of Hinduism to define themselves. Their views and interpretations are considered biased, prejudiced and too subjective.

This is in sharp contrast to the attitude one takes while studying other major religions such as Christianity and Islam. These religions are invariably represented by their followers. Their observations and assessments are accepted as authentic and legitimate. It seems that only Hinduism is expected to be represented by outsiders, mostly its critics, in the name of objective study.

Frawley claims that while Hinduism is open to criticism from hostile forces, no view from 'inside the tradition' is allowed. This has led to a tremendous gap between how Hindus define themselves and how others portray them. As a result, not much good literature is available on Hinduism, explaining it from the perspective of Sanatana Dharma.

Insider Perspective

In this context, Frawley's *What Is Hinduism?* is a path-breaking study in many aspects. It brings new insights. It presents an insider's perspective, looking at Hinduism not as an outsider but as someone who is immersed in the tradition. His views are not of an academician but of a mystic. He is an *acharya* (teacher) in the truest sense of the word. The teachings of Hinduism are reflected in his *acharana* (behavior and action). He reminds us of the great yogis and masters of Indic tradition, who perfected the art of explaining the sublime philosophy of Hinduism in a very simple language.

In the present work, Frawley offers an 'inside the tradition view'; exploring Hinduism in the light of Sanatana Dharma. It is an attempt to define Hinduism as Hindus feel, perceive and think. It is an endeavour to discover the universal principle of Hindu Dharma which has sustained it through millennia.

The book is divided into two parts. The first part contains essays on religion, spirituality, dharma and Hinduism. It is meant for seekers who wish to explore the universal and eternal traditions of the world including Hindu Dharma. This section also sheds light on the crucial difference between Dharma and Religion.

The second part contains over hundred questions and answers resolving a wide range of queries on what Hinduism truly is. It is interesting to note that these questions are not limited to Hinduism as such but encompass everything that we can think of under the umbrella of spirituality and dharma. It provides a concise but profound explanation of basic questions that agitate a seeker's mind.

Ultimately, this book explores the human aspiration for eternal tradition and the role of Hindu Dharma in it. It explains the tradition of spiritual inquiry in India, which gave birth to the finest spiritual ecosystem in the world. It is quite illuminating to explore these ideas briefly here.

Hindu Dharma: An Inquiry into the Eternal Tradition

Frawley's definition of Hindu Dharma is the most comprehensive; yet like all universal laws, can be stated in a few words.

He defines Hindu Dharma as an art and science of Self-realization, an outcome of the individual quest of a seeker to understand his own Self. This quest ends not with theological dogmas and assertions but with the realization of divinity deep within one's Self. The basic quest is not to ask 'Who is God?', but to dive deep into our own selves and ask, 'Who am I'?

In such a quest, it is not sufficient to believe in God; to know God is to become God. This dictum might sound offensive to those who believe in the permanent separation of the Divine and human. Yet this is the foremost goal of Hindu Dharma; to liberate oneself from the illusion of separate identity by merging in universal consciousness. It is this emphasis on spiritual experience, at an individual level, that allowed the most diverse spiritual teachings to flourish in India without coming into conflict with one another.

Frawley also examines the root of spiritual abundance in India; a unique heritage, unparalleled elsewhere. He explains that it is the spirit of an open inquiry in every sphere, from mundane to spiritual level, which laid the foundation of spiritual pluralism in India. Hindu Dharma, like science and unlike dominant religion, is the pursuit of truth and nothing else. He boldly claims that 'if it is a question of religion or truth, we should always follow truth'. He encourages all of us to examine claims of spirituality and dharma in 'the fire of Self-enquiry'.

Applying the same spirit of an open enquiry, Frawley probes into the most intractable question of our time: Are all religions the same? And what does this sameness mean? Are all religions good or are all religions worthless?

A majority of scholars, writing on religious issues, parrot the slogan of the sameness of all religions. But Frawley brings to our attention that we don't follow this dictum of sameness in any other sphere of life. We always discriminate in what water we drink, what food we eat and what clothes we wear. We can't imagine living a good and healthy life without discriminating even at such mundane levels. Frawley encourages us to practise and apply the same discriminative intellect in the sphere of spirituality. He himself adheres to this dictum in the sphere of religion and spirituality and clears the mist surrounding it. He warns that it is a fallacy to assume that all religions are same.

Religion, as it is understood in the Western world, cannot be simply equated with dharma. The former is belief oriented, centred on one preacher, one book and one institution. It is an exclusive belief system claiming a monopoly over truth. It assumes human beings to be inherent sinners and in urgent need of salvation. Religion divides mankind into two antagonistic camps—believers and non-believers. They divide time into two opposite directions, before Christ and after Christ. They also split geographical space into two mutually hostile regions, the land of the pure and the land of the impure or heathen. Thus, space, time and mankind stand permanently divided in their consciousness. All prophetic religions are dualistic in their theory and practice even though they claim themselves to be monotheistic. It teaches theological ethics based on belief. Anyone who does not hold the 'right' belief and shows even a slight skepticism toward dogmas of religion is labelled irreligious. Christianity and Islam belong to this category.

Frawley compares and contrasts religion with dharmic traditions that define themselves through Self-knowledge, not through dogmas and exclusive belief systems. Dharmic traditions recognise the innate divinity in every human being, every creature and even in inanimate objects. They recognise the Supreme Consciousness which is indivisible. Dharma teaches universal ethics based on action. One becomes adharmic by living in disharmony with the universe and contrary to the nature of things. All indigenous, tribal, native and dharmic traditions of the world belong to this category.

On the basis of this distinction between dharma and religion, Frawley makes the position of Hindu Dharma amply clear; not only by defining what it is but also by discriminating what it is not. He states that Hindu Dharma never believes in institutionaliszing spirituality and claiming a monopoly over truth. According to him, 'Even calling dharmic traditions as religions is misleading.'

This discrimination in the realm of the religious and spiritual sphere is the most important contribution of Frawley's book. It places Hinduism in its proper dharmic context and shows its rightful position among the world's spiritual traditions.

The Significance of Frawley's work

David Frawley's *Hinduism* was first published more than two decades ago. Since then, it has trained a whole generation of Hindus to define their spiritual tradition in the light of their own living experiences, reflecting their daily rituals and practices. It has inspired seekers to express the core essence of Hindu Dharma as propounded in their sacred scriptures. The new edition notably updates the work and makes it equally relevant to a new generation, with its new concerns of the information technology era.

Frawley urges us to look at Hinduism from a fresh perspective. The foremost requirement for this is to see Hinduism in the light of Sanatana Dharma, reflecting the universal tradition of inner knowing.

It is ironic that someone who is born outside the Hindu tradition could lay bare the essence of Hindu Dharma so lucidly and coherently, much better than the majority of its own practitioners. Frawley's elucidation restores pride among Hindus as an inheritor of the most comprehensive spiritual tradition in the world.

Yet Frawley's writing on Hindu Dharma is useful not only for Hindus but for every spiritual seeker in the world. In the present times, people are tired of organised religion and are looking for experiential spirituality to gain a deeper understanding of their own Self and consciousness. More people, across the world, are exploring a form of spirituality that teaches a direct experience of the reality. These seekers are looking beyond fixed dogmas and standard commandments in search for true spirituality, based upon the cultivation of higher consciousness.

What Is Hinduism? provides guidance to such spiritual seekers by defining Hindu Dharma, at its core, as an art and science of Self-exploration culminating in Self-realization. True seekers, for their inner development, can choose from a variety of individualised spiritual practices available in Hindu Dharma without formal conversion.

In this context, it is pertinent to mention that Frawley's own spiritual journey is a fascinating example of a true seeker in search of ultimate reality and the nature of consciousness. For him, this discovery of Sanatana Dharma is like going home and rediscovering one's true Self.

May Frawley's book continue to inspire Hindus to present their tradition from a dharmic perspective. May his journey become an inspiration for seekers to search for a universal tradition of exploring divinity in their own Self.

Ram Sharma
Centre for Indic Studies
Indus University

Preface

Hinduism as a religion is coming once more into the light today. There are several reasons for this. First, Hindu-based teachings of Yoga, Vedanta, Ayurveda and related disciplines have gained popularity worldwide. Second, Hindu immigrants, particularly to North America and the United Kingdom, are now among the best educated and affluent immigrant groups and are honouring and not rejecting their religion by doing so. Third, the current Indian government of Narendra Modi and Bharatiya Janata Party (BJP) has been promoting a much more positive view of the Hindu-majority culture as the basis of national development; a view that other political parties, including the Congress, are taking up and showing more respect for Hindu traditions.

Yet Hinduism is not just a local religion of India, its people or culture. Hinduism is the basis of the oldest and most diverse of the world's great religions, whose original name is Sanatana Dharma, 'the eternal tradition of Truth'. To understand it we must go back to its broader principles and adaptable practices, which can far exceed what most of the world regards as a religion today, being more akin to experiential spirituality than to any dogma or commandment.

Though born in the United States, I have been fortunate enough to connect to the Hindu tradition from its ancient Vedic roots to its many contemporary gurus. Over several decades, I have written extensively on important aspects of Hindu thought, including Yoga, Vedanta and Ayurveda, in a number of books and articles. This Hindu experience has compelled me to write on the underlying system that has provided the inspiration for my writings and my inner quest.

My examination of the world's spiritual and religious traditions, East and West, led me to Hindu-based teachings of Yoga and Vedanta that I found the most compelling, comprehensive and articulate. This culminated in an encounter with the universal view, Sanatana Dharma, behind these. As few people today—including a great majority of Hindus—understand the profound background of this complex tradition, I have tried to present it in a contemporary idiom, so that others might share in the discovery.

I am not writing about Hinduism from an academic perspective, which, however interesting, is a second-hand view that is often artificial in its presentation. The academic approach is not the view of the artist but the art critic. It is not the view of the practitioner in the field but the critic peering in the distance, often with a different agenda and his own biases. Hinduism, with its subtle and mysterious teachings, affords endless ground for academic investigation, but such an approach will not provide a first-hand understanding of this vast tradition that antedates by millennia the views according to which it is usually judged.

I am writing about Hinduism as someone who has become immersed in the Hindu tradition, discovering that tradition at the core of his own being, not as a novel identity but as a doorway to one's true Self. Many Hindus have requested me to write a book expressing their vast tradition to the contemporary mind, particularly for the sake of modern educated Hindus among whom it is fashionable to denigrate their own tradition without having really studied it, and for their children, particularly those in college, to help them appreciate their heritage in a society that has little understanding of it.

Fortunately, I have been able to meet people in India from all backgrounds, including swamis, yogis, traditional Brahmin priests, social activists and political leaders, Ayurvedic doctors, Vedic astrologers, musicians and modern Hindus of all types, including businessmen, writers and journalists, extending to the Marxists. India contains probably a greater diversity of points of view—spiritually, intellectually and politically—than any country in the world, as it contains all the views of the modern West along with those of its own ancient teachings extending back thousands of years.

I have endeavoured to study the Hindu tradition from its Vedic and Puranic roots including the Vedas, Vedanta, Samkhya, Yoga and Tantra, examining original Sanskrit texts and having discussions with traditional teachers. In the process, I discovered that a tremendous gap exists between how the Hindu tradition formulates itself and how others view it. What people in the West think characterises Hinduism is often inaccurate, prejudiced and contrary to its real teachings.

Inside the Tradition View

To address the many distortions about Hinduism, this book offers what could be best called an 'inside the tradition view', attempting to portray the higher side of Hinduism that has sustained it through the ages while many other religions have come and gone. The book attempts to reveal Hindu Dharma in its greater beauty, profundity and significance. Such an inside view naturally differs greatly from the usual 'outside the tradition view', which is all what most people have encountered in the accessible books on the subject.

In this regard, we should remember that such inside the tradition views are easily found relative to Christianity, Judaism and Islam. They are accepted as representing these traditions directly and in an authentic manner. It is only in the case of the Hindu tradition that the West and even modern Indians wish and insist that while being presented by its critics and detractors, it should be looked at objectively and fairly. Therefore, an inside the tradition view of

Hinduism is important to create the necessary balance, though it has its own value as well.

If there were only outside the tradition views available on Christianity—presenting it according to images of the crusades, inquisition, witch burning, slavery and the colonial genocide of native peoples—Christianity would look gruesome, and not the religion of love that its followers believe it to be. Similarly, if Islam was presented only according to the impressions created by Islamic terrorism and the records of the peoples it conquered, one can only imagine how negatively it might be judged.

The Hindu tradition is usually portrayed according to social evils in Indian society, especially the caste system, though caste by birth is not universal to Hindu thought and is a distortion of earlier Hindu social orders. At the same time, Christianity and Islam are seldom judged according to the inequalities in their societies, though many of these have existed over the years. Meanwhile, Hinduism's lofty Vedantic philosophy, deep yoga practices and towering modern gurus, which are almost unparalleled elsewhere, are usually ignored in academic studies or denigrated in media presentations. For those who may claim that my view is slanted in favour of Hinduism, I ask them to take it as a counterweight for the many books slanted against it.

Naturally, much of this vast ancient tradition cannot be dealt with in a single volume. This book does not attempt to discuss all the teachings of Hinduism, its different branches, teachers and scriptures. It is aimed at understanding the Hindu view of the universe and the orientation of the Hindu mind. It is meant to address the questions that people may have in trying to understand what is behind the Hindu tradition in its several dimensions.

I have written various books on Hindu Dharma and on various aspects of its thought which cover other aspects of this venerable tradition, including texts on historical, social and political issues, as well as details on Hindu worship, Yoga and meditation. This particular book is part of one such longer series of related titles.

The book consists of a series of reflections in the first section, and questions and answers in the second, addressing Sanatana Dharma, the universal tradition behind Hinduism and the yogic spirituality that derives from it. The book portrays Hinduism as both a universal approach and as a well-defined tradition with a complete spiritual science and culture of its own.

I have written this book as one who is Hindu not by birth but by inner affinity and deeper experience. I am not hesitant to identify myself with the Hindu tradition, though some people may think it is politically incorrect and culturally backward, particularly for a Westerner to call himself a Hindu. On the contrary, I think that joining the Hindu tradition is the most transformative spiritual association that one can make, acknowledging its great teachings and connection with the cosmic mind that is perhaps the jewel in world civilization.

This yogic universalism of Hinduism is not a superficial unity of accepting all religions as they are as true but providing an appropriate place for every type of spiritual practice. In this regard, Hinduism reflects the spirituality of the future, after which humanity has moved beyond all dogmas to a greater art and science of Self-realization. It is likely that the West's encounter with Hinduism will eventually transform not only Western religious and spiritual systems but also its science and philosophy, reformulated under the umbrella of the universal view that we find within Hinduism. Hinduism can provide the basis of a cosmic spirituality and planetary dharma, not by converting people to a new belief but by incorporating all human spiritual knowledge into an experiential spirituality at an individual level.

Acknowledgements

I have drawn an inspiration from many Hindu leaders and organizations, including Sadguru Sivananda Murty of the Shaiva Mahapeetham, Sivaya Subramuniyya Swami of *Hinduism Today* magazine, Ram Swarup and Sitaram Goel of the Voice of India,

Swaminarayan Organisation (BAPS) and Pramukh Swami, Swami Dayananda of the Arsha Vidya Gurukulam, Swami Chinmayananda, and Dr. B L Vashta who, besides being my primary teacher of Ayurvedic medicine, brought me into the fold of Hindu thought.

This book is meant to encourage deeper thought and inquiry. If it succeeds in this regard, its purpose has been fulfilled. Compared to the Eternal Dharma, we as human individuals are but dust and must always look deeper to understand its profound and many-sided message.

Let us examine humanity's most ancient, intricate and enduring spiritual and mystical tradition which, of all the religions of the world can most rightfully be called 'the Eternal Tradition', in order to better understand our own deeper, spiritual potential at a personal level. The eternal teaching begins and ends with the Self, the revelation of our true being, which is pure consciousness, freedom, bliss and immortality beyond time and space, birth and death, suffering and limitation.

May all beings recognise that Supreme Self!

May all cultures build their new societies upon It!

—**Dr. David Frawley**
(Pandit Vamadeva Shastri)
February 2018

Part I

Hinduism, Sanatana Dharma and Religion
An Overview

Truth alone wins, not untruth. By Truth is established the path that leads to the Divine, by which the seers, who have fulfilled their desires, reach to the Supreme abode of Truth.

Mundaka Upanishad III.1.6

There is no attainment higher than Self-knowledge.

Shankaracharya, Upadesha Sahasri

The Search for a Universal Spiritual Tradition

Human Aspiration for the Eternal

Throughout history, wise and discriminating individuals from all lands have sought a truth that is universal and eternal. This has been a quest not only of philosophers and mystics but also for all of us in our deeper moments, as we aspire to know the ultimate meaning of our existence. Deep inside ourselves, we long for an absolute truth through which we can permanently transcend suffering and death and gain lasting bliss and immortality. Many great thinkers, looking beyond the names and forms of historical religions and philosophies, have envisioned an enduring tradition of inner knowledge that reflects this universal truth and allows people to access it without any external boundaries limiting their search.

Truth, in the higher sense, is that which is immutable and unchanging. It remains the same for all times and for all people. It is not a fad or opinion of the moment, but the very ground of existence. Such an eternal truth must be honoured and respected in society for civilization to have any real meaning or higher values.

The quest for universal truth, and a tradition to sustain it, is not merely a spiritual quest, but the essence of all knowledge. In any field of knowledge, we are striving to understand universal laws, which like the law of gravity are common to all human beings regardless of their backgrounds. Science formulates itself as an understanding of universal physical laws. Art portrays the underlying creative forces behind life.

All religions have some sense of the eternal within them, however imperfectly this may be formulated or expressed. After all, religion is the field of life meant to address the spiritual reality behind the universe, which is not limited by time or space. The attempt to connect human beings with the eternal is the essence of true religion and experiential spirituality. Yet, as they have been institutionalised, religions have limited this eternal truth to a particular leader, book, or church as the ultimate, which removes them from universality and consigns them to partiality.

Religion has too often been turned into dogma and authority, a vested interest in the outer world in which the discovery of truth at an individual level is set aside. Such a reduction of the spiritual to particular time-space coordinates is the denial of any transcendent reality. However, this belief-based view of religion is easier for the human mind to appreciate as it looks for quick and convenient answers to life's vexing problems. It is also easier for society to regulate a belief and so this belief based view of religion has remained dominant historically, particularly in the Western world.

Because of the tendency of organised religion to become a social control mechanism rather than offering a real spiritual path, discerning individuals have looked beyond it to mystical and yogic teachings. For this reason, the search for universal truth has been conducted more beyond organised religion, than through it. This inner search has taken Western people in the direction of dharmic traditions like Hinduism and Buddhism, which are more experientially based, less dogmatic and offer more individual freedom of approach to the ultimate meaning of life.

The Universal Tradition and the Synthesis of Religions

In the current global age where the different cultures of the world are in constant communication, there is a new movement towards a universal spirituality. This has led to an effort to combine the religions of the world into a global or planetary religion that encompasses all religions and affords each an honoured place. Many Hindu teachers and thinkers from India have had such ideas. This seeking for the unity of world's main religious traditions is a valuable endeavour and can provide much insight. It is an important factor in interfaith dialogue. However, it is not without its limitations.

We must recognise that what is originally formulated in a fragmentary manner cannot easily lead to wholeness. We cannot create the universal by putting together particulars. We cannot create the unity of a tree through gathering together its various leaves that have fallen on the ground. We must return to the original root in order to do so.

By validating limited approaches in the religious realm along with their vested interests, there is the danger that we may validate these limitations and strengthen their divisions. It is like trying to create unity in humanity by accepting all the different borders that exist between nations as fair boundaries. True unity occurs when we set aside outer differences and recognise the essence of consciousness as our true nature, in which all external distinctions lose their significance. This manifests when we emphasise the universal Self within us as more important than any outer name or form.

More important than accepting all religions as they are, we should discern what is universal in religion and spirituality, which is the search for a higher awareness, and give credence to that. True unity is Self-existent at the core of who we really are. It cannot be fabricated by emphasizing differences that exist at the surface. The oneness of the ocean exists at its depths, not at the level of the waves, which must remain ever changing. A universal tradition does not rely upon existing dogmas but on the aspiration of the individual, which transcends the forms that society has developed to either help or to control that aspiration.

Other thinkers today, aim to create a universal tradition by discarding the existent religions of the world, recognizing that these have become limiting identities. This approach has the advantage of avoiding the baggage that religions have accumulated historically. Yet it is like trying to create a new science by discarding all that science has previously discovered. Instead, we should embrace what is universal in the religious and spiritual teachings of the world, neither validating them superficially, nor discarding what they may have to offer in an effort to create a clean slate.

Hinduism and its Universal Connections

This seeking of a universal truth has not always been an isolated phenomenon, or something of the modern age only. There is at least one major world religion that has always formulated itself as a many-sided universal tradition, encompassing all the ways of knowledge and leading all individuals to Self-realization and union with the Supreme—embracing all that we know of as religion and spirituality without seeking to reduce it to a particular name, form, personality or institution as final.

This is the religion that the modern world knows of, albeit imperfectly, as Hinduism, whose correct name is Sanatana Dharma—'the universal or eternal tradition'. Hinduism does not rest upon any single formation or particular belief system but remains open to all approaches to the higher truth through a variety of gurus and practices going back to the beginning of history.

On an inner level, Hinduism defines itself through Self-knowledge, not through a personality, book, institution or heavenly goal. This is the basis of the philosophy of Vedanta, the summit (anta) of spiritual knowledge or wisdom (Veda), which explains comprehensively our true nature beyond birth and death. As the higher aspect of the Vedic teaching, Vedanta remains relevant to everyone, including those who may find the representational forms of Hinduism difficult to understand. Vedanta is the basis of both a perennial philosophy and a path of Self-realization that answers all the questions of life and shows us a way beyond all sorrow.

Hinduism has always reflected a universal tradition of inner knowing. However, the outer aspects of Hinduism are important and quite extraordinary in their own right. They add to Vedanta a culture, way of life and most importantly, sacred arts and sciences that can bring this inner vision of unity into all that we do. These outer aspects of Sanatana Dharma need not be discarded as irrelevant, though they may need to be reformulated and updated according to our world today.

This is not to say that Hinduism or even Vedanta is the sole representative of any universal tradition. A universal tradition cannot be owned by anyone or reduced to any region of the globe. The beauty of Hinduism is that it is a religion that allows a universal perspective to flow through it. Hinduism is a tradition of spiritual search without barriers that accepts all true aspiration regardless of name or form. It places experiential spirituality above outer beliefs, dogmas or creeds.

Such a universal view of Hindu Dharma does not mean that everything occurring in Hinduism today is universal. Any formulation of a universal teaching, being bound by time and place, must contain elements that are particular or limited. It must have specific teachings relative to specific peoples, places and cultures, which may or may not be relevant to others. Though truth is universal, there is always a necessary local aspect in its expression, much like the ecological principle to think globally and act locally.

In addition, Hinduism unfortunately still contains unnecessary accretions and distortions that require purification so that its universal essence can be made more evident. Yet in spite of outer limitations, the universal foundation in Hinduism remains intact at its core. This universal aspect of Hindu Dharma is experiencing some sort of resurgence throughout the world. Hinduism is in the process of reclaiming its global relevance as the many modern gurus from India continue to demonstrate. It is important, therefore, for all spiritual seekers to take a deeper look at humanity's oldest religion and most comprehensive way of Self-realization and understanding universal consciousness.

The Conscious Being alone is all this, what has been and what will be.
                                                              Rigveda X.90.2

All this universe is Brahman. The Self of all beings is Brahman.
                                                    Mandukya Upanishad I.2

He who sees the Self in all beings and all beings in the Self, henceforth has no more remorse.
                                                              Isha Upanishad

Hatred never ends by hatred but only by love, that is the eternal law (Sanatana Dharma).
                                                      Buddha, Dhammapada I.5

Sanatana Dharma: The Eternal Tradition

The Himalayan Connection

The Himalayas are the world's highest mountains, extending fifteen hundred miles across the north of India with thousands of massive snow peaks towering over twenty thousand feet. These lofty peaks are the source of the largest set of rivers in the world: the vast river systems of the Ganga, Brahmaputra, Indus, Amu Darya, Yangtze and Mekong, which nourish and enliven Asia, the world's largest continent. Looking at the Himalayas from the standpoint of sacred geography—which conceives the entire planet as a single being—we could say that these mountains at the roof of the world represent the crown chakra or head centre of the planet. We would, therefore, expect powerful spiritual energies to consistently emanate from them.

Not surprisingly, from these towering summits has come the oldest and most comprehensive spiritual tradition in the world— the teachings of the great yogis, rishis and sages who have lived in the region since time immemorial. From the Himalayas, this yogic teaching has spread to many lands and communities throughout the world and taken root there, particularly in India, which, lodged beneath the Himalayas to the tropical South, receives the largest portion of the mountain waters through its sacred rivers.

This Himalayan tradition, perhaps because of its very depth, richness and diversity, has seldom been understood as a whole. The largest part of the tradition—what has been called Hinduism by the proximity of the Himalayas to India—remains the most enigmatic and misunderstood of the world's major religions, largely because it is not a religion in the Western sense of the term as a belief system, but a spiritual path wedded to the whole of life and nature.

Because of the misconceptions associated with the term Hindu—which suggests an ethnic religion rather than a universal teaching—the teachings of this Himalayan spiritual tradition has been propagated in the modern world mainly under the name of 'Yoga'. Yoga, which means union, is the main practice of the Himalayan tradition, which aims at guiding us to our own Self-realization, an inner unity with the Divine and universal, not simply subordinating us to an outer religious identity.

'Vedanta' is another term for the Himalayan tradition because Vedanta teaches the oneness of the individual soul with the universal being, the inner unity that Yoga is aiming at. The original teachers who brought Yoga to the West like Vivekananda, Yogananda and the many disciples of Swami Shivananda of Rishikesh, spoke of Yoga-Vedanta for this reason.

The term 'Vedic knowledge' can also be used for this vast tradition. Veda, which means spiritual knowledge, indicates the full range of spiritual and sacred sciences, as originally set forth in the profound mantras of ancient Vedic texts more than five thousand years ago.

Such spiritual terms as Yoga, Veda and Vedanta probably better communicate the essence of this nameless tradition to the modern mind than does the limited designation Hindu. However, they can also give the misimpression that Hindu culture and spirituality is something different or not relevant, when it is a broader expression of the same tradition and its great gurus.

Sanatana Dharma and Yoga

The original name for the Hindu tradition, Sanatana Dharma, the eternal or universal truth, provides the background for Yoga and its related teachings. Sanatana Dharma is a tradition conceived of as inherent in the cosmic mind, arising with the dawn of creation itself. It is a set of teachings that comprehends all of life, including religion, yoga, mysticism, philosophy, science, medicine, art and culture as part of a single reality in its diverse expression like a great Banyan tree.

The term dharma has been introduced worldwide, not only relative to Hindu teachings but in regard to Buddhism, whose original name is Buddha Dharma. An understanding of dharma, which more specifically means 'natural law', is crucial to all dharmic traditions. Hinduism is sometimes called 'Hindu Dharma' in order to discriminate it from a religion in the Western sense of the word.

Yoga as the practical side of Sanatana Dharma contains a physical aspect, the science of *asanas* or yogic postures, which has been easy for physically oriented Western culture to relate to. Yet while the term Yoga can be helpful in communicating aspects of Sanatana Dharma without confusing it with a religious dogma, it can cause misconceptions.

Traditional or classical Yoga refers to the inner practice of Sanatana Dharma and emphasises on devotion, meditation and introspection to develop a higher awareness within us. Modern Yoga, on the other hand, is commonly reduced to Yoga postures as a fitness system in which the meditation component is secondary. Even traditional 'Hatha Yoga', which is characteristically a Yoga of personal effort, was originally used to prepare the body for the pursuit of higher states of consciousness. The true goal of Yoga is Self-realization, and not merely a health related or tool to gain flexibility. Health and flexibility come as secondary benefits of Yoga.

Having already been introduced to the teachings of Yoga for over a century, it is important that worldwide Yoga students are introduced to the greater spiritual and cultural tradition from which Yoga derives. This includes Vedic arts and science like Ayurveda (Vedic medicine), Vedic astrology (Jyotisha), Vastu (Vedic architecture), Indian music and dance, Vedantic philosophy and, above all, the greater yogic paths of Knowledge (Jñana Yoga), Devotion (Bhakti Yoga), Service (Karma Yoga) and Psycho-physical methodologies (Raja Yoga).

We could call the greater tradition of Sanatana Dharma as a 'yogic culture' or 'yogic science'. The same physical movements that appear in Yoga postures occur in Indian dance forms as well. The same philosophy behind Yoga forms the background of Ayurvedic medicine. The study of the Sanskrit language, which mirrors cosmic sound, is itself a path of Yoga. Meditation is a way of bringing peace and equipoise to the mind, just as yogic postures serve to do so to the physical body. Mantras are like asanas or yoga postures for the mind, allowing it to hold specific patterns of mental energy.

Hinduism in a Yogic Light

To the global audience today, the term Sanatana Dharma is unfamiliar and complex, and lacks recognition. If one looks for the teachings of Sanatana Dharma in libraries and bookstores, one will not find any major section or category. All such topics are covered under Hinduism. *This means that we cannot dismiss the term Hindu, though it is more limited than Sanatana Dharma. We must expand its meaning back to its essence as Sanatana Dharma.* To facilitate it, we must first restore the connection of Hinduism and Sanatana Dharma, so that we think of the two together.

Some Hindus object to the name Hinduism for their religion and prefer the term Hindu Dharma because it is not an 'ism' or an ideology, or a religion like Western religions but a complete way of life. Yet Hinduism is not merely a religion in the Western sense of the term but more. It includes along with religious worship, prayer and meditation all aspects of art, culture, philosophy and science. It is not simply another way of life but a way of the cosmic life.

Hindu Dharma reflects a universal yogic tradition at its core. Even what appear to be the extraneous aspects of Hindu culture—like depictions of deities or temple designs—are based upon an understanding of universal consciousness and are not arbitrary rules or local customs. Those who wish to understand the greater teachings of Yoga should examine Hinduism not simply as a religion, but as a complete spiritual culture. This requires not merely performing yogic postures but establishing a yogic lifestyle, and looking into the yogic aspects of philosophy, art, science and medicine.

Many people throughout the world have adopted Hindu teachings like Yoga, Vedanta, or Ayurvedic medicine. They follow the guru-lines originating from India, if not teachers who were born in India. Many have taken Sanskrit names, which they refer to as their spiritual names. Yet few would formally call themselves Hindus. Some would be opposed to the appellation, considering it to be a foreign or restrictive religious identity. Yet if one explains the concept of Sanatana Dharma to them, most would regard themselves as followers of such a universal tradition.

Hindu as a particular ethnic type born in India, believing in caste and untouchability, perhaps economically, socially and intellectually backward—which is how this religion has been generally presented to the modern mind—is a narrow and unappealing concept to anyone. On the other hand, Sanatana Dharma—the idea of an eternal and universal tradition of Self-realization and higher consciousness—represents the deepest aspirations and perceptions of the human heart, which all inwardly aware people must recognise.

As a formulation of Sanatana Dharma or the universal tradition, Hinduism is not limited to any single messiah, prophet, scripture, or church. It is not restricted to a particular community and it doesn't look forward to any specific historical end or goal. It contains numerous teachings and revelations, and is ever being reformulated in light of the experience of living Self-realised teachers in communion with the infinite. It embraces all aspiration toward the Divine or Supreme Being by all creatures; not only human beings but plants, animals and the inhabitants, godly or ungodly, of subtle worlds beyond our physical senses. It maintains a connection to all worlds and all times, to the ancient past and the most distant future in the vision of an unbounded Self-renewing reality (Brahman).

Sanatana Dharma is a way of knowledge without limits, yet it does possess unchanging principles and defined characteristics. It recognises the great laws of nature and consciousness, like the law of karma—a clear connection of cause and effect in our actions, not only in the present but relative to past and future lives. It respects the cosmic intelligence working through nature and seeks to harmonise human life with the universal energy. For this purpose, Hinduism encourages us to honour and worship the Divine principles (Gods or Devatas) working through the forces of nature, including Mother Earth, making regular offerings and prayers to these living powers of cosmic consciousness. Its deities are universal forces, and not theological assertions.

Hindu Dharma is a practical way of inner knowing, not a theoretical system or ideology that can be embraced on a conceptual or emotional level alone. It aims at providing us with the appropriate tools to discover the higher truth within ourselves, rather than telling us what that truth is supposed to be. Such practices are diverse and cannot be limited to one set formulation or standardised approach. They include yogic postures, breathing exercises, ritual, mantra and meditation. Sanatana Dharma also teaches us the ethical disciplines necessary to use these spiritual tools correctly, like the attitudes of non-violence (ahimsa) and truthfulness. It directs us to Self-realization as the real goal of our lives.

Hindu Dharma and Religion

Hindu Dharma is like a great mother and the other religions are like her children. Like a mother, she does not like to criticise her children but prefers to nourish and support them. Through Hinduism, we can understand the ground from which all religions spring, which is in a way also their ultimate goal.

Hinduism as a universal tradition contains the greatest diversity and freedom in the spiritual life that can be found in any religion. It allows the Divine to be worshipped in any name or form, or beyond name and form. It allows us to see God as father, mother, brother, sister, friend or master and ultimately requires that we see God as everything and, above all, as our very own Self. It says that whatever leads us to our deeper Self, which is the true Divinity, is good, regardless of the form that it takes, which is a matter of personal approach only.

Yet Hinduism, perhaps alone amidst the world's major religions, has yet to define itself to the modern mind. Even Hindus with a modern education usually do not understand their own tradition and cannot explain it to others. Though its teachings have been set forth quite clearly by many great gurus since Swami Vivekananda, their vastness and diversity has caused the underlying tradition to become obscured by the very luxuriance of its growth.

Most of us with a little reading can define the main principles and beliefs of Christianity, Islam, Judaism or Buddhism. We can study the life of Christ, Mohammed, Moses or Buddha as a model for the religion as a whole. But how many of us, even those who may have studied Yoga and Vedanta, can define the essence of Hinduism? How many of us are aware of its true nature as Sanatana Dharma or the universal Dharma? How many of those born as Hindus know the roots of their own tradition? The very beauty of Hinduism is that it cannot be defined in a simplistic manner. It contains all the mystery and complexity, magic, wonder and enigma of life itself.

Hinduism and Colonial Shadows

To approach Hindu Dharma in its deeper truth, we must recognise how much this great tradition has been intentionally distorted and rarely properly presented. For this, we must examine the history of India over the last thousand years.

The British gained a foothold in India in 1757 and finally in 1819 defeated the large Hindu Maratha Empire that dominated most of the subcontinent. Under British colonial rule the Hindu tradition, which the great majority of Indians followed, was undermined and denigrated and strong efforts were made to convert the country to Christianity. This was justified by British imperial power and its colonial exploitation of the country and its vast skills and resources.

When the British came to India in 1757, India had a quarter of the world's economy. When the British left in 1947, India had less than one per cent! This shows how the British impacted the country overall and sought to exploit it. In additions, millions died in India in British created famines up to World War II itself.

India's traditional educational system that was primarily Hindu-oriented in nature was suppressed and closed down by the British, which replaced it with a British-run educational system designed to create British Indians alienated from their own traditions. The British sponsored colonial studies of the teachings and scriptures of Hinduism, which, not surprisingly, portrayed the religion as primitive and needing from colonial guidance. These British views were introduced into the educational system of India as authoritative. India's great gurus were ignored or looked down upon, though a few Westerners bravely became their disciples over time.

Yet British colonialism was not the first or most destructive for Hindu Dharma. Starting in the eight century, India was under the assault of invading Islamic armies from the West. Arab armies gained a foothold in Sindh in the eighth century, and in the thirteenth century under the Delhi Sultanate, Islamic Turks were able to conquer most of India. By the sixteenth century under Akbar, India was dominated by the large Moghul Empire. After the decline of the Moghuls under the tyrant Aurangzeb in the seventeenth century, the Hindus gradually reclaimed their rule over India, a process stopped by the British.

India's long period Islamic rule could similarly be designed as colonial in nature as it tried to replace the older culture of India with an imported and often hostile culture. India faced several waves of Islamic invaders, including Arabs, Turks and Afghans, which gradually made inroads into the country and resulted in the destruction of thousands of temples and schools, include the massacre of Hindu yogis, monks and priests.

During this long assault, Hinduism was actively suppressed and Hindus were routinely humiliated and targeted for conversion often at the threat of death. Hindus were prevented from practising their religion in public and forceful attempts were made to convert them, which under more aggressive Islamic rulers like Aurangzeb resulted in one of the worst genocides in human history. Even in times of general peace, economic pressure was applied to Hindus through an Islamic religious tax (the jizya tax) to promote conversion and take away the wealth of the Hindus. It is a wonder that Hinduism survived, particularly considering that the older religions of Iran and Central Asia of Zoroastrianism, Tengrism, Manicheanism and Buddhism could not withstand the same onslaught for a much shorter period.

The result of these aggressive attempts to convert Hindus was that Hinduism went underground and became contracted within itself. Hindu Dharma withdrew from its universal orientation into a necessary survival mode. Hindus became reluctant to express their religion, much less to share it with others for fear of criticism or attack. Hindu temples closed to Muslims and foreigners who were seen as potential of enemies, as Hindus had witnessed how they looted and destroyed great temples throughout the country. This history of oppression is the basis of the Self-enclosed appearance of Hinduism that non-Hindus feel when they talk to Hindus about religion or what they sense around older Hindu temples. However, it is not the true nature of the tradition or its deeper teachings, which has had an expansive expression throughout most of history.

The New Faces of Anti-Hindu Prejudices

The legacies of the British system of education and that of the Catholic Church, which could not be called sensitive to Hinduism, still influence, if not dominate our view of India today. The old anti-Hindu colonial stereotypes still occur in the global media, even as far as the New York Times. Portrayals of Hinduism remain coloured by the views of the old missionaries and colonial administrators who were trying to rule and convert India, and were certainly not appreciative of its spiritual culture.

The hostile legacy of the Islamic period has continued under the guise of Pakistan and its Islamic allies, extending to the Taliban, the Islamic State (ISIS) and Jihadi terrorist attacks on India—which is to portray Hinduism in a negative light as a culture of darkness and oppression, a religion of 'kafirs' that must be brought back under Islamic rule. The ideas of Hindus as polytheists, idolaters, or even devil worshippers are missionary and Jihadi stereotypes, deriving from those whose motivation is not to understand this profound religion but to discredit it on principle.

Such hostile groups do not honour the great sages of India or seek to learn Yoga and meditation. They cast Hinduism and Buddhism in the same negative light as they have the religions of the Native Americans, Native Africans, or older European and Asian pagan groups, which are similarly denigrated. How many of us would go to Christian missionaries to learn about Islam or Buddhism? Yet most of the scholars we look up to for a definition of Hinduism or its ancient Vedas, starting with nineteenth century figures like Max Mueller, Ralph Griffith, and Monier Williams have been intentionally trying to undermine it and say so in their own writings.

On top of these colonial denigrations, modern India has suffered a strong Marxist and Communist influence, conspicuous in universities like Jawaharlal Nehru University (JNU) and in the mass media, which could hardly be regarded as appreciative of Hinduism either. India's Communists still rule the state of Kerala and honour not only Marx and Lenin but even Stalin who other Communist parties in the world have rejected. The result is that the view of Hinduism taught in India's schools and history textbooks today, though slowly changing in a more positive light, remains distorted by Marxism, and can be said to be as sensitive to Hinduism as the Marxist interpretation of the Bible was to Christianity. Western media and academia often repeat the anti-Hindu stories of India's Marxist left, not realizing the political bias behind these.

If we examine how religions are taught in the West today, we find Abrahamic religions like Christianity, Judaism and Islam presented by authors and teachers who are part of their traditions, who practice it and who promote a favourable view of it. If one looks at departments of Hindu studies in universities—should they exist at all—one finds these dominated by non-Hindus, Christians and Marxists who would never consider themselves allies of Hindu thought.

Western Hindu scholars use Freudian psychology, which reduces human consciousness to physical urges, to interpret Hinduism—something that was once done relative to Biblical religions but has since been rejected as inappropriate. Only relative to Hinduism does such psychological debunking of a religion remains mainstream in its interpretation. Western Hindu scholars like Wendy Doniger openly declare that they are following the views of Freud and Marx and that they are neither Hindus, nor do they accept the Hindu view of Yoga and Vedanta. Their views of Hindu Dharma do not reflect any deep study or practice of this profound tradition of cosmic knowledge.

Contemporary Hindu gurus and their profound teachings are rarely recognised in modern academic studies of Hinduism, in spite of their large global followings, except perhaps in a derogatory manner as cult leaders! Hinduism is mainly looked upon according to ancient texts that few Hindus study and use today, particularly social law codes from many centuries ago like Manu Smriti, as if Hinduism was a fossil from a previous era. This is not to say that one cannot find critical views of other religions in academia but there are inside the tradition views available to balance these out. *It seems that no inside the tradition view is allowed for Hinduism, only criticism from hostile forces.*

Hindus being overall tolerant and spiritually oriented have not mounted major efforts to challenge these stereotypes until recent years. These wrong views remain entrenched in the global media and educational system, though such colonial denigrations against other religions have been removed. It is time for colonial and religious denigrations of Hindu Dharma to be eliminated from our educational systems as well. As there are over a billion Hindus, a significant portion of humanity, Hindu traditions require a culturally sensitive presentation, not the old colonial prejudices.

Global Hinduism Emerging beyond Anti-Hindu Stereotypes

Today Hindu teachings have spread globally in spite of the strong and insidious propaganda against them, and the lack of government or academic support for Hindu studies. There are now Hindu minorities in all continents by way of recent immigration, and Hindu-based spiritual teachings like Yoga and Vedanta have been adapted by people in all lands and from all cultural backgrounds.

Hindu minorities in the USA and UK are affluent and well educated, modern and scientific, and yet still Hindu in their spiritual practices, quite unlike the missionary stereotypes of poor, backward and superstitious Hindus. Yoga and Vedanta have an appeal to affluent and educated groups in the West. Western scientists and physicists have given positive views of Hinduism and its teachings through the Bhagavad Gita, Vedanta or the worship of Lord Shiva. Hindus in the West and Western born people following Hindu based practices show how hollow and wrong the negative views of Hinduism that we see in the textbooks and are slowly causing these to change.

Hinduism is beginning to appear more like a religion of the future, a teaching for the emerging planetary age. Of all religions today, Hinduism is the most synthetic and can integrate all spiritual paths into a deeper quest for Self-realization. Hinduism, as a conscious formulation of the universal tradition, has the breadth to encompass, integrate and transcend all religions. It has a wideness of cosmic vision that can not only embrace but extend the field of modern science into spiritual domains of higher consciousness and cosmic intelligence.

So let us put the old colonial and missionary prejudices to rest and look at this venerable tradition anew according to its value for everyone. Hindu Dharma is a key component of our greater human, spiritual and yogic heritage that we must examine in order to understand our true potentials as a species, not only toward scientific development but towards higher consciousness.

Come together, speak together, together let your minds arrive at a common understanding, just as the ancient Divinities in a common knowing honour the same Good.

Rigveda X.191.2

He who does not know the Imperishable Word of the chant that dwells in the supreme ether, in which all the Divinities reside, what can he do with the Vedas? Those who know That, let them gather together here.

Rigveda I.164.39

Organised Religion and Dharmic Spirituality

Religion—A Blessing or a Curse?

Religion is not only probably the most profound and uplifting aspect of human life, but also the most ambiguous, contradictory and at times, most destructive. Religions, more than any other domain of human culture, have served to instil ethical values and raise human beings to higher levels of sensitivity. We see this in the mystics, saints, sages, seers and yogis who can be found, at least to some extent, in all the religious traditions of the world.

On the other hand, religions have been the main cause of misunderstanding, mistrust and hatred between human beings. They have been responsible for the greatest violence and inhumanity, and numerous instances of genocide, which persist to the present day. We see this in the inquisitions, crusades, holy wars, witch burning and terrorism perpetrated in the name of religion, which show no respect for life, even trampling on women and children along the way.

The term religion originally means 'to unite'. At the deepest level, one can connect it to the unification of the soul or essence of our being with the Divine or the Supreme universal principle. This deeper definition of religion resembles that of Yoga, which clearly refers to uniting the individual with the supreme reality.

Religion—properly understood as a means of union with our fellow human beings and with the underlying Divinity—has brought many people to the awareness of the Divine as their true nature. Religion—improperly understood, as an exclusive belief system that places us against those who think differently—has become the basis for pillage, plunder, wrecking entire cultures, and condemning to eternal hell our fellow human beings, our own brothers and sisters.

Perhaps nothing more than religion stimulates the passions of human beings towards either higher or lower actions. This is because religion introduces absolutes into human behaviour. Religion sets up a standard of judgement for human behaviour that goes beyond life and death.

Such a standard of absolutes can deepen our sensitivity or can breed bigotry, depending upon whether we use these principles to elevate our own behaviour or to become harsher in our criticism of others. While principles like universal truth or Divine love are ennobling and transformative, those like salvation or damnation by belief are divisive and demeaning. True unitary spirituality directs us to an absolute of Being—Consciousness—Bliss, which requires that we cleanse our minds of limited opinions and judgements. False and imperfect religion tries to make absolute the very prejudices, opinions and limitations that separate us into warring camps according to social identity and physical appearances.

To understand the true purpose of religion, we must first redefine religion in the yogic sense of the search for unity-consciousness.

Otherwise we will be unable to extract the essence of religion from its mass of conflicting practices, dogmas and assertions. We must look at religion as a means of connecting with universal reality through our own consciousness, which is the science of Yoga. This is the view of religion that India has given humanity, the land where human beings have spent the most time in pursuit of the sacred, not to convert others, but to realise the eternal truth within our own deeper awareness.

Religion in the Global Era

Some of us may think that it is best not to examine religion, which is after all a matter of faith. Let each person follow whatever religion he or she prefers. However, in the current era of mass communication, we must strive to understand all people and all cultures. To compartmentalise religion into various faiths, each of which leaves the others alone, would be like saying let each country speak its own language, and we will speak our own, but let us not try to learn the language of others or strive to develop any global communication. This superficial sense of tolerance hides a contraction of fear and insecurity. As human beings, all religions and all cultures are part of our human heritage and we should be free to examine each for whatever value it may have, just as art or science are there for all of us to study without boundaries.

Religion in the deeper sense considers the ultimate questions of life and death. To approach it we must question deeply, including questioning religion itself and, above all, questioning ourselves. We must ask: What it is that we are really seeking through religion? Are we really seeking the truth or to know God and our true eternal Self? Or is religion merely something to believe in externally and then stop searching, regarding a dogma or a saviour enough to solve the deeper mysteries of life?

Is religion merely a church to belong to, a new identity, to be a part of a group of people which can provide us comfort and support in our outer lives? Is religion a social movement to take over the world and convert it to a belief that is meant to arouse our missionary zeal? Is true religion the certainty that we will have ultimate salvation and happiness, and those who follow different beliefs will be punished by God?

These are emotional and vital urges that however powerful, have little to do with the search for truth, which cannot cater to human partialities. Such urges cause us to distort reality according to our personal and collective desires. They are not part of a genuine seeking of truth, but a further development of egoistic drives. Religion should be the search within our own being for the truth of this wonderful universe in which we live, its indwelling Spirit and consciousness. Otherwise we should probably call it something else.

What then is the universal element in religion, which like the universal element in art can reveal its essence? Can the essence of religion be found in the churches, holy books, or priests? Does it reside in religious controversies, conflicts and holy wars? Or does it reside in the ultimate aspirations of our deepest heart, which no single group can own or dispense? Is the truth of religion unique to one religion? Is it present to some degree in all religions? Or does it perhaps exist beyond all of them?

Has our religious urge existed because of or in spite of what society has institutionalised and enforced as religion? Is religion, as we commonly think of it, a formulation of spiritual aspiration, or a deformation of it? What is the basis for real inner spirituality and can it be found within the confines of organised religion? These are some of the many questions we must examine and find the answers for within ourselves, through contemplation and meditation.

Divisive Religious Beliefs or Experiential Spirituality?

In the contemporary world, many of us are not really interested in religion, and perhaps wisely so. Business, sports, entertainment, politics and other outward aspects of life are the main focus of our attention, and these are less controversial and divisive than religion, which often appears to be a holdover from the dark and troubled Middle Ages. Given the nature of what we call religion with its sin, guilt, fear, and even vengeance, there appears to be little reason why we should have much regard for it. It can appear as an emotional negativity devoid of common courtesy, not to speak of love, compassion and humanity.

If we are interested in religion, it is not always the inner side of experiential spirituality that concerns us. It is our particular church, the religion of our fathers, our nation or our community, which we are trying to promote at an outer level though politics and conversion. The inner search for truth through introspection and meditation seems forgotten, and in some religions has hardly been there all along.

Fortunately, many of us are able to look beyond the institutionalised religions, which have controlled the world over the last many centuries. Religion as a belief system—the idea that one religion owns the Divine or truth as if it were a kind of property—is a product of a dark age of lack of scientific knowledge and global communication. This division of religions appears at par with the division of races, nations, languages and currencies, not a fundamental truth but a harmful fragmentation of human society.

Religion as it is generally known in the Western world, and its culture which now dominates the world, projects an exclusive truth for a particular leader, book, or group of people and the need to convert the world to it—which is contrary to the idea that there is an inherent universal truth within the hearts and minds of all creatures. Such organised religion formulates truth as an external authority rather than an inner experience and often limits any real inward search for the Divine.

This exclusivist idea of religion may have one God but it has two humanities—the believers and the non-believers—and regards the non-believers as inferior or sinful—to be converted or conquered—which leads to every sort of misunderstanding and exploitation. Its concern is not union with God but elimination of the non-believers. It does not aim at making us better people but at changing those who do not outwardly conform to what we think is religious. As we are beginning to come together as a planet and recognizing our common humanity, such divisions can no longer be accepted. They no longer appear religious but inhumane, not much better than racism or ethnocentricity.

In a number of Western countries today, particularly in Europe, only a small portion of the population attends church on a regular basis. Even although many people may still call themselves Christians, the designation is nominal at best. For many people in the West, religion is a regressive word. They can no longer believe that only one religion is true. Some may doubt whether any religion is true.

Much of Asia is following a similar movement. The younger generation is often more interested in the popular culture imported from the West than in its own traditional religious or spiritual traditions. The educated elite is proud of its modern, scientific, and humanitarian views and often denigrates the religious background of their culture.

In this age of open communication and critical scrutiny, many of us have become painfully aware of the limitations of an organised religion and its herding of people into hostile camps. We have come to recognise that behind the rhetoric of God and religion can be political, economic or sexual exploitation—not an enlightened force. Compared to such divisive creeds, science and humanitarianism, even of an atheistic bent, can appear more compassionate and enlightened.

Yet though the bonds of organised religion are breaking down, the long-term seeking for the eternal and infinite, which is the essence of human nature, is growing. More people are exploring experiential forms of spirituality to satisfy this internal longing. It is not so much that religion has failed us or become out of date, but that religion as we know it is not relevant to our inner needs.

Religion as belief is losing its regard but spirituality as the seeking for direct knowledge of cosmic reality is undergoing a revival. There is a search for a new religion not as a new church, but as a universal spirituality. It heralds a return to dharma, a discovery of the laws of life and the all-pervasive presence of consciousness.

Religious Fundamentalism and Terrorism

However, a contrary and darker trend is also developing throughout the world that is shadowing this global spiritual awakening in a very troubling manner. There has been, over the past few decades, a powerful upsurge in religious violence, extending to global terrorism. This is most obvious in the Middle East, where most of it has been originating, but is also occurring in Western and supposedly scientific countries like the United States and Europe, sometimes by refugees but also at times within the culture itself. Such virulent religious exclusivism is an attempt to return to the rigid religious divisions of the Middle Ages and to continue the old religious wars of conversion as in medieval Crusades and Jihads.

This new religious exclusivism reflects the intolerance inherent in exclusivist beliefs that seek to convert the world and promote their theology as the only truth. This dangerous face of religious extremism should be a clarion call to all religious leaders and insist them to give up the sole claim to truth and affirm pluralism in spiritual practices for all people. This requires Abrahamic faiths should also honour dharmic traditions like Hinduism and Buddhism, and native traditions, as valid spiritual paths.

Even in America, Christian fundamentalism is not just a thing of the past, but a modern media based phenomenon funding a multi-billion-dollar multi-national conversion business. Evangelical Christianity in America is a pop religion of slick TV preachers accompanied by country and Western music singers. It offers instantaneous conversion at football stadiums, with wild prophecies and make-belief miracles. Such so-called religion is accompanied by little true introspection and few spiritual practices like meditation.

Islamic fundamentalism, on the other hand, is more militant and does not hesitate to resort to violence as in the case of Jihadi terrorist groups, not only against those of other religious backgrounds but even against those among its own people who do not agree with its extreme views. It has been growing in numbers and in sympathy, sometimes gaining new adherents who were not born Muslim.

This fundamentalist reaction, terrible as it is, does have a cause—and we must address the factors that make it possible at a cultural level. Modern popular culture with its lack of higher values can lead people into a spiritual and moral wasteland. The weakening of the family system, increased promiscuity and the rampant use of drugs leaves many individuals searching for a religious belief to save them from the chaos of their lives. Such individuals may lack the inner focus to search out a higher spiritual path through meditation, making them easy prey to the absolutist claims of fundamentalist beliefs for a quick answer to their confusion.

The criticism of degeneration levelled against modern consumerist culture by the fundamentalists can be accurate, even when their dogmatic and violent reactions to it are utterly wrong, if not evil. Civilization wise, we need to reconsider our relationship with the Divine and universal, which we have sadly ignored. But the correct force to counter modern materialism resides in a universal experiential spirituality, not a retreat into old religious prejudices. Religious aggression serves to make materialism look more humane by countering it with a force of superstition.

We must pass out of the duality of dogmatic religion and scientific materialism, both of which have their failings. True spirituality is based upon an inner search for higher consciousness, not mere faith and belief but a practice of meditation in which we can learn to perceive the universal truth for ourselves. Its search for the Divine is for an inner reality and its science is one of consciousness, not just a study of the forces of the external world.

Future Trends: The Revival of Dharmic Traditions

One can foresee a future age of world peace and harmony in which serious individuals seek Self-realization through meditation paths beyond the bounds of organised beliefs or any fixed dogmas. We can no longer look upon the time of one ancient prophet and his small following as the last word for all humanity. We have been too exposed to the rest of the world to pretend in a medieval way that our particular community is the only one honoured by the Divine. We can paint our enemy as the devil but it is not so easy to make it believable any more. That we are all human beings with the same basic drives and potential is evident to all open minds.

The ugly head of religious fundamentalism still has a fair amount of bigotry and a number of terrorist tactics left, but this is only a sign that it will be rejected over time. Whether it takes years or decades to go, it remains on the downward side of history. This is not to say we should underestimate its power, which may have yet to reach its maximum, but that we should bring out higher teachings that can effectively neutralise it. As long as we do not remove exclusivism in religious belief—the idea that only one faith is true and all the others are false—such fundamentalism is not likely to pass away.

We live in a global age in which we must come together as a planet. For this we need a universal tradition that recognises the sacred nature of all human beings. Different cultures have developed different spiritual approaches, just as they have developed different types of art, music, literature, and philosophy. We can no longer say that only European art is good and that Chinese or Indian art is barbaric, for example, though even in the last century educated Europeans had such views. We should have the same openness in the spiritual realm as we do in other domains of life. Unfortunately, the spiritual realm is where we have the most intolerance though, as the domain of life that deals with the infinite, it is a place where intolerance has no real place.

In seeking a new spirituality, we must remember that there are traditions that have survived to the present day, which though tainted by time, can help catalyse it. The dharmic traditions of Asia, particularly of India and Tibet, can help us show the way to an authentic global spirituality. They have never formulated themselves as exclusive belief systems, but as universal meditation paths. They have preserved ancient lineages of inner realization, the millennial heritage of a spiritual humanity, with great living masters. Such gurus are necessary guides for us to help develop our own authentic experiential wisdom. As Western science moves to the East, Eastern spirituality and its science of Yoga is coming to the West. This can serve to link up the two sides of human knowledge for the coming planetary age.

The Western world has prided itself in modernity and rationality. Yet if we look deeply, we see that it has also been guilty of various forms of prejudice and narrow mindedness, a Euro-centrism in religion, art and culture, the shadow of which still remains. Today we have been forced to recognise the inhumanity committed in the colonial era by Western powers, which led to slavery and genocide on a global scale. We must similarly recognise the accompanying Western cultural imperialism that has portrayed non-European communities in a negative light, particularly their spiritual traditions, and has reduced their longer and richer histories to mere footnotes to recent events in Europe.

In addition to this, we must recognise a similar genocide and destruction of cultures as committed by Communists and Marxists as in the Soviet Union and Communist China. In fact, communists and radical socialists have promoted the same denigration of traditional non-Western cultures, as did the colonial powers, even to a greater degree. India's Communists, for example, have sustained the anti-Hindu propaganda of the British and Christian missionaries, which might otherwise have disappeared.

The judgement of Eastern religions as pagan, idolatrous, and primitive, appears at par with the judgement of Asian and African peoples as racially inferior—not an enlightened discernment but an embarrassing prejudice. The attempt to discredit venerable and profound dharmic traditions—which is still going on by missionary movements today—is not motivated by any real understanding but by political, economic and religious ambitions toward domination that avoid real dialogue and discussion.

The West can no longer look down upon Asian culture. The Japanese have shown how well the Asians can compete on all levels of modern culture. The Chinese and the Indians are not far behind, as their resurgent economies indicate. The world has come to recognise the value of Asian systems of Yoga, meditation, natural healing, martial arts, music and painting. We have seen the skill of Easterners as scientists, artists, doctors, and businessmen.

Just as Asia is resurgent, Africa and South America in the dawning century will likely learn to apply modern technology according to their own cultural and religious backgrounds. Older indigenous religions as a whole will experience a revival. Europe will once more encounter and integrate its pre-Christian past. The spiritual depth of ancient myths and rituals, especially in pagan teachings, will become obvious to a deeper psychological vision. The Middle East and North Africa will have to face their pre-Islamic past, particularly the Egyptian and Babylonian traditions that modern archaeology has uncovered, and come to recognise the value of their older images and icons.

The mystical side of all religions will become prominent and ideological side will recede. Spiritual, yogic and mystical movements of all kinds will gain interest throughout the world. Syncretic religious movements that combine various teachings will proliferate. In addition, futuristic spiritual ideas will arise which will aim at contacting the magical reality of the mysterious universe in which we live that will take us beyond our intellectual and emotional boundaries.

There are many signs of such a new awakening. The already existing interest in dharmic traditions of Hinduism, Buddhism and Taoism reflects this trend. The upsurge of interest in Native American traditions, Western occultism, pagan practices, and shamanism is an indication. A renewed interest in the mystical side of Abrahamic religions is another and yet another indication is a seeking of higher consciousness through modern psychology and modern physics.

One of the traditions that will greatly benefit from these new trends is Hindu Dharma, whose universality provides for a global integration of culture and spirituality. Modern gurus from the Hindu tradition over the past one hundred years—starting with Paramahansa Ramakrishna, Swami Vivekananda, Aurobindo, Yogananda, Shivananda and Mahatma Gandhi, to mention a few— have been at the forefront of the new global universality in religion and experiential forms of spirituality. Sanskrit terms like Yoga, karma, gurus, mantras, Kundalini and chakras have entered into common parlance in many languages of the world and become the basis for many new insights in science and medicine.

Hinduism—which had appeared as a contracted religion in retreat for many centuries—is expanding its influence throughout the globe with a cosmic vision. Its teachings under different garbs like Vedanta, Yoga, Tantra, and Ayurveda form one of the primary trends of the new planetary spirituality. A Hindu spirit, a sense of universality, tolerance and non-exclusivism, is arising in the minds of many people today. Therefore, it is important that we examine this ancient rishi tradition that has so many dimensions and so many unexplored dimensions. May the inner eye, Lord Shiva's third eye of pure unity, awaken within each one of us!

Where all books of knowledge become one; that is the conscious Self of all beings.

Taittiriya Aranyaka III.11.20

Yoga is the cessation of the disturbances of the mind.

Patanjali, Yoga Sutras I.2

The teacher guides the student in the meaning of the Vedas: Speak the Truth, practice the Dharma, do not be heedless in your Self-study.

Taittiriya Upanishad I.19

Neither agency, nor action does the Lord create for the world, nor the experience of the fruits of action. All this occurs according to the forces of nature. The Lord does not recognize the good or evil done by anyone. Knowledge is covered by ignorance, by which creatures become deluded. But those whose ignorance is destroyed by knowledge of the Self, for them like the Sun, that knowledge reveals the Supreme.

Bhagavad Gita V.14-16

Religion or Dharma: Outer Belief or Inner Knowledge

In the Western world, religion is usually associated with a belief in something unseen, miraculous, perhaps even irrational. For the Western mind, religion is often placed apart from the world of nature, something supernatural or miraculous. Religion thus becomes a matter of faith, even if that faith contradicts our actual experience.

This belief-based idea of religion is not the basis of the traditions of India. The term for any spiritual teaching in India is dharma, which refers to universal principles, not a matter of faith, but of knowledge. What we call the religions of India—like Hinduism and Buddhism—are ways of cultivating dharma and developing higher awareness. To follow dharma requires living in harmony with life, attuned to the consciousness of the universal being.

Discovery of dharma requires direct perception and living experience, in which we understand the nature of things and how they really work. Each thing has its dharma, nature or way of being, whether it is a force like fire, an emotion like love or hate, or an individual human being. If we try to understand the dharma of things rather than assert a belief, we can contact with the essence of existence and discovery the unity and interdependence of all. If we emphasise dharma rather than religion, there will be no more religious conflicts in the world. Religion will dissolve into an inner search for truth through Yoga and meditation.

True spirituality means recognizing the dharma, the underlying universal truth, and to build our life and culture around it. Just as the same physical laws, like gravity, operate for all human beings regardless of race, nationality or religion, so the same spiritual laws, like the law of karma, are in operation for everyone. These are the Dharmas that we must discover. To discover the nature of dharma, we must approach the universe with an open mind and heart, not coming with any preconceived belief or theory.

Dharma as the nature of things is the eternal constant, the Self-existent reality. No one doubts that fire burns; its very existence proclaims it. Everything in the world similarly proclaims its dharma or place in the universal order through the qualities that it demonstrates. Each person has his or her own dharma, a unique place and function in the cosmic rhythm. To know the dharma is to discover not only the unity of truth but also all the variations upon it.

Yet while we can easily perceive the nature of physical objects, like the burning quality of fire, it is difficult to perceive our mental states and their long-term consequences. We do not easily see the results of our own actions because these effects manifest only over time and sometimes not until future lives. To learn the real consequences of what we are doing, we must purify our minds and hearts by right living and meditation. Just as a person who puts his hand in a fire must suffer, though there is no intent on the part of fire to hurt anyone, so when we violate natural law, we must suffer. Greed, anger and hatred are negative forces that harm us as well as those we injure through them.

We have one basic choice in life. We can choose to be dharmic, which is to follow the laws of the universe, or we can choose to be 'adharmic', which is to try to go against them. To be religious in the true sense is to be dharmic, which is to recognise the sacred nature of all beings. Unfortunately, to be irreligious is often portrayed by organised religion as the rejection of some arbitrary dogma rather than living out of harmony with life. This view must be changed if we hope to discover what is truly real. Religion must base itself upon the pillar of natural law and immutable truth, not upon human opinion and transient convention.

The Dharma of the Human Being

As human beings we are in doubt as to our true nature. This is a simple fact that each one of us can observe. We do not know who we really are or what is our real purpose in life. We do not know what happened before we were born or what will happen after we die. We spend our time pursuing outer goals of pleasure, wealth, fame, or power. Yet none of these bring lasting happiness as we can easily observe by examining the lives of the people who have gained them. Collectively, we seek to gain power, territory, or mastery of the external world, which do not lead to real peace in society as the on-going crime and wars in the world reveals. Unlike the rest of nature, we appear not to know our place in the universe or how we can find lasting happiness.

There is a reason for this uncertainty; the true dharma of the human being is to search out and discover the universal truth. We have no fixed outer dharma, no instinctual programming like animals that we cannot deviate from, but an inner dharma to bring a higher consciousness into the world. While the nature of other creatures is evident, our human dharma must be created, must be won as it were, and requires a tremendous labour to bring forth. This is the labour of spiritual practice or sadhana in Hindu thought.

The spiritual life exists beyond the limited names and forms of objective and material existence. Dharma is not a mere name, a belief or an 'ism', but it is the indicator of the eternal truth beyond all opinions. Sanatana Dharma or the universal dharma is not a name and form based belief system. For dharmic spirituality what truly matters is what we are actually doing and thinking on a daily basis. It doesn't matter if we are called pious according to one religious authority or excommunicated by another. The real issue is whether we are introducing a greater consciousness into the world.

Whatever name or form one may look up to spiritual practices is not of ultimate significance but how it is used to approach the inner reality. If concentrating on the Divine or the universal in the form of a rock aids in preparing the mind for meditation, such a rock is a great dharma, a noble truth. On the other hand, if the idea of a Supreme Being encourages only dogmatism and sectarianism, such a deity is an obstacle to our spiritual life, not an intimation of the infinite and eternal.

Dharma and the Religions of the World

The different religions of the world cannot simply be called different Dharmas. What the world calls religions are better described as faiths or beliefs than dharma that is more a matter of knowledge and inquiry. Eastern dharmic traditions and Western monotheistic traditions cannot be simply equated, though they have points of connection. Even calling dharmic traditions religions is misleading.

The spiritual traditions that have their origins in India have always emphasised dharma. Buddhism is called 'Buddha Dharma', the law or truth taught by the Buddha or the enlightened one, the dharma of enlightenment. Jainism is called the 'Jain Dharma', the truth or teaching of the 'Jina' or the one who has conquered his own nature. Sanatana Dharma, or the Eternal Dharma, is the basis of Hinduism and explains its continuity and many-sided nature.

The great sages of Hinduism have never regarded themselves as limited to a belief. They have always looked upon themselves as followers of a universal tradition of truth. The term Sanatana Dharma can be found in Buddhist and Jain teachings as well, as this movement toward universality is part of the culture of India and the Himalayan region as a whole.

Another important term for Hinduism has been Manava Dharma—the dharma of mankind or human beings. Hindu Dharma has examined our full human potential and developed unique teachings for all types and temperaments of people and all aspects of human life. It holds that all human beings must eventually come to the realization of their true nature and provides appropriate teachings and practices in order to facilitate this.

We could say that there are two basic types of spiritual teachings in the world. The first are belief-oriented systems that emphasise sin and salvation leading to either heaven or hell. Their idea of cosmic law is something given from above by the will of God, which may at times appear to be arbitrary. The world of nature is looked upon as an outside reality, a creation of God, to be controlled or conquered, a realm of temptation, not part of our own being. Humanity is given dominion over nature, rather than finding nature to be a part of our own being.

Second, are dharmic traditions that emphasise natural law, meditation and Yoga practices leading to enlightenment or Self-realization. Dharmic traditions seek to know the truth of things and do not set forth any dogma. Indigenous and tribal religions, with their connection to natural law, have affinities with dharmic teachings as they similarly regard all life as sacred.

Yet among the mystics of all countries, who are often rejected by the orthodox, we can find a respect for life and a practice of meditation similar to dharmic traditions. Among these are Jewish and Christian mystics and Sufis that share an appreciation of unity consciousness with yogic traditions. In addition, there are mystical and occult groups outside of organised religion, like the Theosophists, which recognise the doctrine karma and rebirth that characterises dharmic traditions. New-age spiritual movements in the West that are often syncretic in nature also recognise karma and rebirth.

One could argue that dharma as universal consciousness is the real impetus behind true spirituality. Similarly, there are adharmic elements in all spiritual paths, even those of a yogic nature, as the human ego can distort and abuse any higher truth.

Relative to this concept of dharma, Hinduism as Sanatana Dharma remains generic. It is not a particular dharma but dharma as such, reflecting a concern for dharma as a whole. It is not the dharma of any single teacher, nor does it exclude any particular dharma from it. For this reason, Hinduism is not so much a particular religion but encompasses all that could be called religion and spirituality. Sanatana Dharma is an attempt to embrace all Dharmas, not to set up one against another.

Religion and Belief in One God

Religion, as generally known in the Western world is, defined rather simply, but narrowly by the formula of a belief. Religion is a belief in One God, one primary representative of him, and one book of revelation. Accepting the right belief is said to be the best of all good actions and to bring about salvation. The wrong belief is thought to be the worst of all sins and bring about condemnation or damnation. Such religions try to convert the entire world to their belief, which they view as salvation for all humanity.

While such monolithic systems can state their beliefs in clear and uncomplicated terms, they often sound like slogans or stereotypes—absolute statements that appeal to an emotional need for security but fail to deal with the real complexity of life. Can eternal truth be made into a formula, or have we narrowed it down according to a bias, which however well intentioned, falls short of what life in its abundance truly reflects?

Why should God have only one Son when all things come from the Divine and transcendent? Why should there be a final prophet when there were previous prophets, when there are innumerable gurus, and the capacity of spiritual knowledge can be found in all people? Why should there be only one final bible or religious book when any number of books on other subjects is possible? Is the 'Divine Word' so limited that it can be put into one book for all time and made sacred on a piece of paper? Can the Divine Word be reduced to human language at all? And is it salvation that we need or Self-understanding and Self-realization? Does mere belief fundamentally change our consciousness or must we learn to take our awareness beyond the mind and intellect?

A statement of exclusive absolutes is not possible for dharmic traditions like Hinduism, or even regarded as desirable. From a universal perspective such restrictions are arbitrary. They reflect not as a deep understanding of the infinite that satisfies our inner aspiration, but a mental or emotional formulation that mirrors the ego's need for certainty and control.

Only that which is absolute can be absolute. The eternal can be absolute, but to assert finality for a particular person or event in the historical realm is to try to make absolute that which is relative. This process lends itself to spiritual materialism, confusing the absolute, which is formless with particular forms in the outer world.

And why should a belief be asserted at all? Rather the dharma should be recognised. Does not the truth of things speak for itself if we are open to it? We don't have to shout to the world that the sun shines. It is an experiential fact. So too, spiritual realities should be experienced. The insistence on belief usually indicates lack of experience and can prevent people from developing a direct experience of their own.

Let us be clear: Belief is not knowledge. A belief is an assumption; at best it is a working proposition that can help us strive to find the truth. But if we take a belief as true in its own right, it becomes a preconception that clouds our vision. For example, in order to climb a mountain, I must first believe I am capable of it. But if I regard believing I can climb the mountain is the same thing as actually climbing it, then my belief is a delusion that breeds not only incapacity but unreality.

Belief in God is not the same as knowing the Divine, infinite and eternal, though it may assert what God is supposed to have said. And how can we know what someone has said if we don't know who they really are? If we ourselves do not know God or the Divine within us, how can we fulfil any Divine purpose? And how can we know any Divine reality on the outside?

To know a particular food, like grapes, we must actually eat them. It is not enough to believe in grapes or believe in another person who once ate them. Belief is no substitute for experience and by itself it cannot destroy our ignorance. The process of belief building can reinforce the ignorance of the mind that asserts its mental and emotional patterns as truth.

Any numbers of beliefs are always possible because beliefs are speculative, with no ultimate certainty. One religion has its set of beliefs, which are said to be the absolute truth. Another religion has a different set of beliefs claimed to be equally true. One religion asserts that God is only this and another proclaims that God is only something else. One religion makes a particular representative of God as final; another does the same with another figure who may have a different teaching. This process of belief building leads to division. As belief is not knowledge but emotional assertion, belief often ends up on the battlefield, not to determine which belief is true but which will dominate the world. Belief removes us from spiritual experience, which inherently takes us beyond beliefs.

Theological Ethics and Universal Ethics

Exclusivist religions erect theological standards for judging human behaviour, which may be apart from or even contrary to ethical values. They hold that if a person does not believe in a particular formulation of God, in one specific representative of him, in one book which contains his word, or other such dogmas, that the person will suffer or go to hell, however good, kind, compassionate, generous, or selfless he or she may otherwise be. This can be called 'theological ethics', judging people not by their actual behaviour but by their beliefs, which makes not accepting certain beliefs into a moral failure on par with actually committing harmful actions.

Some theologies teach that not believing in a particular saviour or prophet is a mortal sin, along with crimes like theft or murder. Theological morality unfortunately easily gets confused with universal ethics. It causes people of one belief to consider that those who do not accept their belief must be morally depraved or even subhuman in their values and actions.

Hindu Dharma cannot accept any such theological morality. It holds that we raise ourselves up in life by good actions and lower ourselves by actions that are harmful. It does not matter what we believe in but what we actually do. Hinduism says that a person, who leads a good life, even if he or she has never come into contact with any scripture and has no religious beliefs, will come to a good end. On the other hand, a person who leads a bad or harmful life will come to a bad end, even if he believes in what some regard as the true religion.

It is not going against the codes of belief, ritual or prayer of a particular church that we should be afraid of, but adharmic actions, living out of harmony with the universe and contrary to the nature of things. Regarding only one belief alone as true is contrary with the bounty of life, which includes all beings, and like the sun shines on all alike.

Theological morality divides humanity into the believers and the non-believers, the people of God and those against God, including condemning different sects within one's own religion as heretical. This division is equated with a real division in behaviour between good and evil, holy and unholy, as if only the members of a particular religion can be truly good and those of other beliefs must be evil.

Dharmic traditions differentiate human behaviour into dharmic and adharmic, actions that further the truth and those that promote ignorance and illusion. There is no division of humanity into dharmic and adharmic souls because our soul or inner nature is inherently dharmic. Our soul or inner being is our dharma. The difference is between those who know their true nature and those who do not. Knowledge or ignorance is a capacity of all human beings, and we must all strive to move from the ignorance to the knowledge.

If there is only One God or divinity, then there cannot be two humanities, the believers and the non-believers, the saved and the condemned. If reality is one, then humanity must also be one. To connect with the unity of reality, we must first recognise the unity of human beings. If we cannot recognise the unity of human beings—including our unity with those of different religious persuasions—then we cannot talk of the unity of the Divine. True unity requires recognizing the common dharma of our inner being, which is to seek the eternal, not to accept limitations under restrictive religious identities.

The Culture of the Dharma

Culture appears to be an outward thing, the changing codes and customs of different peoples, times and countries. If we look at the world, we see every sort of cultural variation in terms of language, clothes, diet, art, and religion. The spiritual path or way of Self-realization as something timeless and universal appears to be beyond culture and begins only when we set transient cultural practices aside.

However, culture has a deeper meaning that must also be considered. To be cultured implies a certain level of refinement and sensitivity beyond ordinary behavioural compulsions. The spiritual life is a type of cultivation, what in Yoga is called a sadhana or yogic practice. Culture also refers to how we live, the field created by our thoughts, feelings and actions. This is called 'Samskriti' in Sanskrit, like the term for the language itself. It refers to constant introspection and contemplation leading to an inner transformation. To reach a higher state of awareness, we must cultivate a lifestyle that supports it, with daily practices to bring consciousness into all that we do. Dharma as a way of life is a higher type of culture, a culture of consciousness, not our ordinary cultural practices that that bind us to the outer world.

Many modern gurus have tried to purify their teachings from extraneous cultural considerations like the need to have a certain type of name or wear a certain type of clothes in order to follow them. They have provided practices that can be applied irrespective of the cultural context or social background of a person. They teach universal meditation approaches that can be adopted without asking people to change the outer aspects of their life, work, appearance or even the religion that they follow. Gurus from the Hindu tradition have shared Yoga and meditation practices with people throughout the world without requiring that their followers become Hindus. This reflects the universal approach behind Sanatana Dharma.

While this non-cultural approach has its value, it does have limitations that must be considered as well. The culture we follow impacts our lives on all levels, colouring our values and perception in a way that may limit our awareness. Many people today who reject the cultural side of spiritual or yogic teachings remain immersed in materialistic or intellectual cultural patterns contrary to these. They do not take up a spiritual culture—like the study of yogic teachings, chanting, ritual and spiritual art— but continue with the popular culture of entertainment or an intellectual culture of politics, art and materialistic science. Many of us practice spiritual teachings but remain otherwise immersed in a materialistic cultural matrix. In this process, we are coming under the influence of outer cultural influences that may inhibit any inner dharmic culture from flowering.

We must recognise the nature of the culture we follow, and be clear as to its values and how these affect us. While we can apply spiritual teachings outside of cultural limitations, this does mean we can ignore the nature of the culture we are immersed in. We cannot graft spiritual teachings onto a non-spiritual culture and expect them to flourish. Nor do we need to reject the cultural side of spiritual teachings when it may be useful in enriching our lives.

Different spiritual traditions have created various cultures. India has developed a culture of Yoga and Dharma pervading the whole of life from the family and community. The culture of the Dharma is the richest of all cultures because it is based upon honouring nature and recognizing a single consciousness behind the universe. It promotes the civilization of the cosmic mind that transcends the limitations of mere human social structures. It integrates systems of physical, mental, and spiritual culture. It contains art, music, poetry, philosophy, medicine, and science as yogic paths. It provides a rich field in which all parts of our being can grow toward the light.

We should examine our own lives and discern how much of our time is spent in areas of culture that do not foster any higher consciousness within us. If we do not nourish a dharmic culture, then we may not be able to lead a dharmic life or create a dharmic society. If we are going to immerse ourselves in a culture, which to some extent we must, let it be the culture of Dharma. This may require daily Yoga practices, mantra, meditation, chanting, devotional singing, pujas, havans, satsangs and pilgrimages (yatras). It may include studying or practicing the dharmic systems of music, dance and poetry, or following an Ayurvedic lifestyle or healing discipline. Hindu Dharma provides us the resources in order to do this so that we can adapt at an individual level.

As rivers flowing to the sea discard their names and forms, so the person of spiritual knowledge, liberated from name and form enters into that celestial Being who transcends all.

Mundaka Upanishad III.2.8

That which they call Indra, Mitra, Varuna, and Agni, as also the celestial beautiful feathered eagle - That which is the One Being, the sages declare in manifold ways.

Rigveda I.164.46

He whom the Shaivites worship as Shiva, whom the Vedantins call Brahman, whom the Buddhists call Buddha, whom the Nayakas call the creator, whom the Jains call the Arhat, whom the Mimamsakas call karma, may that Vishnu, the Lord of the three worlds, grant you the object of your desire.

Stotra to Vishnu

The Divine Immortal Fire gives power to the Gods, so the Eternal Dharmas cannot be violated.

Rigveda III.3.1.

The Vast Tradition of Hindu Dharma

Hindu Dharma is the oldest, most complex and enigmatic of the world's major religions and the most different as compared to Western monotheistic traditions. Hinduism, we could say, represents the other side of religion—the ancient, imagistic, occult, mystical and yogic side that Western monotheism has tried to supplant, if not exterminate. Hinduism is the largest of the non-Abrahamic religions in the world and the third largest religion overall after Christianity and Islam, with over a billion followers. As the oldest religion in the world, through history, probably more people have been Hindus than any other religious domination.

Non-Abrahamic and pagan religions, of which Hindu Dharma is the largest representative in the world, are not simply primitive, immoral or oppressive as portrayed by their detractors. As the unknown, the other, the opposition as it were, monotheistic traditions have projected their own fears and suspicions upon the pagan traditions followed by their own ancestors and borrowed heavily by them for their languages, culture and sciences. Western religions have similarly judged Hinduism according to the limited perception caused by their beliefs, which like a set terminology, condition us to a particular point of view.

Dharmic traditions are open, creative and meditative in approach, an attitude often shared by Western pagan religions and philosophies, notably the Greeks or the Celts. Such experiential traditions have a tremendous appeal to the inquiring spirit, with their insight into deeper levels of consciousness. They possess a long history of tolerance and respect for other views, a necessary attitude in the multicultural world order in which we live today. Hinduism, as Sanatana Dharma, has always been able to accommodate many different religious and spiritual approaches. From its standpoint, spiritual teachings are not absolutes but working models and guides to practice, which must eventually be left behind once we reach the goal of direct realization.

Hindu Dharma abounds with every possible name and form for truth or the Divine. This is because Hinduism requires that we see the same reality in all the diversity of life—that we see the same Self in all beings. It is not because Hinduism is trapped in differences of name and form but because its sense of unity is inclusive of all possible variations. Hinduism is not limited even to its own names and forms, however diverse. It can accommodate the names and forms of other cultures into a comprehensive view of the Divine that accepts all that is true in human aspiration to transcendence. It allows the teaching of Hinduism to encompass forms of knowledge, and affords it a characteristic tolerance and syncretic view of life.

The Western mind, used to historically based monotheistic creeds, tends to reduce religion to distinct names and forms. It tries to compartmentalise Hinduism into a religion the way Christianity and Islam have been designed, seeking to find in all religions a particularised belief system and its personal and historical application. Looking for such a code of beliefs, many people regard the diversity and freedom of Hinduism as confusion, contradiction, or showing a lack of any real identity. They take it to mean there is no defined tradition of Hinduism as such but just a collection of unrelated cults. Yet this seeming chaos of Hindu Dharma reflects the broad field of a universal tradition that is ever adaptable.

Sanatana Dharma as an open tradition does not exclude any useful way of approaching the truth of the vast universe in which we live. It does not define itself against something else but includes all that is helpful to the spiritual life. Yet this does not mean that Hinduism can accept all other religions however they formulate themselves to be. This is not possible because exclusive systems that insist their point of view alone is correct are mutually contradictory. In accepting the value of all sincere approaches to the Divine or universal, Hindu Dharma cannot sanction the exclusivism of any particular group. Hindus may honour the good work that Christians may do, for example, but this does not mean that Hinduism accepts the Christian claim that Jesus is the only Son of God.

The Name Hinduism

It is a great irony that Hinduism—the main religion in the world that defines itself as a universal tradition—has come to be viewed as a narrow ethnic belief system. Perhaps the main factor that causes us to misunderstand Hinduism is that Hinduism is originally a religion without a name, a religion in fact beyond names.

The name Hinduism suggests a belief limited to a certain geographical region, ethnic group or nation—the religion of the people who inhabit the Indian subcontinent, who were colonially regarded as a primitive dark-skinned racial type. This is a misconception that reflects little knowledge of Hinduism or of India and its inhabitants. It would be like calling Islam 'the religion of the Arabs', or Christianity 'the Greek religion', which were terms historically used for these religions when they were more circumscribed in the regions that followed them.

India is not a small and homogeneous country like France, Germany or Great Britain, but a subcontinent like Europe. In fact, India contains more different ethnic groups and languages than that of Europe as a whole. Modern India has fourteen official state languages that have a variety of scripts. The Punjabis of North India and the Tamils of the South are as distinct people as the Swedes of Northern Europe are from the Greeks of Southern Europe. Yet India has maintained a cultural and even political unity better than Europe, largely because of its common Hindu and dharmic culture.

Hindus come from a number of ethnic groups within India. The people of Nepal, though a Mongolian type like the Tibetan and Chinese, are predominately Hindus. The tribal groups of India, which include those of an Austroasiatic language family, are predominately Hindus. Hinduism remains in the island of Bali in Indonesia, where it once predominated, and has left an important imprint upon the culture of the region. Hinduism once dominated Indochina where the massive Angkor Wat temple complex abounds with Hindu temples. Vietnam was a Hindu country up until the seventeenth century. Hinduism dominated Afghanistan till the tenth century. A Hindu influence existed in Persia, Central Asia and the Middle East.

The Term Hinduism and India

The name Hinduism goes back to ancient times. The Sanskrit name of the Indus River, Sindhu, gave rise to the terms Hindu, Indus and India.

In the Vedic age India was called Sapta Sindhu, the land of the seven rivers. The same name appears in the *Zend Avesta*, the holy book of the ancient Persians, as Hapta Hindu, with the Sanskrit 's' replaced with an 'h', a sound shift that occurs in various Indian dialects as well. The Greeks called the land India or Indika, which also derives from the term Sindhu, removing the initial sound altogether. So clearly, Sindhu or Hindu has been a name for India going back to very ancient times. India was Sindhu Sthana, the land of the rivers or Sapta Sindhu Sthana, the land of the seven rivers, which later became Hindustan.

Sindhu has three meanings in Sanskrit. First, it means a particular river called the Indus, second, a river in general or third, the ocean. Clearly, Sindhu in the land of Sapta Sindhu refers to river in general and not simply to the Indus as a particular stream. It meant India as a vast land of many extensive river systems. The main river in Vedic India, was the Sarasvati River and in later times the Ganga. So Sindhu Sthana is also Sarasvati Sthana and later Ganga Sthana, not simply the region of the Indus.

Hindu Dharma, Sindhu Dharma or Hinduism is the name of the culture and religions of this great and diverse subcontinent. Hinduism as Sindhu Dharma has three meanings following the meanings of Sindhu.

1) It is the river religion (Sindhu Dharma). It flows and develops like a river. Not limited by an historical revelation, Hinduism continues to grow and develop through time without losing track of its origins in the eternal.

2) It is a religion of many rivers and streams, a pluralistic tradition that accepts the existence of many paths, many sages and many holy books and is always open to more.

3) Sindhu means the ocean. Hinduism is a religion like the ocean that can accept all streams without overflowing. This is also the meaning of Hinduism as Sanatana Dharma or the universal tradition.

Hinduism is thus originally a geographical term. *Yet even this idea of the land of the seven rivers has a mystical meaning relative to the seven planes or lokas of the cosmic existence from gross matter to pure Being.* The Vedic Sarasvati River is also lauded as the cosmic river with forms on Earth, in the atmosphere and in Heaven.

Sindhu became Hindu not only among the Persians but also in some dialects in India, particularly in the West of the country. By the twelfth century, in the poem Prithviraj Raso by the poet Chand Baradai, probably the oldest work in the Hindi language, we already find the term Hindu proudly used in India for the religion and people of the region.

Vedic Dharma is also called *Manava Dharma*, or the Dharma of all humanity. It teaches all human beings how to develop health, happiness, creativity and liberation. It is not simply a tradition of the Brahmins, which gave rise to the distorted colonial term Brahmanism for Vedic Hinduism. The Vedas not only laud great rishis but also great kings and emperors, merchants, along with the people and the country overall.

The term Hindu is not found in the classical texts of Hinduism, in the Vedas, Upanishads, Bhagavad Gita, or classical books on Yoga, the recognition of a single and continuous tradition is clearly there. What came later to be called Hinduism defines itself as Dharma, or more specifically as Sanatana Dharma. As Sanatana Dharma or the universal tradition, Hinduism does not need to represent itself as one religious identity as opposed to others. If we live in the ocean, for example, do we have to give water a name? Hinduism has never separated itself off from the universal truth and formulated itself as one point of view regarded as exclusively true. *While the convenience of modern language may require that we use the term Hinduism to identify this great tradition in the world today, let us not forget its vaster implications.*

Sanatana Dharma and the Movement of Time

From the eternal vision of Sanatana Dharma, history is not a linear progression but a cyclical process, a spiral indicated by the lotus that is the most enduring symbol of Hinduism. We are ever moving around the great centre of truth that resides within us as our true Self or Atman. While we may divide people by separate identities, religious or otherwise, we are only fragmenting our own deeper unity with all. While we may place human beings on a progressive time line leading to heaven or utopia, we are only removing ourselves from the eternal present, in which alone is liberation.

The timeless view of Sanatana Dharma affords two aspects to its teachings:

1) First, the same foundational eternal teaching of cosmic knowledge and Self-realization prevails throughout all its diverse layers, like a single thread on which many gems are woven.

2) Second, and complementary to this, the teaching is reformulated anew with every generation relative to the needs, capacities and temperaments of time, place and person.

The teachings of Sanatana Dharma in this way are both eternal and ever new. This is its two-fold beauty. It abides in timeless reality.

This means that the Hindu tradition is not only the oldest of the world's religion; it is also the newest. On one hand, having no founder, it goes back to beginning-less time. On the other hand, being recast by living sages in every generation, Hindu Dharma is always adjusted to the present moment. The Hindu religion provides not only the oldest teachings in the world but living exponents of it in every age, great gurus who have realised the Divine Self. Sanatana Dharma teaches us that we are all the same Divine Being and that we must realise it within our own lives. It is a religion that is coterminous with life itself.

Seeing no final goal within the realm of time, Hinduism is thought by some to stand outside of the progressive movement of history, or to oppose it. However, being oriented in the eternal, Hinduism sees the final goal as present within each moment of time. It is not bound to a history that makes us look to the future, but teaches that the eternal itself pervades all the waves of time.

A New Look at Hindu Dharma

There is not much good literature available in Western languages on Hinduism that explain its true meaning as Sanatana Dharma. Most of the existing literature attempts to fit Hinduism into the mould of Western religions, which it does not resemble. Those who do this criticise Hinduism for not living up to a standard it never had, expecting Hinduism to also have a clearly defined dogma of One God, one representative of Him, and one book. While there is a significant amount of literature on the different branches of Hinduism like Yoga, Vedanta, Vaishnavism or Shaivism, there is little that explains their position within the greater Hindu tradition.

Hindus, with an open and inclusive view, have seldom found it necessary to define what Hindu Dharma is as opposed to different religions. For many Hindus, Hinduism as a universal tradition includes everyone except those who wilfully exclude themselves from it. Some Hindus do not even like to be called Hindus because they think the name detracts from the universality of their tradition.

Academic views of Hinduism focus on particular aspects of this broad tradition and seldom address it as a whole. They rarely discuss the idea of Sanatana Dharma and they seldom comprehend its true scope. Few books have attempted to define what all Hindus have in common. Hinduism, like its motherland, India, is like a tropical jungle, extending up to the highest mountains in the world, which no simplistic view can adequately characterise.

Most of the studies of Hinduism available remain limited and unreliable. They fail to see the unity of the tradition and merely examine formal differences between different Hindu sects or practices, often placing one teaching in conflict with another. Instead of looking for the common thread, they try to divide off Veda and Tantra, or Vedanta and Yoga, often on what are little more than semantic grounds. These are largely exercises in the discriminating intellect of academicians who miss the real truth of the teaching. Another vision is required, not merely for better understanding Hinduism but for understanding our own reality, which is what Sanatana Dharma is all about.

Hinduism and Organised Religion

Hinduism is not an organised religion such as the West ordinarily considers one to be. There is no dominant Hindu church, no Hindu Pope, no Hindu Rome, Jerusalem or Mecca that all Hindus should go to or bow towards. There is no Hindu messiah or prophet all Hindus must revere and no one Hindu Bible all Hindus must read. Hinduism has no single type of worship or no prescribed mass, ritual or call to prayer that everyone must do. The different sects within Hinduism have their different ashrams, temples, leaders, holy places, festivals and holy books. Many of these are common but there is no one set for all.

Hinduism does not rest upon external organization but on internal freedom. It has never structured itself along monolithic lines, with a set dogma and specific canon of beliefs. It has remained decentralised and localised, which is perhaps why of all the ancient mystical traditions, it alone has survived throughout the ages. Hinduism as an open tradition is relevant to all who are looking for a religion with a wide diversity of teachings that does not require an exclusive belief. Hinduism is the religion of the individual and allows each person to choose his or her own approach to Divinity.

However, Hinduism is probably the best organised of all religions in that it contains systematic teachings for all temperaments of people and all stages and aspects of life. As

Sanatana Dharma, it has teachings that encompass all of human life and culture including medicine and science, art and music, occultism, spirituality and Yoga. In this regard, Hinduism has probably the most extensive, best-organised and complete teachings and literature of any religion, addressing all aspects and levels of our existence, including those considered to be outside the domain of religion. The literature of Hinduism is older and larger than that of any other religion, and much more extensive. Unfortunately, most of it has not been translated or understood properly, and much of it has not been examined at all.

Some people have wondered if Hinduism is a religion at all. They state that its very absence of organization and its non-seeking of converts disqualifies it from being a religion in the common sense of the word—that it fails to have a worldview and is a purely local phenomenon. They would reduce Hinduism to a collection of local cults from the Indian subcontinent, holding on to every sort of primitive ritual and superstition that has long been discarded in the Western world.

On the other hand, Hinduism contains many of the world's most profound spiritual philosophies, like Vedanta, which have inspired great Western thinkers, including a number of important modern physicists. These are certainly not haphazard in their formulation or the product of local folk cults. They reflect the greatest minds of humanity and a state of spiritual realization rarely achieved in the Western world and not yet understood by it.

Hinduism accepts the validity of all aspects of human spiritual aspiration, from the use of simple images to formless meditational approaches. Those who judge it by one side only reveal their own lack of comprehension. Hinduism is a multidimensional tradition that no form of linear thinking, whether scientific or theological can grasp.

Certainly Hinduism stretches our limit of the idea of religion. Yet the very things that make Hinduism different from organised creeds provides it with perhaps a greater claim to be a religion in the true sense of the word, a teaching that helps us to unite with truth or the Divine. Though Hinduism is not a religion as a convenient and exclusive set of dogmas, it is a monumental spiritual tradition that addresses all the prime issues of life and death, God and immortality. Hinduism contains a comprehensive set of insights, principles and practices that reveal the highest truths of Self and cosmic knowledge. It provides specific and well-developed methodologies or paths of Yoga to enable us to perceive this truth in our own consciousness.

Hindu Dharma has its characteristic spirit, universality and yogic view, which affords it its own identity among spiritual traditions, and provides it its own authoritative voice. This goes back to the most ancient Vedic texts and their ability to identify any name or form of the Divine with all others, as when the Vedas proclaim that the sacred fire, Agni, includes within itself all the Divine powers as the very essence of light. Hinduism is a vibrant ocean of spiritual, religious, artistic, philosophical and cosmological insights and practices, woven into a vast culture that includes the entire world of nature. It has the complexity of life itself, which cannot be reduced to a formula, understood in a single book, or controlled by any organization.

The Religions and Sects of Hinduism

There is perhaps a greater diversity of religious teachings and practices inside of Hinduism than outside of it. The different religions of the world do not contain any more extensive variety of forms and practices than what occurs among the different sects of Hinduism. We could say that as Sanatana Dharma or a universal approach, Hinduism is a collection of religions rather than a particularised religion as it is commonly understood. However, these different sects within Hinduism are integrated into a greater universal truth, not haphazardly thrown together. Each of the main sects of Hinduism can be viewed as a religion in its own right. Several sects of Hinduism, like the Shaivite and Vaishnava, have a longer tradition and a more extensive literature than the predominant Western religions. Yet all of these direct us to a common goal of higher consciousness and accept the law of karma.

Whatever can be found in any religion by way of forms of worship, including rituals, prayers, yogic practices and meditations of all kinds, or view of reality, including monotheism, pantheism, polytheism, agnosticism, atheism and monism can be found in Hinduism. Hindu Dharma respects each according to its place in human development and none is allowed to serve as the last word for all people. This is not to say that all views and practices are regarded as equal or the same—generally meditation is the highest practice and Self-realization the highest goal—but each practice is given its appropriate place and the freedom of inquiry is honoured.

One Christian fundamentalist group has said that there are only two religions in the world, Hinduism, which absorbs everything, and Christianity, which excludes everything. One can be a Hindu and practice whatever spiritual teachings one finds beneficial, whether they arise from the Hindu tradition or outside of it. Hinduism defines itself as a pursuit of truth, not the insistence upon a particular belief. Another of its names is the 'religion of truth'—Satya Dharma. It says that truth alone wins, not untruth. One does not cease to be a true Hindu by pursuing truth in different forms but only by ceasing to pursue truth and instead promoting dogma.

India, the Land of Dharma and Yogic Spirituality

The universal spirit of Hinduism is manifest in India, which probably contains more different religions than all the rest of the world put together. All the main religions of the world are present in India as in no other country. Besides the many branches of Hinduism, India contains the Sikhs, Jains and Buddhists, who originated in the country. India has also become the land of refuge for many religious groups. It contains Parsees, representatives of the ancient Zoroastrian religion of Persia, which itself is similar in language and deities to the ancient Vedic religion of India. There is an ancient Jewish tradition in India going back to pre-Christian eras, and a Syrian Christian tradition going back to the fourth century.

Surprisingly, there is a greater diversity of Islamic groups in India than in any Islamic country in the world, which includes Sunnis, Shias, Ahmadiyya, Ismaelis, Bohris, and Sufis, a number of which, as unorthodox Muslims, are banned in orthodox Islamic countries like Saudi Arabia and Pakistan. The largest Bahai temple in the world is in Delhi and the Theosophists have perhaps their largest following in India. The acceptance of such diversity is explicable only through the open tradition of Hinduism, as non-Hindu countries do not have such diversity of groups.

The Worldview of Hindu Dharma

The Vedantic worldview, which is the main philosophy behind Hinduism, rests upon an ultimate and impersonal reality or Brahman, and sees the world as a manifestation of Brahman, not as a separate reality. It states that Brahman is the supreme truth. For this view, Hinduism is sometimes accused of rejecting the world, denying life, and not giving proper importance to the individual, while religions that fail to recognise such a transcendent reality are considered progressive because they rest upon a personal and historical concept of the Divine and try to convert all people to their beliefs.

Yet Hinduism does not reject the reality of the outer world, only the idea that it exists apart from universal consciousness. Hinduism abounds with reverence for the Divine in all the forms of life and all aspects of nature, including animals, plants, rivers and mountains. It honours all aspects of the personal worship of the Divine with forms of the Divine Father, Mother, Lover, Friend, and Lord. Moreover, it says that the individual is God (*aham Brahmasmi, ayam Atma Brahma*). It emphasises on the full realization of the 'Universal Being'—that is our true nature.

These two most salient features of Sanatana Dharma—seeing of the Divine in innumerable forms and recognizing the Divine reality that transcends all forms and actions—are not contradictory but two sides of the same vision which not only recognises the 'absolute' but finds it reverberating in all existence. Those who see Hinduism as either caught in the formless or confused in the diversity of forms only reveal their inability to understand the wide scope of its teaching. How can the same teaching be criticised in such opposite ways? It is like criticising a person for being both too impersonal and too personal at the same time.

Owing to its orientation to the eternal and rejection of mundane goals as final (including heaven, which as another world is also a mundane goal), Hinduism is sometimes said to be pessimistic or anti-life by its detractors. They emphasise the image of Hindu ascetics mortifying themselves, closing their senses, fasting and weakening their bodies. This is another misinformed judgement. Hindu Dharma teaches that we are all God and we contain all time and space within ourselves—that our very nature is infinite bliss or 'Ananda' inherently transcending all sorrow and limitation.

To call a teaching that says that our nature is infinite bliss as pessimistic, while religions that teach we are born sinners or materialistic science that teaches we are only biochemical reactions, optimistic, is absurd. Hindu Dharma teaches that all life arises from joy or Ananda and that we will all eventually return to eternal joy, however many mistakes we may make along the way. Religions that teach damnation or an eternal hell are the real pessimists, and those that teach an eternal heaven that still depends upon a body (which can never be eternal) are also pessimistic. Those who limit our being to this transient life are perhaps the worst pessimists of all.

Universality in Religion and Conversion

Hinduism is often criticised as not being a universal religion because it does not proselytise or aggressively seek converts like Christianity and Islam often do. Its very universal view that honours the Divine in all prevents it from becoming a religion seeking world domination. From its point of view, the organised seeking of converts to an exclusive belief is a sin against the Divine in others, a kind of salesmanship, which fails to recognise the Divine presence inherent in everyone. However, Hinduism shares its teachings with all those who are receptive. Its concern is with communicating the essence of truth not merely getting people to change religious labels. It regards truth as something we should search inside ourselves, not try to impose on others as if it were an external thing.

Religious proselytizing is actually the denial of universality and an assertion of partiality. If truth is universal who are we going to convert and to what belief? Hinduism emphasises recognizing the Self-existent truth. We cannot be converted to truth but only to a belief, which is limited. A universal teaching does not need to run after converts because it recognises that we are always part of universal reality. No one can be excluded from it, though we may try to live apart from it.

From the Hindu standpoint, attempts at religious conversion are implicit forms of violence, first at a psychological level of harming the feelings of others, but often outwardly as well, harming them at a physical or material level. They attempt to impose an external belief or code upon a person, not to help them understand their inherent nature. They do not serve to awaken the Divine Self in people but to subordinate them to an institution or dogma instead. This violates the principle of ahimsa, or non-violence and reflects a lack of understanding of the deeper consciousness in all creatures. A truly aware individual honours the Divine in others, rather than trying to impose his or her own belief upon them, which is to insult the sacred nature of the person.

Hinduism has not sought to convert the world by preachers or by armies. It grows organically among people as part of a spiritual culture and way of life that affirms the inner truth over outer appearances. Wherever Hinduism has gone, it has preserved the indigenous cultures of the people. It has sought to promote nature and the Self everywhere, to help all beings develop their highest potential. It is concerned with a genuine spiritual development, not merely with a change of names or clothes.

Formally Becoming a Hindu

Yet it is wrong to think that people cannot formally become Hindus, regardless of their land of birth. This begins with a special preparation, including study, meditation, and following a particular lifestyle and ethical discipline. It is usually not given instantaneously or overnight. Once these preliminaries are fulfilled a simple ceremony called 'Shuddhi' is performed which makes one into a Hindu. There are a number of groups who do this, like Vishwa Hindu Parishad, Arya Samaj or Hinduism Today.

Shuddhi means purification, not conversion. According to Hindu Dharma we cannot be converted to anything, just as we cannot change our nature. Becoming a Hindu is not a question of becoming converted from one identity to another but of acknowledging what our real identity has always been. To become a Hindu all that we need to do is purify our minds and hearts, so that we can recognise our eternal being. This is not to assume a new identity but to discover the Divine within us. Such conversion does not require denying any truth. It only requires giving up exclusive beliefs that cloud our perception.

Today Hindu gurus travel all over the world to share their knowledge with disciples from all countries. Many Westerners practice Yoga and meditation, chant Om and other Hindu mantras, and visit sacred sites in India but have not had to become Hindus in order to do so. This is because Hindu teachers see more value in sharing spiritual practices than in getting people to assume different identities.

However, by formally becoming a Hindu one does have the additional advantage of a stronger connection to this vast and profound tradition that can make its teachings and practices more efficacious. One embraces the greater Sanatana Dharma, rather than just one branch of it, and the inner connection to innumerable rishis and yogis can become our own heritage, lineage and family, drawing us to the cosmic mind and the highest Self-realization.

Universality in Religion and Monotheism

Western religious thinkers generally identify universality in religion with monotheism—the idea that there is only One God—and hold that all truly religious people should worship this same Supreme Being. However, this insistence on monotheism is exclusive, not universal. It may claim that God is one but does not accept any diversity of religion or spirituality. It rejects polytheism, pantheism, monism (the idea that there is only One Reality), and other forms of spiritual experience that are common to many human beings and cultures. Exclusive monotheism reduces the Divine to a single formulation, insisting on one saviour, one final prophet or one book. Such a One God is not a truth of unity, which is universal, but the assertion of a single belief, which is opposed to all else. True unity is universality; it is not one thing as opposed to another, but the One that is all.

The partiality inherent in exclusive monotheism is revealed by how it tends to denigrate other views. It fragments itself further into warring creeds, with different monotheists fighting with each other as to whose One God, or view of the One God, is correct. Such extreme monotheism is often a religion of warlike people. It promotes conquests and aims at the building up of empires. The religion of One God becomes reflected in one state and one leader, and the denial of dissent. Not surprisingly, Western monotheism has appeared historically as the religious counterpart of political imperialism. History has revealed how monotheism has been allied with invasions, colonialism and genocide, which may be the unfortunate end result of a rigid, one-sided and ultimately violent view of the Divine.

The One God can become an abstraction to which actual people are sacrificed. He can become jealous and wrathful and encourage intolerant attitudes among his followers. He is portrayed as opposed to individual inquiry and experiential spirituality and insists upon his law, ritual and theology as the unquestioned truth. While this may not be the intention of the mystics in these traditions, it has often become the behaviour of literal-minded followers. Such monolithic views are out of harmony with the cultural diversity of the modern world and represent a medieval and authoritarian standard.

Hinduism, on the other hand, contains the diversity needed for a global age. Following a pluralistic view of truth, Hinduism as Sanatana Dharma cannot be limited to belief in One God, though it does acknowledges theism as an important approach to the spiritual life. Hinduism is a theistic religion but not exclusively so and has created a number of theistic approaches. While accepting theism as one major aspect, some Hindu groups do not regard it as the highest. Many Hindu teachings regard monism, or the idea that there is only One Truth, as the highest truth, transcending any theistic view or personal God.

Hinduism recognises the 'Divine' in many names and forms— as possessing both unity and multiplicity, and as both personal and impersonal. It does not see any ultimate contradiction between Divine as One and as many. It honours the many as various appearances or manifestations of the One, which is not one in the sense of one thing opposed to others but a unity that includes diversity without being limited by it.

Hindu forms of theism exist in abundance. There are Shaivite and Vaishnava forms of theism with the Supreme Divine called Shiva or Vishnu. But Hindu theism is different from Western monotheism and much richer in its forms. It contains a theism of the Divine Mother, with the Goddess as the One Deity that is the creator, preserver and transformer of all. Hindu theism is a yogic path that emphasises devotion to the deity and personal communion with it through meditation and samadhi. It is not a monolithic belief system but an experiential theism of the Divine Beloved.

Hinduism is noted for the complexity of its views of reality, which seem bewildering for a mind trained to think that there is only One God. Its many names and forms for the Divine, its numerous great teachers from the most ancient times to the present generation, and its many paths of Yoga encompassing all human temperaments—is difficult even for a broad mind to comprehend. While other religions seem to have a single strand, Hinduism appears like the tail of peacock.

Great Teachers of Hindu Dharma

Hindu Dharma recognises many great spiritual teachers, sages, seers, incarnations, yogis and siddhas throughout the millennia. There are several figures—like Krishna and Rama, the avatars of Vishnu, or Shankaracharya, the great teacher of Advaita Vedanta— who are particularly important but none that dominate Hinduism so much as the figure of Christ, Mohammed or Buddha dominate their religions. Each region of India has its important Hindu saints and sages of recent centuries like Tulsidas and Kabir in the north, Narsi Mehta and Mira Bai in Gujarat, Guru Nanak for Sind and Punjab, Jnaneshvar and Tukaram for Maharashtra, and so on.

Hinduism has many new sects, and does not limit itself to the teachers of the past. The Swaminarayan movement starting in Gujarat in the late eighteenth century, the Ramakrishna-Vivekananda movement starting in Bengal in the late nineteenth century, the Arya Samaj movement founded by Swami Dayananda Sarasvati in North India in the mid-nineteenth century, are only a few of such groups that now have wide followings of their own. Overseas, Hindu groups are also emerging, like the Hinduism Today magazine and its mainly Western devotees, a phenomenon that is bound to increase dramatically in coming years.

Many modern Hindu teachers have become known in the modern world like Ramakrishna, Vivekananda, Yogananda, Aurobindo, Ramana Maharshi, Anandamayi Ma, Mata Amritanandamayi, Sai Baba and Shivananda. Yet they are not known as mere propagators of a mere religious belief but as world teachers, proponents of Yoga, meditation, and universal spiritual principles. Such great gurus see themselves as part of a universal tradition, not the proponents of one particular religion against others. This is no accident. It is part of the universal formulation of Hindu Dharma that is not closed along particular lines.

Liberation of Consciousness: The Supreme Goal of Life

Hindu Dharma wisely holds that freedom or liberation of consciousness is the true goal of life. True freedom is freedom from all external conditioning influences, whether of body or mind. This is the freedom of Self-realization, complete independence from time, space and karma. We are all seeking freedom. No one is happy with boundaries or limitations. No one wants to live in a small and cramped room, or have no space in which to move.

Unfortunately, we normally seek freedom in the outer world, through possessions, power or pleasure, which are all ultimately forms of bondage and limitation. Hindu Dharma teaches that we need to redirect this seeking of freedom within, where alone it can be truly realised. True freedom is not the ability to have more things or gain more experiences but inner fullness which no longer requires such external supports for our happiness. A universal tradition emphasises freedom, which includes freedom from religious domination as well as spiritual, as a means of gaining freedom. If we remain limited to a church, book or saviour our religion has failed us, or we have failed our religion.

Hindus have great freedom in their spiritual life. They have any number of holy books to choose from and are not required to literally believe in any one of them. They have any number of avatars and gurus to choose from, and aren't required to follow any of them exclusively. They have their sacred sites everywhere that they live. Their spiritual practices are done in their own homes on a daily basis and require no church.

In the modern world, we pride ourselves in our freedom of choice. We can choose where to travel, where to work, what to read, and so on, but in religion we still have little choice. We may be able to choose what church to join, but how much freedom do we have to choose our relationship with God? If we want to worship the Divine as Mother, what choice do we have in Christianity, for example? We can worship Mary as the mother of Jesus but she can never be at par with him. And how many churches teach us to contact the Divine within ourselves as our own true being, all names, forms and institutions aside?

As part of Sanatana Dharma, Hindus are not restricted from respecting truth wherever and in whomever they see it. Hinduism does not have any word like heretic, pagan or kafir. Hindus have never invaded any country and tried to force people to adapt their religion, nor do Hindus ever condemn anyone to damnation. Hinduism does not require that we all have the same view of Divinity but encourages unique and diverse views for the full unfoldment of our creative intelligence. Hindu Dharma teaches that there each person is unique and has a special connection with the Divine, and that there should be no standardised religion for everyone.

Hindus are not required to agree with one another on religious matters but are encouraged to follow their own insights. If two Hindus do not follow the same guru, worship the Divine in the same form, or study the same scripture, it is not a problem. They will not fight with or try to convert the other person. They respect their diversity as part of the great abundance of life.

Hinduism has developed an unparalleled freedom in the religious and spiritual realm, as Western culture has done in the scientific and material realm. It would be of great benefit to humanity to combine these two forms of freedom. To the Hindu, the spiritual realm is an inner universe to be explored, not merely a dogma to believe in and stop one's search. Hinduism provides the tools of Yoga and meditation so that we can make this exploration for ourselves and discover the truth within us.

On the other shore of the waters, in the centre of the Earth, on the ridge of Heaven, greater than the great, by luminous seed having entered into the lights of the senses, the Lord of Creation stirs within the child.
Mahanarayana Upanishad I.1

There is only One Divinity hidden in all beings, who pervades all, the Self of all beings. He is the overseer of all actions, who dwells in all beings, the witness, the sole consciousness beyond all attributes.
Svetasvatara Upanishad VI.11

The Self is the Divinity that exists in all directions, born in the beginning, he moves within the child. He alone has been born and he alone will be born. He faces all creatures whose face is to every side.
Svetasvatara Upanishad II.16

Who One only like a magician rules all the worlds with his ruling powers, who One only exists in the arising and birth of all beings: those who know Him become immortal.
Svetasvatara Upanishad III.1

Hindu Dharma and the Religions of the World

As a tradition that honours all spiritual aspiration and higher knowledge, Hindu Dharma has room for numerous views and practices regardless of the time or location of their origin. Yet it does evaluate spiritual teachings relative to the ultimate goal of Self-realization, in which alone is true liberation.

Hindu Dharma recognises that much of spiritual aspiration will always remain unknown, undefined, and outside of any institutionalised structure. It values individual spiritual experience over formal religious doctrine. Wherever the universal truth is manifest, there is Sanatana Dharma, whether it is in a field of religion, art or science, or in the life of a person or community, regardless of the time, place or circumstances. Wherever the universal truth is not recognised, or where it is scaled down and limited to a particular group, book or person—even if done in the name of God—there Sanatana Dharma ceases to function, whatever the activity may be.

The Religions of India

India has been a great land of spirituality and mysticism since time immemorial. It is not merely a nation in the modern sense of the word but a land, a formation of Mother Earth into a cosmic culture, held together not by a force of arms but by a common spiritual aspiration. The great beings of this land have focused on the development of higher consciousness as their primary pursuit, giving economic development, intellectual pursuits and religious ritual—the primary goals of other cultures—a secondary role. Because of the emphasis on spiritual experience in all its forms, India has promoted the idea of a universal tradition and has given birth to the greatest number of religions and the widest diversity of spiritual teachings and yogic practices in the world.

Hinduism itself is not a single religious belief, but a harmony of different spiritual teachings that have maintained a peaceful coexistence with one another as integral parts of a universal tradition, encompassing the whole of life. Hindu Dharma has not moulded or forced these different teachings into uniformity. It has nurtured their diversity through a respect for all paths to the Divine. It has allowed many different sects to come into being, expressing various approaches to the inner truth.

One could divide Hindu Dharma into a Vedic religion, a Shaiva (Shiva) religion, a Vaishnava (Vishnu) religion, a Goddess (Shakta) religion, a Ganesha religion, a solar (Saura) religion, and various local or regional systems, including new spiritual movements that have no defined affiliation. These different teachings have neither merged into one common belief, nor separated off into conflicting creeds. They have come together while maintaining their particular approaches, in the recognition that true unity includes the fullness of diversity. They have realised that the truth of any religion need not exclude the truth of others because all religions are merely aids to the unfolding of the universe, which is the real goal and origin of all. This harmony between the different sects of Hinduism can be used as a model to integrate the different religions of the world. It would not require any religion giving up its distinctive spiritual flavour but only recognizing the validity of other approaches to the spiritual life.

Hinduism's Spread through History

Hinduism is often erroneously looked at as restricted to the subcontinent of India. However, historically Hinduism has been practiced in many parts of the world, and teachings of similar nature to Hindu Dharma have flourished everywhere. Hinduism has never formulated itself as restricted to a particular geographical region but as relevant to all humanity. Nor has it frozen itself in time. It has continued to grow and absorb additional spiritual and cultural impulses into itself, developing in an organic way.

Hinduism has spread in three main waves through history. The first occurred during ancient history and prehistory. It is difficult to define owing to its tremendous antiquity but is clearly evidenced by the common languages, culture and spiritual traditions found from Bengal to Ireland among people speaking Indo-European languages. Regions of this ancient Indo-European culture consisted of Eastern and Western Europe (including Greece, Rome, the ancient Germans, Celts, Thracians and Slavs), Anatolia (Modern Turkey, until the Turkish invasions of the Middle Ages, with Hittites and Greeks), Syria (the Mittani era, second millennium BC), Iraq (the Kassite Era of the second millennium BC), Armenia, Persia, Afghanistan, Central Asia (Scythians), Western China (the

Tarim Basin and Tocharians), and North India (to the Krishna river). Even South India, though its Dravidian languages do not have any simple affinity to the Sanskritic, retains a common Hindu culture with North India going back as far as any historical records exist.

In addition, similar practices to the Hindu can be found in many ancient cultures, including the Egyptians, Babylonians, Sumerians, Chinese and Native Americans (Mayas) with their common solar religions, fire offerings, and threefold social system of priests, warriors and common people. This early phase of Hinduism or Vedic culture existed from perhaps as early as 8000 BCE lingering to as late as 500 BCE. It was the early ancient phase of Hinduism, evidenced by the Vedas, the oldest books in the world, but even looks to times before the current Vedic compilation was made.

The second phase involved the spread of Indian civilization, including a diversification of Sanatana Dharma, with the development of religions, philosophies, yogic, monastic and spiritual movements through Hinduism, Buddhism and Jainism. Its main movement was to the East with Buddhism spreading to Tibet, China, Korea and Japan, and both Hinduism and Buddhism spreading to Burma, Thailand, Indochina, Indonesia, to Borneo and the Philippines. At the same time, there was a secondary spread of dharmic teachings to the West into Central Asia, which was predominately Buddhist but had Hindu elements as well, as among the Kushanas. Another diffusion occurred to Persia and Europe, mainly through various mystical movements, like the Manichean and Zoroastrian, but moves of trade as well.

This was the classical age of Hindu-Buddhist culture, which came to dominate Asia for many centuries and through it the majority of people in the world. It began before 500 BCE, overlapping with the first wave of Hindu-Vedic influence. It started to decline with the Islamic invasions of India around 700 AD and came to an end around 1500 AD with the Islamic domination of India and Indonesia, that caused the Hindu religion to contract in order to preserve itself and which largely eliminated Buddhism from India as it did from Central Asia.

The third wave of Hinduism is beginning today as part of one of the most important spiritual movements of modern times, the expansion of dharmic teachings throughout the modern world. It also shows a combination of Hinduism and Buddhism, as well as aspects of Taoism or all the main Himalayan traditions. This phase began slowly with the dissemination of Hindu teachings to the West through the eighteenth and nineteenth centuries. Vedantic influences reached many Western thinkers including Goethe, Schopenhauer, Emerson and Thoreau, mainly through translations of the Upanishads and Bhagavad Gita.

This new phase manifested in earnest with Swami Vivekananda's first trip to the West in 1893, and has been followed by a steady stream of Hindu gurus traveling and teaching worldwide. There are now Yoga, Vedantic, Vedic, Tantric and Buddhist centres in most countries and most major cities of the world. The Theosophical Society included an acceptance of dharmic views into new Western mystical movements and New Age groups, notably, a wide acceptance of the ideas of karma and rebirth.

Along with this worldwide dissemination of Hindu and dharmic teachings has occurred a modern migration of Hindus to many countries, leading to significant Hindu populations in North America, Great Britain, the Caribbean, parts of South America, Africa, Asia, Polynesia and Europe.

In addition, India since independence in 1947, is continuing its Hindu tradition that includes building new temples and a revival of Hinduism and its rich traditions of art and culture, as well as its philosophy and teachings. Combining all these factors, it is clear that Hinduism will remain a dominant influence on the entire planet for the future, in spite of the continued efforts by many outside groups against it. Sanatana Dharma is entering a new and expansive era of flowering that can help transform civilization as we know it into a spiritual adventure in consciousness. Yet, this phase is only beginning and has much resistance to face and very far to go for its full manifestation.

Hinduism and Particular Religions

In this section we will examine the history and connections between Hindu Dharma and the other main religions of the world.

Buddhism: Buddhism formulates itself as Buddha Dharma, 'the way or Dharma of enlightenment'. It also used the term 'Arya Dharma' or the teaching of the noble, which Hinduism and Jainism have also used. Starting as a likely monastic reform movement within the field of Hindu teachings, Buddhism gradually developed a separate identity of its own apart from the common stream of Sanatana Dharma, though it never entirely separated from its roots. Indian Buddhism and its direct offshoots like Tibetan Buddhism, use Sanskrit mantras, Yoga techniques, Vedic fire rituals, Ayurvedic medicine, Vedic astrology and share a common iconography and temple worship with the Hindus. Buddhist traditions of more distant lands, like China and Japan, maintain many of these same practices but as adapted to their own local cultures.

Buddhism and Hinduism have much in common, like the ideas of karma and rebirth and the practice of mantra and meditation, and their differences are often semantic or variant lines of approach. There are perhaps greater differences between teachings within each tradition than between the two traditions overall, as both traditions contain considerable diversity. Tibetan Buddhism in particular shares much in with the Hindu tradition. While Hindus and Buddhists may disagree as to the precise nature of enlightenment or liberation, they accept spiritual realization through meditation as the goal of life.

The Buddha is not portrayed as the only Son of God, the last prophet, or the only Buddha. He is regarded as the main representative of enlightenment in this era, the ideal sage. He is often looked at as an inner archetype than an historical person. There are said to be Buddhas, teaching in all worlds in this vast universe, not just on this Earth. Previous Buddhas are recognised and some of these, like the previous Buddha Kashyapa, which is the name of one of the seven seers of the Vedas, suggest Hindu connections. Hindus recognise Buddha as an avatar of Vishnu, and in the same way, Buddhists recognise the Hindu avatar Rama as a Bodhisattva or enlightened being. There are many sages and yogis honoured in both traditions, like the Nath Yogis and Siddhas. Sanatana Dharma or the eternal tradition can be called Buddha Dharma or the enlightenment tradition, and the term also appears in some Buddhist texts.

Jainism: Jainism is another great religion of India that did not entirely merge into the common fold of Hinduism, though over the course of time it has become closer to Hinduism than Buddhism did. Mahatma Gandhi has been called the greatest modern Jain, for his championing of non-violence, though he was actually a Hindu. The Jains base their teachings on various Tirthankaras, who like Buddhas, are great enlightened teachers going back to ancient times. Jains have similar yogic values and practices as other Hindu and Buddhist teachings. In fact, much that is regarded as typically Buddhist, like the emphasis on non-violence, karma, and the rejection of a personal God, are Jain teachings, which may predate the Buddhist by some centuries.

Jainism can also be viewed as an aspect of Sanatana Dharma, not a separate religion. Jainism has fostered some of the greatest minds of India, including poets, mathematicians, astronomers and philosophers. Many of the most beautiful and ornate Indian temples are Jain temples. Many Jains consider themselves to be part of the greater Hindu culture in India.

Sikhism: The Sikhs were originally a sect of Hindus. It was a custom to make the eldest son into a Sikh or a defender of the faith.

This was done to counter the Islamic invaders who tried to force conversion upon the people of India. The Sikhs arose as defenders of Hinduism or Sanatana Dharma against the Islamic invasions from Central Asia. Guru Nanak, regarded as the founder of Sikh Dharma, is also honoured as a great Hindu teacher and Yogi. Guru Nanak begins his teaching with 'Ek Omkara' or there is only One OM, which is the most sacred mantra of the Hindus, the source of the Vedas and represents the Adi Guru of the Yoga tradition.

Some modern Sikhs consider that they have a separate religion outside of Hinduism. However, if we examine the sacred books of the Sikhs, we find these filled with references to Hindu names for the Divine, like Rama and Hari, and Hindu holy books, like the Vedas and Puranas, and are composed by various saints and sages, like Nanak, who are equally revered by the Hindus. Sikh holy books are written in the language, of Gurumukhi that has much in common with Sanskrit and have frequent references to Hindu teachings and stories. Many Sikhs still consider themselves to be a sect of the Hindus and hold to the idea of Sanatana Dharma.

Philosophically speaking, the Sikhs accept the main teachings of Hinduism including karma, rebirth, liberation and Self-realization. They follow practices of Yoga and meditation much like mainstream Hindu practices. Though Sikh temples worship their holy book, rather than a representative form, they follow the same types of ritual practices as the Hindus, and share many of the same religious festivals like Diwali. Sikhs also use Ayurveda and other aspects of Vedic culture.

Some people think that the Sikhs combine Hinduism and Islam, which is another misunderstanding. Sikh holy books have very few references to Islam, Allah or Mohammed. The Sikhs fought against the Muslims and were their main opponents in Northwest India, particularly against the Moghuls. However, Sikhs like Hindus have accepted Muslims into their culture, if they were peaceful and respected other spiritual traditions, particularly certain Sufi groups.

Taoism: Taoism is an ancient Chinese tradition, yet there were considerable contacts between Taoism and India, and both arose in the Himalayan region throughout history. Buddhism and Taoism in China influenced each other considerably and often merged into a single teaching. Hinduism had contact with Taoism from a pre-Buddhist era, which was maintained throughout the Buddhist era.

Taoism can be regarded as a dharmic tradition, as it contains yogic and meditation practices much like the Hindu and Buddhist, and many Taoists accept karma and rebirth. Like the Vedic tradition, Taoism looks back to an earlier enlightened age of humanity, before what we know as civilization began. Like Hinduism, Taoism is a religion of life and nature that seeks to grow organically. It does not proselytise or seek converts. It has no dogma or ideology and promotes a universality of vision. Like Hinduism Taoism has its folk religion of various Gods, Goddesses and nature spirits, with similar forms of temple worship offered to them.

The Shinto religion of Japan, which has much in common with Taoism, and has also become intertwined with Buddhism, can similarly be regarded as part of dharmic traditions.

Zoroastrianism: The Zoroastrian, the ancient Persian religion, still survives in India as the Parsees, who took refuge in India in the eighth century after the Islamic conquest of Persia. Their religion is similar to the older Vedic in terms of language, concepts and practices, particularly in its emphasis on fire worship (Agni), and can be seen as another dharmic tradition. Their scripture, the Zend Avesta, has much in common in language and teachings as the Vedas.

Zoroastrianism had a strong influence on the Greeks, Romans, Jews, Christians and Muslims and brought many Vedic ideas to them. The Zoroastrian Magi were famous mystics for the ancient Greeks and Romans. Even medieval European mystical movements looked to Zoroaster as the greatest spiritual master. The influence of Zoroastrianism spread as far to the East as China. Western India was often under Persian rulership in ancient times and brought about yet a further exchange of ideas and practices.

Correlating Vedic and Zoroastrian texts is an important area for research in order to understand the spiritual heritage of humanity.

Pagan Religions and Native Traditions

The pagan religions of Greece and Rome, and those of the ancient Celts, Germans, Slavs and Baltic peoples (Lithuanians and Latvians) have much in common with the Hindu, particularly through their similar Indo-European languages and cultures. The ancient Greek culture has many affinities with that of ancient India. Both had temple worship of Gods and Goddesses, many with common names or characteristics, elaborate mythological systems, deep philosophical traditions and a love of astrology. Much of this older European religion can be better understood through looking at Hinduism.

A study of Hinduism—where these traditions are still alive— can aid in the restoration of this older European tradition in which many of the keys to Western mysticism, Goddess worship, spiritual art, philosophy and science lay hidden and are ready to return. This same Hindu type worship of Gods and Goddesses, temples, magic and mysticism can be found among the Egyptians and Babylonians and many other ancient peoples. Hinduism as the best surviving religion from that most ancient period can help us understand and recreate other ancient traditions from throughout the world.

While Christianity looks down upon pagan religions, we should note that Christian theology and philosophy relies heavily on Plato, Aristotle and Plotinus, who were pagan philosophers. The philosophy, medicine and science of both Christianity and Islam have a pagan Greek basis from which came modern science and most of modern European intellectual culture, art and poetry. Science and its empiricism developed from a pagan basis, reflecting the concern of indigenous traditions with understanding of the world of nature. Pagan cultures are not simply primitive but capable of great spiritual, philosophical, and scientific sophistication.

Native and indigenous religions of the world; whether in Africa, America, Asia or the Pacific Islands similarly have much in common with Hinduism and other pagan traditions and are often lumped along with them. Many of them have oral as opposed to written traditions. Most are pluralistic and wrongly called polytheistic, though they recognise a unitary nature to the Divine or the sacred. They have highly developed rituals, images and interactions with the world of nature. Hindu Dharma can be seen as the world's largest, oldest and most diverse native tradition.

Judaism: Judaism as an ancient religion resembles Hinduism in a number of respects. Ancient Judaism employed similar fire offerings as the Vedic tradition. Its emphasis on Torah or the Law is similar to the Hindu emphasis on Dharma. Judaism actively promoted mysticism in its Kabalistic tradition. Some Jewish mystics teach karma and rebirth and promote yogic teachings and practices.

The Jewish people, like the Hindus, practice religious tolerance, not promoting conversion, viewing religion as a culture and way of life, not merely a belief system. They have never sent armies on crusades and holy wars or sought to impose their religion on others by the force of arms or propaganda. The Jewish people respect other religions and do not claim that theirs is the only true religion.

Historically, there was an ongoing trade between ancient Israel and India through the Phoenicians as early as the reign of King Solomon, three thousand years ago. During the second millennium BC, Syria was under the rule of the Mittani, an Indo-European people worshipping Vedic Gods who had contact with the Jewish kingdoms as well. This means that the connections between India and Israel are quite old. Jewish traders had colonies in India throughout medieval history up to modern times.

The main difference between Hinduism and Judaism is theological, with Judaism largely opposed to the use of images that most Hindus follow. However, there are Hindu groups, like the Arya Samaj, who also do not prescribe images.

Christianity: Christianity in its early days exhibited a degree of mysticism and a practice of non-violence that may derive from a yogic or dharmic influence. There are stories that Christ came to India to study during his lost years, or that he retired to India after the crucifixion and died in Kashmir at a very old age. There is an additional story that St Thomas, one of the twelve disciples, and sometimes called the brother of Jesus, died in India. We are not certain how true all this may be and much exaggeration or even distortion may have occurred. Yet, for certain we do know that India admitted Christian refugees into the country as early as the fourth century AD, giving them a land to practice their religion without persecution.

Hindu and Buddhist ideas spread to ancient Greece and Rome long before Christianity and influenced the Hellenistic world and culture. Greek and Roman philosophers studied the teachings of India and some visited there. Indian traders had colonies in the Greco-Roman world including at Alexandria, a tradition going back to earlier eras of ancient Egypt and Babylonia. Some of the early mystical traditions of Christianity along with others in the greater Greco-Roman world, accepted karma and rebirth and a seeking of Self-knowledge. Plotinus is a good example of this side of the Greco-Roman world.

However, with the development of Christianity as a state enforced religious institution, the later Roman Empire gradually opposed and restricted these yogic elements which were soon marginalised as heretical, sometimes suppressed by force. The early Church formally rejected the doctrine of rebirth as heresy and along with it many Eastern influences were suppressed.

Yet Christianity, alone among the main Western religions, developed monastic orders like Hindu and Buddhist traditions. This is true not only of the Catholic, but also of the Greek

Orthodox and other Eastern churches, though the Protestants of later times rejected them. The robes, rosaries and use of statues in ecclesiastical Christian orders reflect the older practices of Hindu and Buddhist monks.

Trade between India and Europe continued through the Middle Ages up to the time of the Turkish conquest of Constantinople (the fifteenth century). Columbus journeyed to America seeking India, searching for an alternative sea route to the land route closed by the Turks. Not surprisingly, great medieval Christian mystics like Meister Eckhart and Hildegard arose in the Rhineland region, which was at the end point of the trade route with the East. No doubt spiritual ideas came along with the trade. There is a possible Hindu and Vedantic influence on Christianity into the Renaissance, when thinkers like Marcilio Ficino mention Hindu teachings with respect.

However, Hinduism and Christianity can be very different in their teachings, with the Hindu approach being inclusive and Christianity exclusive. Catholicism, though having a mystical and devotional side like the Hindu, has an authoritarian structure and missionary militancy quite different than the diversity and tolerance of Hinduism. Catholic theology through St Thomas Aquinas is different than Vedanta, not teaching any Atman or higher Self, any Brahman or Absolute, or karma and rebirth. Protestant Christianity is yet more removed from Hinduism in its orientation. Like Islam, it is against all use of images and generally anti-mystical, emphasizing the authority of the book over inner experience.

Naturally, as long as Christian missionary activity and its propaganda is directed against Hindu Dharma, it is difficult for Hindus to respect Christianity as a whole, however much they may appreciate certain Christian mystics or the figure of Christ himself. Otherwise there can be a helpful dialogue with regard to Yoga, Vedanta and Christian mystical traditions. The Catholics have mostly preserved the worship of the feminine in the form of

Mother Mary. In this regard the Hindu worship of the Goddess or Mother of the Universe in all of her forms, aspects and depth can broader that appreciation.

Islam and Sufism: Long before the advent of Islam, Arabia received a considerable influence from Hinduism and Buddhism. Hindu traders lived in Mecca and contributed to the culture and welfare of the city. The Pre-Islamic religion of Arabia, like the Pre-Christian religions of the Middle East and Europe, resembled the Hindu, using a multiplicity of names and forms for the Divine. Mecca was a site where the Goddess was worshipped and contained 360 icons, following a solar symbolism. The stone of Mecca is an ancient sacred stone much like the Shiva *lingas* or Shiva stones of Hindu worship. Islam has formally discarded most of this earlier type of worship but its imprint in the psyche of the region still remains.

The first part of India to come under Islamic influence was the province of Sind by the mouth of the Indus River. From there, mathematics, astronomy, medicine and other arts and sciences better developed in India were taken back to the Middle East as, for example, the Hindu decimal system that the Arabs introduced into Europe. Vedantic teachings were sometimes adopted by Sufis, the mystics of Islam, who are defined even today by the *Dictionary of Islam* in India as Muslims following Vedantic ideas.

Afghanistan and Central Asia came under Islamic influence in the period around seven hundred and one thousand AD. These were originally regions of Buddhist and Hindu predominance and preserved aspects of these older teachings. Even today many Sufis look to this mountain area as their holy land, particularly eastern Afghanistan and its portion of the Himalayas, which links them back to the greater Himalayan tradition. Some non-Islamic groups have survived in the Middle East, like the Druze in Lebanon and the Yazidis in Iraq, whose traditions have connections to India and follow ideas like that of rebirth, showing other religious trends like Hinduism from the Middle East.

However, Hinduism and Islam are often opposite religions in orientation, with Hinduism presenting the diversity and creativity of the tropical jungle and Islam the stern absolutism of the desert. Islamic rulers in India were largely intolerant of Hindu Dharma, taxed Hindus heavily and prevented them from building or renovating temples. Islamic armies destroyed Hindu temples in great numbers, sometimes building mosques upon Hindu temples or out of temple materials. These events were lauded in Islamic historical accounts and sometimes in Sufi poetry as well. There were exceptions like the Emperor Akbar and Prince Dara, son of Shah Jahan, who were more tolerant. Unfortunately, their influence remained limited, while that of the intolerant Aurangzeb prevailed, leading to the downfall of his empire.

Even the Sufis have had among them teachers who were militant and anti-Hindu in their views and actions. This means that Hindus cannot uncritically embrace the Sufis, though there are many points of connection with them. As long as Hindus are the targets of Islamic conversion efforts, just as the case with Christian conversion efforts, it is difficult for them to forget the history of Islamic aggression against them.

Dharmic Versus Belief-Oriented Religions

There are two general types of religions in the world. The first are belief-oriented religions centred on a particular teacher and an exclusive formulation of the Divine through a particular book or scripture. Most typical in this respect are Christianity and Islam in their predominant and orthodox lines. These religions have an historical revelation, a time bound vision of their mission and insist upon the same belief system for all human beings. They are strongly monotheistic and recognise only one life for the soul followed by an eternal heaven or hell. They tend to be aggressive, proselytizing and at times militant. They often impose their beliefs upon existent cultures and either subordinate or destroy them in the process, intentionally or unintentionally.

The second type consists of religions that arise from nature, which include indigenous, tribal and native traditions, and dharmic traditions in general. They have many names and forms of the Divine, with no set dogma or seeking of converts. Such groups include the native and tribal beliefs of Africa, Asia and America, and the pagan religions of Europe. These religions are connected to nature and to the Earth, and are overall peaceful and passive. They are part of an organic unfoldment of life, not the imposition of an ideology or dogma upon it. Hinduism, Buddhism, Jainism and Taoism belong to this category as they have an organic basis, emphasise meditation experience rather than belief, and have a great respect for nature and the sacredness of all life.

These native spiritual cultures breathe the cycles of eternity and are not based upon any historical revelation. They are interwoven with the culture of the people and must be taken up as part of the whole way of life. They aim at an inner experience, a greater awareness of both the cosmos and oneself. They often believe in rebirth or reincarnation. They contain experiential traditions of Yoga, shamanism, dance, chanting and knowledge of higher states of consciousness, both occult and spiritual.

Judaism contains aspects of the second type of religions as it is rooted in a people and a culture, and not seeking world domination. Liberal and mystical aspects of Christianity and Islam can have features of the second type, though their majority groups are mainly of the first.

Of the nature-based traditions, Hinduism, which integrates together the indigenous religions of Southeast Asia, is the largest, best organised and best preserved. Therefore, Hinduism can provide a key to the preservation of these organic religions and show us their relevance as part of a universal tradition of global spirituality.

Today, with a new interest in mythology and shamanism, we are rediscovering the validity of native religions and their spiritual practices. We are finding in the native religions of Africa and America, much psychological sophistication and the greater connection with nature that we all need in this ecological age. Unfortunately, most of these native cultures have been overrun, and those few that have survived are still fighting for their existence.

Christianity and Islam spread historically mainly by converting people from their indigenous beliefs, teaching them that their indigenous religions and the culture on which they are based, are wrong, inferior or evil. Hinduism, on the contrary, teaches people to preserve their indigenous customs and beliefs, to cherish their native heritage, not simply on a mundane level but as a spiritual path. Hindus are seeking to help such indigenous cultures revive themselves and flourish in the modern world. Those following native traditions should examine Hinduism and form a common alliance with it. Those seeking to preserve indigenous religions and native cultures will find a common cause with the Hindus.

A Hindu Critique of Religion

Though Hinduism finds some affinity with the mystical traditions of Christianity and Islam, it cannot accept the exclusivism that too often characterises these traditions. Vedanta has been critical of different philosophies and theologies on a number of important points, particularly where they fail to understand the higher levels of consciousness and universal laws like karma and rebirth.

Hinduism is not afraid of criticism by other religions, which it has already received in abundance. Yet other religious groups seem offended if Hindus criticise them in return and, particularly, do not like their dogmas and miracles questioned. We should approach religion and spirituality like science, in which debate is encouraged and experiments are required. Yet, in spirituality the experiments consist of the pursuit of higher consciousness through meditation, done within our own minds and hearts.

Above all, Hindu Dharma cannot accept religious divisions as real. Truth, after all is 'One'. This means that there are no separate religious compartments that we ultimately belong to, Hinduism for the Hindus, Christianity for the Christians, and so on. The law of karma and the seeking of Self-realization are common to all souls. *No soul is born into any religion. All souls are born into the Dharma, not into religions that are manmade.*

In Sanatana Dharma, like science, truth is a matter of reason and perception. Truth is a universal fact that each objective observer can discover by probing to the depths of his or her own psyche. We must question and examine all that we call religion in the fire of Self-inquiry. Otherwise we are not searching out the truth but merely attempting to uphold various vested interests in the outer world. This means that we should question what religion and spirituality are meant to be, even if it requires questioning our own traditions and abandoning those aspects of it that fail to reflect the truth.

There is no reason for us to feel offended if our beliefs are questioned. If they are true, like the heat of fire, any objective examination will affirm them. If they are not true, like fire being wet, we have lost nothing in discarding a false belief. In this respect, any true examination must include deep questioning in order to be valid. Let all doubts be brought out. But let us question in order to find out what is true, not merely to refute or uphold one belief or another. The ultimate truth is beyond all theories, names and forms. It is our own inner nature divested of limiting concepts and conditioned thoughts.

There is a common human spiritual striving for all that we must recognise. Yet there is nothing wrong with the idea that our path is best for us, if it is accompanied by openness, tolerance and respect for the views of others who think differently. It becomes a problem when associated with militancy and the attempt to impose our beliefs upon others, when it becomes Self-righteous.

Hindu Dharma does not regard it as necessarily a sign of greatness if all the people in a particular country hold to the same belief, follow the same religious leader, read the same holy book, or perform the same prayer. It may be a sign of spiritual poverty and repression. It would be as if the people in a country all wore the same style of clothes, produced the same style of art, ate the same food, and all tried to look like each other.

Hinduism states that religious identities are not separate or Self-contained, but at best, aspects of a vaster universal tradition. Let us accept all great teachers and teachings and integrate them together into a universal science of Yoga and Self-realization. Let nothing of any true spiritual aspiration be rejected wherever it might occur, which includes preserving native, tribal and indigenous religions as a common global treasure. Let no real spiritual aspiration be destroyed in the name of conformity to a belief or modern progress. As human beings we should all share our spiritual knowledge, not to convert others, but to unite with the infinite.

From non-being lead us to Being, from darkness lead us to Light, from death lead us to Immortality.

Brihadaranyaka Upanishad I.3.28

I was the father of the human race and I became the Sun.

Rishi Vamadeva, Rigveda, IV.27.1

All this in the beginning was Brahman. It knew itself as 'I am Brahman'. Therefore, it became all. Whoever among the Gods, seers or men has awakened to That, he also became That.

Brihadaranyaka Upanishad I.IV.10

Idolatry and Dogmatism: The Veils of Maya

The main charge that Abrahamic traditions have made against Hinduism, as also done with pagan traditions, is that of idolatry—that Hindus worship Gods and Goddesses other than the One True God and are therefore making a great error or committing a great sin. On the other hand, the main charge that pagan and dharmic traditions make against Abrahamic traditions is that of exclusivism—that they are trying to impose an arbitrary set of beliefs upon all people, which favours one group over another and leads to oppression, exploitation and genocide such as history has often recorded.

There is no doubt we should question our attachment to the outer world of name and form and missing our connection with the Divine and our inner Self. We should not worship the false Gods of material forms and transient enjoyments. Yet when religion mistakes the inner Divine reality for a particular belief, it becomes guilty of the same outwardness it is criticising. It becomes dogmatic, which is another form of false worship, or trying to limit truth, which is infinite, to a particular fixed form in time and space.

To insist that God or the Divine should only have one name or be worshipped in only one manner indicates ignorance of the unlimited nature of universal truth. True spirituality reveals the limitations of our outward seeking but it does not seek to impose an outer standard on our inner search. The search for the infinite and eternal cannot be limited by any social, emotional or intellectual formulation. There can be no outer group that owns or dispenses the inner truth, as if it were a limited material or intellectual commodity. Such so-called religion is not a true seeking of the universal and eternal, but the assertion of a personal point of view that divides humanity into hostile camps.

Idolatry charges people with literally regarding as Divine some material thing like a stone, a piece of wood, or a picture. Yet even the so-called primitive tribal knows what we call his idol is not the real deity he worships but only a means of communication with it. The core human problem that limits our inner awareness is regarding something other than the Divine as the true reality— valuing money, sex, power, or any other outer object over the spiritual being or pure consciousness underlying the universe. In Hinduism, this belief in the reality of something other than God or the Self is called ignorance (avidya).

Hindu Dharma teaches we should regard the Divine as the true reality in all creatures and honour everything as sacred. We should not grant a separate reality to anything apart from its Divine essence. This, however, is a matter of inner discrimination, not a simple process of banning the use of images in religious worship. The Divine dwells in all beings as our true Self. What is important is to honour the Divine in all things, rather than trying to possess material objects for our personal enjoyment only.

Hinduism and Idolatry

As a universal tradition, Hindu Dharma has a place for all forms of worship from complex rituals to the highest meditation. This includes worship both with and without form—which catalyse our spiritual awareness in different ways. Hinduism employs a vast array of beautiful and powerful representational forms as well as every sort of formless approach and philosophy of the Absolute as Being-Consciousness-Bliss (Sat-Chit-Ananda) beyond time and space.

This abundance of Hindu forms has been criticised by aniconic (anti-idolatry) traditions as the idol worship of primitive or ignorant people. The idea has often been that whoever uses images in religious worship is somehow unethical, perhaps a worshipper of the devil, and does not know there is only 'One God'. Image worshippers may be lumped together with criminals, perverts, or whoever at the moment is regarded as representing deviant behaviour in society, as if the use of images led to moral depravity and every sort of human failing.

Such intolerant ideas easily give rise to prejudice, if not bigotry, and are akin to racism and its negative stereotypes. People who hold to them never take the time to communicate with so-called idolaters and find out what they are truly worshipping, to discover that they are also human beings often with more love and tolerance than the religious zealots who attack them. Not surprisingly, the charge of idolatry is often levelled as part of a campaign of conversion, invasion and conquest. It has been used as an excuse for smashing statues, robbing and demolishing temples, for plunder and genocide, all conveniently done in the name of God. Such a God is but a personification of intolerance and greed and his worship is built on the blood of innocent people. There is nothing wrong if a religion wants to develop its approach to the Divine apart from image worship. But to denigrate and attack those who use images has nothing holy about it.

Western missionaries through time, and Christian fundamentalists today, have used a charge of idolatry to misrepresent Hinduism and other pagan religions. They never mention that the images are looked upon only as vehicles or communication devices, not as real in themselves. Their statements would be equivalent to Hindus calling Christianity a religion of human sacrifice owing to the Holy Communion ritual of drinking the blood and partaking of the body of Christ.

Hindus use a variety of images in their religious worship, which include statues and pictures of deities, great teachers and avatars. Hindu worship consists of burning incense, lighting lamps, reciting prayers, chanting and singing devotional songs around these sacred images, including rituals in which the statue may be bathed, fed or dressed. Yet Hindus also worship symbolic and geometric forms, like *yantras* and mandalas. They honour sacred places in nature like mountains, rivers and lakes. In Sanatana Dharma, all things in the universe are objects of worship as the Divine presence pervades all life.

Hindu images of Gods and Goddesses have supernatural characteristics to show their higher reality. Deities may be depicted with several heads, many arms, and various unusual weapons and adornments. Sometimes they may have animal aspects, like an animal head or body with Ganesha. Usually they have animals as vehicles or *vahanas*, like Vishnu riding the eagle Garuda. Sometimes they are shown with frightening features as in the form of wrathful protective deities.

Such dramatic deity forms may appear strange to those who come from anti-idolatry traditions. However, to a deeper vision—which anyone can gain by a little open-minded study—these images are great archetypes of life, embodiments of the great truths of the eternal and the infinite, in which our ordinary mental constructs must be broken down. Those who make the charge of idolatry against such images only demonstrate their ignorance of symbolic language and mythology. Not surprisingly, anti-image traditions are often opposed to mysticism and have stifled artist expression as well.

Such a worshipper of images was Paramahansa Ramakrishna, who millions throughout the world have been inspired by. Ramakrishna was a priest at a Hindu temple in Kolkata and worshipped the Goddess Kali, who has a terrible form, replete with an outstretched tongue, serpents as adornments, a girdle of hands, and a garland of skulls, as she represents the Eternal Mother who stands beyond all the limitations of time and death. Let those who are opposed to the use of images show among their members an individual of such spiritual realization of Ramakrishna.

We should note that religions that use images have not historically been more violent or sensual than those that deny them. Hindu and Buddhist communities maintain strong ascetic and monastic traditions, as well as an emphasis on non-violence, even though they use images. Image-denying religions, on the other hand, have often been guilty of violence and destruction in the name of destroying idols and converting infidels, adding captured infidel women to their homes and harems for their personal pleasure. The denial of images in worship has not increased our human sensitivity or respect for other cultures or peoples. It has destroyed some of the greatest artwork of humanity, including innumerable great sculptures in India. It has burnt books like the great Indian university city of Nalanda.

Icons and Idols

All religions use images and forms to some degree. Catholic and Greek Orthodox Christianity have many images, icons and statues as an examination of their churches reveals. Hindu, Buddhist, Taoist and Shinto groups routinely employ them. Native American, African and Asian religions all have them, often in forms that we may find hard to understand. The ancient religions of the entire world from Mexico to Greece, Egypt, Babylonia, Persia, India and China used images extensively, as archaeology so clearly has uncovered. The use of images is an integral part of religious practices and no universal spirituality can be regarded as complete without them.

Most Protestants and Muslims do not use any images and accuse the Catholics of idolatry for using of them. No statues or images can be found adorning their churches or mosques. Yet, we do find that many Protestants have a picture of Christ or at least wear a cross, which is still a usage of images and symbols. Muslims honour Mecca and worship a special rock placed there. They pray only in the direction of Mecca, which is the limitation of the Divine to a place. Muslims often have pictures of their religious or political leaders in their homes or offices. Shia Muslims have pictures of Ali, the grandson of Mohammed, though they do not allow pictures of Mohammed. Both Protestants and Muslims regard their holy books, the Bible and Koran, as the Word of God. This is also a worship of objects.

However, there is a strange dichotomy in how religious images are judged. When images are part of the Christian tradition, they are called 'icons' and classified as works of art and sacred in nature. However, when they are part of non-Christian or pagan traditions they are called 'idols', a derogatory term that indicates not the sacred but mere superstition. In the case of Native American and African images, even when done by a culture as advanced as the Mayas of Central America that built great pyramids and had many large cities, they are lumped along with so-called 'primitive' art.

By this logic what makes for idolatry is not the use of representational forms in worship or their sophistication artistically, but only the use of non-Christian images, which is obviously a gross prejudice. An image of Krishna as the good cow herder is on par with that of Christ as the good shepherd, the Divine as the caretaker of souls. To make one into a superstitious idol and the other into a sacred image is hypocritical and intolerant. It is like saying that only spices used in American cooking are legitimate spices, while those used in Indian cooking are food adulterants!

What Christian would accept a depiction of Christ being called an idol? Would Christian religious leaders approve of it in the press or mass media of Christian countries? Yet Hindus and other non-Christians routinely are made to accept that depictions of their deities—who represent such high truths as Self-realization—are demeaned as idols, which is how news groups still call them today.

To call such images idols implies that those who worship them take the image itself as a God. This adds yet more prejudice and error to the judgement. The use of an image—whether we call it an icon or an idol—does not imply belief in the reality of the image. That we keep a photograph of our wife and children by our office desk does not mean that we think our wife and children are the photograph!

The use of the term idol further inflames the sentiments of anti-idolatry religions like Christianity and Islam, as both the Bible and the Koran instruct their followers to destroy idolaters and their temples. The use of the term idol in the media is careless, insensitive and inflammatory. It should be removed in an effort to promote understanding and good will between religious groups.

Idolatry and the Book

One may confuse the Divine, which is unlimited with any number of limited things, not merely representational forms. Books can also be invested with the illusion that they are the truth. The written word is arguable the foremost of all false Gods, the confusion of spirit and matter, because as the most evident form used in human communication, it is the foundation for many other dogmatic constructs. The idolatry or blind worship of the word, idea, name or book, is perhaps the worst of all prejudices. It confuses reality with a verbal representation, which is worse than mistaking God for an idol.

Verbal constructs are less real than ordinary realities. For example, the word tree is not as real as an actual tree. So too, the word God is not only less real than God, but less real than an actual object. It is less real than even one human being. To sacrifice one living human being for such a mere concept is not only a sin against God, but a crime against life. To identify the Divine or truth with a particular name or phrase is to fall not only from spiritual reality but to alienate ourselves from the world of nature. For this reason, Vedic texts emphasise that truth is discovered only where all speech turns back without reaching.

Many religious groups insist that their book is literally the word of God. They have identified God's word with a material thing, a mere book. How can the infinite and eternal reality have speech or words? God is not a physical person who has a mouth. His Word is at best a metaphor for the cosmic creative intelligence. This Divine Word is a vibratory state of awareness, not something that can be found in a dictionary or made into a dialect.

To regard an actual book as the word of God is a form of matter worship. This worship of a book creates literalism, taking statements, however metaphorical, as actual facts: like the belief that the world was created six thousand years ago because this is the literal age of the lineages of the prophets given in the Bible since the time of creation. It creates dogma—the idea that something is true merely because it is found in a book that is said to be the Word of God.

A book itself does not say anything. It has to be read and interpreted. Usually any book is capable of multiple interpretations. Scriptures, which are written in archaic and symbolic languages, and often reflect many authors, time periods and points of view, are capable of numerous interpretations as is obvious by the disagreements between religious scholars. A book is a passive object that if used properly can yield knowledge, but if used improperly can yield half-truth or falsehood. We can compare a book to a musical instrument. The person who plays it is as important as the instrument itself.

Art and the Use of Religious Images

The use of images as an artistic approach to the Divine is part of what we could call the 'Yoga of Art'. For this purpose, sculpture uses statues, painting uses coloured surfaces, music uses sound, and poetry uses verbal images. To deny these things as idolatry is only to banish art and beauty from our relationship with the Divine. For this reason, anti-image traditions have remained artistically limited or suppressed. Where, for example, can we find great religious sculptures or paintings among orthodox Muslims or strict Protestants?

Both the Bible and the Koran, though they reject graven images, abound with poetic images, which are responsible for much of the beauty of these books. If a poetic image is acceptable, why is a formal image not allowed? Is not a picture worth a thousand words? Why is a poetic form of art acknowledged as sacred, but not a plastic form like painting or sculpture? It could be argued that the literalism of certain religious traditions in worshipping their books has only occurred because they deny the use of images. The book becomes a substitute image to fill our spiritual aspiration that looks for a symbolic object to worship.

The religious traditions that reject the use of images only make themselves incapable of representing the full spiritual aspirations of humanity, which must include all forms of sacred art. Hinduism as a universal tradition includes all forms of art as valid approaches to the Divine. It contains music, dance, poetry, drama, sculpture, painting and architecture, not as ends in themselves but as different languages of worship and meditation. Yet this has not prevented it from having formless approaches as well, with a worship of the Absolute pure consciousness beyond all time, space and person that it has developed to a degree unparalleled in anti-image traditions.

Idolatry and Dogmatism

Many great teachers and gurus have existed throughout the world over the course of time. The higher truth can never be limited to a single person, however great he or she may be. To insist that God has only one son or that he has a final prophet is itself a form of idolatry—an attempt to limit ultimate reality to what is only an appearance in time and space. We are all sons of God and all potentially God-realised sages. Whatever good or evil that has ever existed in any human being exists in each one of us. Whatever greatness has existed in any human being is also part of our own potential. There is no special prophet, messenger or incarnation that is set apart from who we really are.

Vedanta holds that the individual as the bearer of consciousness is the most important factor in the spiritual life. The teacher is only an aid and a guide to our own Self-realization. Hindu Dharma does not sacrifice the sacred nature of the individual for any final prophet or saviour, however great, but directs each one of us to our own Self-realization as the highest goal. When we set up something outside ourselves as the truth, we fall from the spiritual path, and end up creating a cult, an illusion that blinds us to the inner reality.

The very religious groups who have most condemned others as idolaters have themselves been the most guilty of dogmatism, of an authoritarian insistence upon the sole truth that does not allow any objective examination, much less any other point of view. They have regularly suppressed any criticism of their views, which they make true on the grounds of faith alone. Dogmatic beliefs use the spectre of idolatry to condemn those who think differently. But their dogmatism itself is a form of materialism, the limitation of truth to a particular form, person or idea.

Exclusivism in religious belief—the belief our God, saviour or holy book alone is true—is itself materialism, the limitation of truth to a construct in the realm of time and space. It holds an inherent violence of partiality and intolerance. Unless we transcend this spiritual materialism of religious exclusivism, we are only following a divisive creed, which breeds conflict and can never lead to peace.

We must honour all the various ways that human beings have used to approach the Divine, the infinite and eternal, and allow for their free exploration, which must flow beyond the boundaries of any particular religion, whether it uses images or not. We are not puerile children that religion must threaten or cajole to keep in line. We are intelligent beings, centres of cosmic awareness, with the potentials of the entire universe. If we treat ourselves like animals to be herded in a particular line, we only stifle our deeper consciousness.

However, if we recognise our true Self and provide it with a rich field in which to grow and the freedom to discover the truth, then there is no limit as to how much each individual can flower in the cosmic reality. This requires honouring the Divine as dwelling in human beings, not a God set apart from ourselves, who being separate from us can never truly uplift us.

Part II

What Is Hinduism?
Questions and Answers

A single wheel revolves with a single rim, with an unlimited number of spokes moving both before and behind. With half of itself it generated the universe. Where has its other half gone?

Atharva Veda X.9.7

Encompassing all beings, all worlds, and all directions of space, approaching the original being of Truth, with the Self he entered into the Self.

Going around Heaven and Earth in an instant, going around all the worlds, the directions, and the enlightened realms, breaking the extended line of karma, he saw That, he became That, he was That.

Shukla Yajurveda XXXII.11-12

The infinite Mother is Heaven. The infinite Mother is the Earth. She is the Mother, the Father and the Son. The Infinite Mother is all the Gods and the five peoples of humanity. She is all that has been born and all that will be born.

Rigveda I.89.10

Questions on Hinduism 1: Hindu Dharma and the Spiritual Life

In this section, we will examine the issues of faith, religion and spirituality, extending to Yoga, enlightenment and Self-realization, relative Hindu tradition, which often has different views on these subjects than dominant Western religions. For Hindu Dharma, Ananda, the supreme bliss, and samadhi, the state of absorption within it remains the highest goal.

A. Hinduism and Religious Issues

What is the Origin of Hindu Dharma?

Sanatana Dharma, which means the eternal tradition, as the original name for Hinduism, has no specific origin in time. Its origin coincides with the beginning of the universe itself. Sanatana Dharma as the universal dharma arises anew with each cycle of creation, being inherent in the very laws of nature.

Because it has been formulated in terms of Sanatana Dharma, there is no specific point in history when we can say that the Hindu tradition began. As it does not have an origin, Hinduism has no end either. It does not look to any end of the world or last judgement. It will continue throughout the future of this and all other possible worlds as the expression of the cosmic life and its underlying laws.

Hindu Dharma is based upon universal principles like the law of karma, which are true in all places and all times. Though its names and forms may vary, its principles are unchanging and must be discovered by all creatures in every world of existence. The origin of the true Dharma is within us as the root of our deepest thoughts and the basis of our highest aspirations. This is because we contain the entire universe within our own hearts as Vedic teachings proclaim.

What is the Goal of Hindu Dharma?

The goal of the universal life is Self-realization, the experience that the entire universe dwells within us at the deepest level of our consciousness. The goal of universal truth is to become one with this Supreme Reality, which is to become one with all. This state of cosmic unity brings liberation from all bondage based upon the dualities of life, birth and death, pleasure or pain. If we are one with all, what else could exist for us to fear or to desire?

Ultimately this goal of Sanatana Dharma is realised because the universe is inherently one with our inmost nature as the essence of all. To reach this goal is to recognise its Self-existent reality, which is to merge into the ocean of unlimited Being-Consciousness-Bliss. It constitutes freedom from all bondage and sorrow, not simply knowing God but merging into the Divine within us.

Yet besides this ultimate goal, Sanatana Dharma recognises the universal manifestation, including the organic unfoldment of the various potentials of all worlds and all creatures. While this process leads all creatures to the ultimate goal of Self-realization, each stage has its appropriate place, displaying the full beauty and glory of existence, including all the wonderful life forms in the world of nature.

What is God or the Divine?

God is the term most often used in Western thought to describe the Supreme Being or spiritual reality behind the universe. The term God is originally a Germanic word and relates to the idea of the good, what is most beneficial in life. God in the Jewish, Christian and Islamic sense stands for the Creator of the universe, who has a personal nature, and is often conceived of as a father who resides in Heaven above.

Sanatana Dharma teaches that there is an ultimate spiritual reality, which one can call God, but that this reality transcends all names and forms and is the nature of Pure Consciousness. As such, Hinduism has its own terms like Atman (Self), Purusha (Cosmic Person), Ishvara (Cosmic Lord) Brahman (Supreme Reality), or Bhagavan (the Beloved) among many others, with their varieties of indications. As a Hindu I do not like to use the term God for such Hindu formulations of universal consciousness, though it can be helpful some instances. The term God carries a lot of Biblical baggage and connotations that may not apply to Hindu terms for divinity, which we should learn to examine in their own right.

The highest truth of Non-dualist Vedanta, the main teaching of the Yoga of knowledge, is monism—not that there is only One God but that there is nothing but God. Such a Divine reality is not merely the Creator. It is the creation itself as well as the Absolute that transcends time, space and causation, the pure consciousness that Vedanta calls *Brahman*. All creatures are in essence that supreme Divine reality. Our soul is one with it and can experience it within itself.

Is the Divine Personal or Impersonal?
Hindu Dharma distinguishes between the Divine with qualities or *Ishvara*, the cosmic Creator, and the Divine without qualities as the Supreme Brahman, the Absolute behind creation. Ishvara is viewed in a theistic sense. Brahman transcends creation, which consists of the surface waves on its infinite sea.

Hindu Dharma with its universal view recognises the full range of personalities of the Godhead. It is not limited to any single personal God, prophet or incarnation. It honours all relationships to the Divine as father, mother, friend, beloved and master. Yet the Divine is impersonal and personal, the formless Being-Consciousness-Bliss as well as the cosmic Lord and Creator.

There is no contradiction between these personal and impersonal aspects of the Godhead. The impersonal Divine in its creative play assumes various personalities as the Creator, Preserver, and Transformer of the universe. It is the same reality with or without qualities. One can honour both aspects or one can focus on one aspect. All possibilities are worthy of exploration relative to that which both contains all time and space and transcends all time and space.

What is Our Relationship with the Divine?
Our relationship with the Divine or universal being is our only enduring relationship, as it is not limited by death. The Divine is our true origin and goal, our ultimate friend and companion. The Divine is our father, mother, son, daughter, brother, sister, friend, and master. Whatever we are related to in essence is Brahman as the true Self of all, the Divine presence in the hearts

of all beings. We are not merely related to God, the Supreme Being is our true nature. In the highest truth, we don't have a relationship with God; we are God. There is no God apart from who we are.

All that we experience in life is part of our own eternal and infinite consciousness and its creative capacity. The love we feel for others is only a portion of the love that is eternal, which is our own immortal Self. All relationship is an attempt to see our Self in the other and the other in our Self. There is only One Self in all beings, seeking to rediscover its universal wholeness. All our relationships are in the Self and of the Self, which is neither you nor me but all.

Why Do Many Religions Refer to God only as He?

The Divine is both male and female, and beyond both male and female. One can call the Divine 'He' relative to the masculine qualities of the cosmic being like strength, justice, will or discernment. One can call it 'She' in reference to its feminine qualities like love, devotion, beauty and receptivity. One can call the Divine 'It' relative to its neutral qualities like infinity, impartiality or pure existence.

If one only calls God 'He', then such a Deity is not the Supreme Being but a personification of a male centred view of reality. As our culture is dominated by male energy, not always of a higher order, we may project this idea upon God as well. Such a one-sided conception of God is reflected in exclusivist religions, which claim that they alone have the truth. It can lead to imbalanced views or even violent actions, including denying the worship of the Goddess or Divine Mother.

While we can call God 'He', we should not limit how we conceive the Divine reality. The Divine is all beings and all relationships. Whatever entity or relationship we conceive is our very own Self. Without this Self no name, pronoun or gender is possible.

What is the Importance of the Divine Mother?

In Western religions, the Divine is not usually worshipped as the mother. Protestant Christianity and Islam have all but banished the Divine as mother from their religions. Catholic Christianity has accepted the feminine principle of Mary but only as the mother of Jesus, not as Divine in her own right or as the Mother of the universe.

Hindu Dharma has always recognised the importance of the Divine Mother. According to Hinduism, the deepest relationship that we can have is with the Mother. No human relationship is closer than that of mother and child. It best mirrors our relationship with the Divine. The land of India itself is regarded as a mother, often viewed as the Goddess Durga who saves us from all danger. The Hindu religion is regarded a mother and its teachings are her milk. The Vedas are called 'Veda Mata' or Mother Veda.

In our current era in which we are accepting the equality of men and women, we can no longer reject the feminine aspect of divinity. The rejection of the feminine aspect of the Divine— which is loving kindness, tolerance and caring nurturance—and the promotion of a stern male-only father-sky God, has arguably contributed to the religious animosity that has devastated humanity for many centuries.

What religion has ever aggressively promoted a belief in the Divine Mother? What form of religious fundamentalism or exclusivism has ever been made in the name of the Goddess? Who could ever kill people in the name of a God called Mother? What Mother would allow her children to be hurt; no matter how far they may have fallen? What Mother would condemn her children to damnation as sinners? Who could say, 'Believe in the Divine Mother or you will be punished with eternal pain?' Not surprisingly, Hindu Dharma, the world's major religion that has honoured the Goddess, has never promoted wars of religious conversion or theologies of damnation.

The female is the form side of the Divine. Woman represents the Divine embodied. The Goddess holds all the beauty, wonder and magic of the world of nature. Her worship requires the creation of appropriate forms to revere her, which is why an-iconic or anti-image religions have little place for the Goddess. We must once again create magnificent images of the Divine Mother to allow her healing grace, which is essential for world peace, to descend unhindered. Without acknowledging the many forms of the Divine Mother of the universe, our religions will likely remain imbalanced and lead to conflict.

What is the Relationship Between the Divine and the World of Nature?

Some religions place God and nature apart or in conflict with one another. Others see nature as God's creation, which he owns and rules from above and for which the glory belongs only to him. The Hindu view is a little different.

According to Hindu Dharma, the world of nature is the manifestation of the Divine Being that is our very Self. Nature is our own greater body. The entire universe is our manifestation, the reflection in form of the formless truth of who we really are. We not only exist in nature, all of nature exists within us. We are the Cosmic Being that expresses itself through all the forms of creation. Nothing is alien to us or apart from us. Each thing is but an aspect of the totality that we are. God has not merely created nature; nature exists in God as God. Nature is the expression of the Divine Word that is the vibratory power of pure Consciousness. It is the Divine Message and teaching vehicle through which we can come to know our true Self. The true scripture is nature itself, without being able to read we cannot know truth or divinity.

What Hinduism teaches is not pantheism, the idea that nature is God, but monism, the truth that there is only One Reality, which includes the world. Hindu yogis and sages have always revelled in the world of nature, communicating through her with the transcendent, divine existence of Brahman. Nature is the Divine Mother who, if we are open to her beauty and wisdom, will unfold all the mysteries of higher awareness. Besides the outer nature is her inner form, the power of yogic knowledge, the intelligence that directs the evolution of consciousness, which ultimately takes us to the Supreme.

Nature and the Divine are one reality like the ocean. The manifest world is the outer waves, the formless Absolute the inner depths. But it is all the same water, all the same Being that is our own true nature as well.

Why Do Hindus Worship Many Gods?

Human beings through history have formulated many different names and forms for the Divine or eternal, which different cultures have adopted and made important. The Western world has prided itself in monotheism, the idea that there is only One God or Creator as the highest truth. Western religions have said that only the names and forms that refer to this One God are valid but those that appear to worship another God, or a multiplicity of divinities, must be false. They have restricted the names and forms they use in religious worship, and insist that only one set, which is theirs, is true and correct and others are wrong or unholy.

As a universal formulation, Hindu Dharma accepts all sincere approaches to truth. According to its view, there is only One Truth or reality, but it cannot be limited to a particular name or form, or owned by any person or group. Though truth is One it is also infinite, not an exclusive formulation. It is an inclusive not an exclusive Oneness. The highest truth is a spiritual reality of Being-Consciousness-Bliss, which could be called God but which transcends all names. What are called the different Gods and Goddesses of Hinduism represent various functions of this One Supreme Divinity, not separate deities.

Having many names for something is not necessarily a sign of ignorance of its real nature. On the contrary, it may indicate an intimate knowledge of it. For example, Eskimos have many different names for snow in their language because they know snow intimately in its different variations, not because they are ignorant of the fact that all snow is one. Similarly, the many different deities of Hinduism reflect an intimate experience of the Divine according to various levels and aspects. It is hardly a crude polytheism, but an exalted pluralism or many-sided understanding of the One that is Infinite. Such an all-encompassing approach to Unity reflects deep wisdom and profound experience over many generations.

Why Do People Worship the Divine in Different Forms?

The Divine, though formless in essence, assumes various forms in its cosmic play. We ourselves have a complex form, a body and mind, yet behind that we have a continuous sense of our own being.

Different people worship the Divine in different ways because the minds of human beings differ according to their life experiences. The ultimate way to the Divine is to worship the Divine as the Self of all beings. This means that God or the Supreme Being can be found in rocks, mountains, rivers and stars as well as beyond the world. Actually every form is a Divine form worthy of worship. This is not merely to bow down before the form but respect its Divine essence.

What is important is to allow the free use of forms so that the doors to the Infinite are open to everyone. We must not only see the Divine beyond the world but God in the world, in every form and flower, to really know the omnipresent reality. Everything you see is a manifestation of the Deity looking back at you to remind you to discover your true Self. Do learn to recognise your own all-pervasive reality, which is the answer to the mystery of life.

Can the Divine Be Portrayed in Animal Forms?

The Divine pervades all nature and its many life forms. Animals are manifestations of the same cosmic spirit as are human beings. Animals also have a soul, a mind and a personality. We should honour this Divine presence in animals, not merely look at their bodily characteristics or limitations. Hindu thought honours animals according to the Divine Being expressing through them. It does not look up to the animal state as the highest. Unless we can see the Conscious Being in all creation, we do not really see at all. We do not know ourselves, nor will we function as a humane and compassionate presence in the living universe.

Hindu Dharma recognises that animals project certain cosmic energies as manifestations of the universal life. Animal images appear in Hinduism for their archetypal and poetic value and their place in the cosmic order. Respect for the Divine in animals, which includes representing the Divine in animal forms, is part of any universal teaching. It is not a sign of lack of spirituality but of a greater sensitivity to the sacred nature of all life. If we refuse to recognise God in animals, it only shows that we have not yet come into contact with the real Divinity, that our God is a human prejudice, not a universal truth. It indicates we will probably abuse and exploit animals for our own personal pleasure, not treat them with respect.

Not only Hinduism, but all other pagan and native traditions recognise the cosmic meaning of animal forms and use them in their rituals and their artistic expression. Each animal has something to teach us about the nature of reality. Unless we know the inner meaning of our creaturely companions, we will not know what life is really all about.

What are Divine Names and Their Importance?

There is only One Divine Reality or Supreme Being, which is both beyond all names and also possesses an unlimited number of names. In the Hindu tradition, one can call the Divine Shiva, Vishnu, Divine Mother, the Creator, or whatever one likes. No forms are rejected, nor is the formless. Each Hindu deity has many names, commonly a thousand names for worship, which indicate how it connects to the whole of existence. Among these many names is Atman or our own highest Self.

We don't think that the English word for grapes is the only legitimate word for grapes and those who call grapes by any other name know nothing about this particular fruit. Yet some religious groups may insist that the name for God belonging to their particular community is the only true name and should other people call upon that spiritual reality by another name, they must be calling upon something else or even worshipping something undivine. The name is not the thing. Even a person cannot be reduced to a single name. The Divine has all names and transcends all names. What is important is to know that reality is not trying to impose one name or one idea about it on all humanity.

A name for the Divine enables us to establish a relationship with that transcendent Reality. Generally, the name reflects various Divine qualities—like love, peace, or truth—which allow us a means of access to the higher truth. Repetition of Divine names is perhaps the easiest method of concentrating the mind. However, when we limit that transcendent reality to a mere name, which is a collection of letters, then the name becomes a factor of illusion and separation. We must use the name as a means to contact the inner being, not merely worship. Ultimately, we are that Being and its name is our name, which our every breath and heartbeat proclaims.

Is Atheism Wrong?

Atheism, the idea that there is no God or Creator, is a conception of the human mind that occurs at various stages of human development. It appears in unevolved minds that are unable to perceive any deeper reality than what is evident through the physical senses. Yet atheism also appears in developed intellects that see through the dogmas of organised religion and can no longer accept these as true.

Some dharmic traditions, like Buddhism, are not theistic in the sense that they do not posit a creator, God or a cosmic Lord. Yet, it would be wrong to call them atheistic in the sense of those who deny any higher reality to the human being beyond the body. Such non-theists are not materialists but have a trans-theistic view of reality.

It is wrong to say that atheists are bad, whereas those who believe in God are good. True believers have done much harm and among atheists there are many noble people. The important thing is our inquiry into truth. If this inquiry is more alive in an atheist than in the dogmatic follower of a particular religious belief, such an atheist is a better seeker of truth and therefore closer to God who is truth than the so-called religious person. God does not punish atheists; rather those who do not seek the truth become limited in their understanding, regardless of their beliefs.

Actually, most of us are atheists in our behaviour, including those who may regard themselves as religious. What we believe in is not spiritual reality or higher consciousness but money, pleasure, power, converts and ideologies, all of which are material. If we hold to the reality of the Divine, we will not run after such outer aspects of life as the most important.

How Should True Spirituality Be Propagated?
True spirituality spreads itself by the force of truth and the sharing of consciousness. It does not rest upon overt efforts to convert others and transcends organizational endeavours, which should aim at disseminating knowledge, not promoting dogma. True religion (unity) is reflected in universal interdependence. It is spread by promoting unity consciousness in thought, word and deed. Without recognizing this universal truth, to seek to promote a particular belief is only to promote a separative and warring creed.

True spirituality is the recognition of the eternal and the infinite. This religion of truth is inherent in nature. The wind blows it. The sun shines it. The rivers make it flow. Flowers bloom through it. What is important is that we take it up and let it spread through our awareness, and through it let go of the limited identities and opinions of the mind.

In promoting spiritual teachings, we must avoid propaganda, which tries to influence the mind through emotions and slogans, instead of emphasizing calm thinking and meditation. Religious propaganda is a denial of any ultimate truth. Spirituality should be a means of connecting us with a higher reality. This cannot be done through appeal to the lower aspects of the human mind—greed, fear, anger, hatred and division—which propaganda aims at.

How Should Spiritual Life Be Organised?

According to Hindu Dharma, there should be no one religion, church, religious leader or institution for everyone. True spiritualty is an inner experience that cannot be organised as a dogma, creed, or social institution. It should not be standardised or stereotyped or it loses its depth and creativity and becomes rigid and artificial.

Religion should direct us to spiritual knowledge through inner practices of Yoga and meditation, functioning as an expedient means to inner spirituality, not an end-in-itself. It should be developed as a system of higher wisdom, not as a vested interested in the outer world. It should not be oriented externally to gain a mass following but focused within to afford access to higher levels of awareness.

The Hindu model is of a diversity of gurus, spiritual groups and organizations in a general alliance or federation, respecting a unity of truth but a diversity of approaches. In this manner, experiential spirituality can grow in a natural and organic way in which the individual, the real bearer of the sacred flame of consciousness, is honoured and nurtured. The real teachings are passed down orally from teacher to disciple, not made into a creed to be promoted in a rigid external form.

Spirituality is not something that we should personally attempt to organise. True spirituality reorganises us, as it were, restructuring our own nature as body, mind and consciousness, placing us in harmony with the universal Being. Unless our inner being has gone through this integrating process, our efforts to propagate religion outwardly will remain caught up in partiality and illusion.

What is Karma and Rebirth?

Those who follow yogic traditions, as well as many nature-oriented religions, teach that the soul takes many births in its evolution toward Self-realization, Divinity or enlightenment. The soul must reap the fruits of its actions, experiencing the consequences of the energies it has put forth. Just as there is an evolution of form (the body) through the world of nature, so there is a corresponding evolution of consciousness (the mind) through repeated births of the soul. The soul is nature's vehicle for the evolution of intelligence, which occurs through its development in repeated births.

The law of karma is very scientific. The effects of our actions must be of the same nature and extent as the original actions themselves. It is not a question of reward and punishment but of energetics. Our actions set in motion a subtle force that propels us along in life. If we act in a violent way towards others, for example, that violence becomes embedded in our psyche and reflects upon us, causing us to act and to be acted upon in a violent way. If we act in a loving and compassionate manner, on the other hand, that energy carries us along the stream of love and brings the forces of love into our life to the same degree and manner as the love we have put forth. Whatever we set in motion through action, even if that action is directed toward others, we first must come to experience within ourselves. When we die we take with us the essence of our actions and the will behind them, which becomes the basis of our next life.

Karma is the residue of past actions that follows the soul along its journey until it is able to transcend action which, based on desire, is always limited. The goal for dharmic traditions is liberation into or union with the higher truth. This arises from knowledge, not action, because action that occurs in the realm of time cannot bring us to that which transcends time. We must learn to look beyond action and give up the sense of being the doer. Then the fluctuations of action and its result cannot disturb us, and whatever we do, being detached, will be inherently good.

Is Life Predestined?

There is a karmic pattern to our lives. Whatever exists in the realm of time must follow the rhythms of time and the law of cause and effect. The present fruit must be of the same nature as the previous seed. Whatever we are today in body and mind must be the result of our previous physical and mental patterns. This karmic destiny for some people is very fixed. For others it is capable of modification, though its basic features cannot always be changed. For example, we cannot change our parents, nor can we alter the country or time in which we are born. However, some people have such a developed nature along a particular line that we can say that they were destined to be great or destined to be a criminal, almost regardless of circumstances.

This is not to say that our inner Being is predetermined but only the outer pattern of our actions is, and even that is capable of some modification. Our consciousness, not being a product of time, is inherently free. Karma and destiny belong only to the body-mind complex, which is not really ours anyway but belongs to the world of nature. Our ultimate destiny, which is inherent in everyone, is to realise our immortal Self. Everything else is a movement towards or deviation from this supreme goal.

Are We Punished for Wrong Actions?

The Divine Being is not some great parent or judge in Heaven dealing out rewards and punishments. There is a natural law (dharma) and its consequences according to the law of cause and effect (karma).

If you put your hand into a fire you get burnt. God is not punishing you for the sin of putting your hand in a fire by burning you. It is not a sin but a matter of ignorance of natural law and a consequent experience of pain or limitation. Just as there are physical laws, like fire's capacity to burn, so there are mental and spiritual laws. Violence, for example, brings eventual destruction upon its perpetrator. But one is not punished for violence, violence as a negative state of mind with negative consequences creates its own punishment.

The problem is that the long-term effects of our actions are not as obvious to us as their immediate results. For example, if we eat the wrong food, like too much sugar, which tastes good but is bad for us, its negative effect will not manifest immediately, like fire burning us, but will take time, causing eventual disease through poor digestion that may manifest as diabetes, heart disease or any number of problems. Because of the time lap involved between the cause and effect of our actions, we may not recognise the connection between the wrong food and the disease.

On the level of behaviour, anger is destructive to our finer sensitivities and prevents us from developing any higher awareness. However, if our minds are not properly evolved, we may not recognise this pain; we may indulge in anger and find pleasure in it. But eventually we must experience the consequences of the forces we set in motion, both on short term and long-term levels. Our anger, fear and attachment must lead us into situations that make us suffer. Wrong action itself is its own punishment because it causes the constriction of our consciousness, which always results in unhappiness.

Do Heaven and Hell Exist?

Hinduism recognises that the individual soul (Jivatman) or reincarnating consciousness is inwardly one with the Divine and eternal reality. The soul is immortal and by its very nature ever blissful, free and happy. However, veiled by ignorance, it falls into darkness and confusion, making wrong judgements that lead to suffering in different incarnations.

Souls by their karma, the power of their own actions, create their own destiny, which leads to various happy or unhappy states of existence. A very happy state could be called heaven and a very unhappy state could be called hell. Yet there is no eternal or absolute heaven or hell. Any embodied state is bound by time and must come to an end after a certain period of time.

An unlimited result cannot arise from a limited action; any more than a limited seed can produce an unlimited plant. Therefore, an unlimited or eternal heaven or hell can never result from limited creaturely actions, such as occur in human life. Our limited actions must lead to repeated incarnations, not to any final heaven or hell. Wrong actions lead to suffering but such suffering is equal to the nature of the action, which produced in time, must be limited. There cannot be an eternal result for transient actions. The idea of an eternal heaven or hell is irrational and shows an ignorance of the laws of the universe. Hindus believe in a loving Deity who would never condemn any creature to an everlasting damnation, moreover, who is our own true Self.

Heaven and hell have been used by various priests to entice or frighten people into certain beliefs. Such heavens and hells do not exist. This heaven and hell idea appeals to the basic reward-punishment conditioning mechanism of the immature mind. It does not promote real ethical behaviour so much as creating emotional imbalance and sometimes, religious fanaticism. It is important to recognise that our actions have consequences in both this and future lives, but to place the spectre of an eternal heaven or hell over people is to promote fear and ignorance. Only inner knowledge can release us from the cycle of karma, not any belief. This is a state of higher awareness, not a world that one can go to.

Does Evil Exist?

There is an absolute good, which is in fact the nature of consciousness, but there cannot be any absolute evil. Evil being a form of ignorance and limitation can never be absolute, though it can be a powerful force in this material realm. All souls are inherently good and can only temporarily become evil owing to ignorance, which leads to various wrong and harmful actions.

Various negative forces exist in the universe that can be called evil. Just as there are toxins and pollutants in the physical environment, which are harmful, so there are negative forces in our psychic and mental environment. Wrong actions create a negative force, which like mob-action, can appear almost demonic. Yet, however strong evil appears, it can never win in the realm of truth and eternity. Only in the outer realm of temporary appearances can evil appear to have any real power. Inwardly in consciousness, it does not really exist.

The idea of a Devil or that of an entirely evil being is fundamentally mistaken. No creature exists that is inherently evil or can act in an entirely evil manner. However, the evil or harmful actions of people can create strong negative force that appears to have an existence of its own and can be almost overwhelming under certain circumstances. Such negative powers and entities do exist and must be reckoned with but can be transcended.

These negative forces are not the product of religious unbelief but of wilful egoism. The way to transcend evil is to transcend the ego, which is to go beyond the barriers of belief and identity. Unfortunately, the spectre of evil has been used to dominate or destroy people who think differently than a particular group. Such an idea of theological evil is itself one of the most evil things the human mind has invented, as the violence perpetrated in its wake throughout history has demonstrated. It turns other human beings, who are also the Divine, into demons who have to be destroyed and are not even worthy of human consideration.

Can Human Beings Be Reborn as Animals?

Human and animal evolutions are generally distinct. Once a soul has advanced to the human level, which affords easier access to higher states of consciousness than the animal state, it seldom falls back into animal births. Yet souls that are in the transitional phase between animal and human births may go back and forth for several incarnations. Human beings who have done much harm may also temporarily sink into painful animal births owing to the density of their karma.

However, while the general rule is that animal and plant evolution is lower than human evolution, there are exceptions. Sometimes great sages can take animal births like that of a bird, monkey or deer, or plant births like that of a great banyan tree. Such births allow the sage to devote more time to meditation, as they are less likely to be bothered by other people. Realizing the same Self in all beings, they can experience these lower forms of life as part of the same Divine existence. For example, the great sage Ramana Maharshi brought his cow to a state of liberation or Self-realization, demonstrating that spiritual practice is not achievable only for human beings.

Deities or liberated sages can also manifest in or communicate to us through plants and animals, and through the whole world of nature. This is because they themselves have become the entire universe. The forces of nature become their vehicles, though they might not actually take birth within them.

Do Hindus Worship Human Beings as Gods?

Given the prominence of Hindu gurus as well as the many Hindu avatars, some people think that Hindus worship human beings as Gods. Sometimes we note the term Godmen or Godwomen used to refer to Hindu gurus in a derogatory manner. Hindus may worship the Divine through the medium of great human beings who have realised the truth. However, in such cases it is not the human personality or physical body of the person which is revered but the Divine qualities manifested through them.

Hinduism holds that one of the best ways to worship the Divine is through honouring Self-realised sages and living according to their teachings. This is because realised souls provide examples of how to realise the Divine in life, which can be more meaningful than a mere idea or image of God. Yet, if we literally worship a human being as Divine, we fall from truth, as the supreme divinity is the Self of all, not a particular person. And if we consider that God can only manifest through one human being, we fall into yet greater error because God manifests through all beings. Ultimately to know God we must see all beings in the Self and the Self in all beings.

Are Gurus Necessary?

The Hindu tradition places a great importance on the role of the guru or spiritual guide, the man or woman who has realised the Divine and can lead others to it with experience. In Hindu thought, the guru is more important than the holy book, prophet or saviour with whom our contact is only indirect. Hinduism does honour the teachers and avatars of centuries ago but directs us towards great masters that exist in our own time period to show us the way to the Divine within us.

Hindu Dharma discriminates between Self-realised souls and religious teachers, who are propagating a faith or belief based upon the teachings, experience or realization of another. Yet even relative to religious teachers, the Hindu idea is different. A Hindu religious teacher is first of all a teacher of dharma or right living, not a preacher promoting conversion to a particular faith or creed. True gurus and realised souls are necessary to sustain our inner connection to the Divine as our own Self, without whom it is likely to become a matter of belief rather than inner experience.

Teachers are necessary in all fields of life. We have many different teachers during our education and attend many different schools. Similarly, gurus are of utmost importance because the spiritual path is the most profound, subtle and difficult of all endeavours.

Some of us may have prolonged personal contact with a guru. For others a short or indirect association may be enough. It is not always possible to spend time with great teachers, who may have many disciples. Yet modern gurus have provided us access to their teachings through books, audios, videos, camps and courses. Above all, we should remember that the real role of a guru is to help us understand ourselves. This means that it is not sufficient to honour the teacher outwardly, we must practice their teachings in our own lives.

Can One Change Gurus?

We all have many teachers in the different fields of learning that we take up in life. We don't have only one grade school teacher, or only one science teacher. Being exposed to a variety of teachers allows us a wide horizon of learning and we cease to identify the teaching with a mere single person.

Yet it is very helpful to have a special relationship with a particular teacher who serves as our prime mentor or role model to help us integrate the knowledge that we gain from various sources. This is particularly important on the spiritual path because inner knowledge relates to the eternal aspect of our nature and is not just a short-term subject of study. We may have one primary guru whose teaching serves as the central focus for our inner practices, just as an artist or a doctor may have a primary mentor or tutor. In the spiritual life, we should follow a teaching that leads us to the realization of the Divine within us, and a teacher, who provides a model for it. Such a Self-realised guru or Sadguru is central to Hindu practices and dharmic traditions.

It is also important to maintain a connection with the same spiritual tradition and approach even if we follow more than one guru at times. If we mix teachers of different traditions, even if they are proficient in what they know, and jumble different practices together based upon our own inclinations, it can cause confusion. While we can honour many teachers, we generally need to focus on a single teacher or line of approach in order to move directly to our goal.

What is the Place of Priests in Hinduism?

Hindu Dharma has various priests like pujaris who perform rituals and sacraments, and teach the principles of dharma. Some are employed in temples and schools. Others work independently. They are particularly active relative to Hindu festivals like Navaratri or Diwali.

Yet unlike Christian priests, they do not take confession, preach, proselytise, or function as missionaries. Nor do they serve as intermediaries between the lay population and the Divine. These priests can be married and usually have families of their own. Such Hindu priests may be different from yogis or swamis and are generally regarded as fulfilling a lesser role than great gurus. Yet many gurus know how to perform rituals as well so that these functions can overlap.

In Western religions, there has not been a proper understanding of the importance of Self-realised gurus. This has given priests and ministers the assumption that they can speak in the name of God, which has led to various distortions in the name of religion.

B. Hindu Dharma, Yoga and Spiritual Practices

What is Yoga?

Yoga arose originally as a Vedic system of spiritual practices to enable us to realise the unity of the individual soul (Jivatman) with the Supreme Self or supreme reality (Paramatman). There are many different yogic approaches in the Hindu tradition including the Yoga of Knowledge (Jnana Yoga), the Yoga of Devotion (Bhakti Yoga), the Yoga of Service (Karma Yoga), and the Yoga of Technique (Kriya Yoga). The latter can be divided fourfold as Mantra Yoga, Laya Yoga (the Yoga of the Sound Current), Hatha Yoga (the Physical and Pranic Yoga) and Raja Yoga (the Yoga of Meditation Techniques).

Yoga is a complete and integral science of spiritual development with methods and approaches for all temperaments and all levels of aspirants. The most specific system of traditional Yoga is the Raja Yoga of Patanjali, explained in his great compilation, the Yoga Sutras, which is the prime text for the Yoga Darshana, Yoga as one of the six schools of Vedic philosophy. The founder of the Yoga Darshana is said to be Hiranyagarbha in the Mahabharata, who passed his teachings down to the Rishi Vasishta.

The main traditional teachings of Jnana Yoga are those of the great sage Shankaracharya. The main text of Bhakti Yoga is the Bhakti Sutras of Narada. Jnana, Bhakti and Karma Yogas are all dealt with in the Bhagavad Gita of Sri Krishna, which is perhaps the most important and comprehensive of all yogic texts. Sri Krishna is Yogeshvara, the Lord of Yoga, and Yogavatara, the avatar of Yoga. Many Yoga traditions like Hatha Yoga and Siddha Yoga go back to Lord Shiva who is Adi Yogi and Mahayogi, as well as Yogeshvara among the deities. Most modern Yoga paths are rooted in the work of the great Yogi Gorakhnath of the Nath Yogis, who followed Lord Shiva. The practice of Yoga is the essence of true action for all human beings, which is to seek transformation within.

Isn't This a Different View Than Yoga in the West?

Yoga in the West has come to emphasise asana or Yoga postures, which is a small and preliminary part of the larger Yoga system. The Western world is physically oriented and so more concerned with the outer practices of Yoga. As such, it is Hatha Yoga, which has a greater emphasis on asana, this become most popular in the West.

Yet even traditional Hatha Yoga includes pranayama and meditation, as well as internal purification disciplines. It is a part of sadhana or spiritual practice meant to lead one to Raja Yoga or deeper meditation practices. These meditation aspects of Yoga are recognised by many people, even in the West, particularly those who are interested in higher awareness, and go far beyond any exercise class or fitness system.

What is Vedanta?

Vedanta is the culminating portion of the Vedas, the main source books of Hinduism, which deals with the ultimate truth of Self-realization, the supreme goal of life. Vedanta teaches the great truth that the Self is God, that our inner being is one with the supreme reality.

There are several schools of Vedanta but all seek realization of God or truth within us. Vedantic schools discuss the nature of the Absolute (Brahman), the Creator (Ishvara), the Soul (Jiva) and Nature, as well as karma, rebirth, bondage and liberation. Vedanta contains philosophy, theology and yogic approaches. It is a vast treasure house of wisdom that explains all the mysteries of life and comprehends all worlds and all states of consciousness.

Yoga is the practical side of Vedanta. Without yogic practices, Vedanta remains a mere theory. Without Vedantic knowledge, yogic practices remain superficial. Vedanta is the real essence of Hinduism and Yoga is its practice. The great teachings of Yoga-Vedanta are the core of Sanatana Dharma or the eternal tradition and should be spread all over the world.

What is Non-Duality (Advaita)?

Non-duality (Advaita) is the understanding that there is only one truth or reality, and therefore only one Self in all beings. This one truth is Being-Consciousness-Bliss Absolute (Sat-Chit-Ananda Brahman). It exists equally in the Creator (Ishvara), the soul (Jiva) and in the world (Jagat) and transcends all three. Such pure unity is not merely a theory but the experiential unity of the perceiver, the action of seeing, and the object perceived. Advaita or non-dualistic Vedanta is the main school emphasised by Jnana Yoga or the Yoga of Knowledge.

Without knowing the One, we remain trapped in duality, ignorance and sorrow. To know the One is to become it, which is to recognise the Self-existent reality. This requires profound meditation, which in turn is only possible if we have first purified our minds of egoism and learnt to live in harmony with universal law. Non-duality is often called the highest goal of all religious seeking. In Advaita Vedanta, it is explained with impeccable clarity, crystal clear logic, and the most powerful insight, covering the foundation and meaning of our entire existence.

What is the Importance of Meditation?

Meditation, like religion or spirituality, is a word that can be used to mean a number of things today, several of which may have little to do with what meditation truly is. The word meditation may be used for prayer, contemplation, visualization, affirmations, pranayama or mantra. So too, the goal of meditation has taken on different meanings. Meditation may be used for stress relief, for fulfilling one's personal desires and other limited objectives.

Meditation (dhyana) in the true sense refers to the ability of uniting our consciousness with the object of our perception. Its goal is liberation from the dualistic currents of thought and unification with the Divine as the ultimate ground of own Being. Meditation occurs when we empty our minds of extraneous thoughts and focus on the Divine Presence that is our true Self (Atman or Purusha).

Meditation is the main method of the Yoga of Knowledge (Jnana Yoga), but is part of all other yogic methods as only through deep meditation can we achieve the state of unity that Yoga aims at.

Meditation techniques work to harmonise the mind and body to allow for the state of meditation to proceed without obstruction. Yogic postures (asanas) calm and relax the body. Yogic breathing practices deepen and calm the breath. Mantra, visualization and concentration techniques control and focus the mind and draw it within. Then meditation, which is the natural state of the mind, can flow more easily. The silent mind has the power to heal itself and connect us with the highest consciousness in the universe.

Does Meditation Have Prerequisites?

Deep meditation is not something that anyone can do at any time without any preparation. Like any profound practice, meditation requires a way of life to support it. Meditation, which is directing the mind towards mergence in the inner reality of Consciousness, cannot occur unless there is order and harmony in our minds and in our actions.

To properly practice meditation requires first a foundation of ethical or dharmic living. One should hold to the universal yogic ethics of non-violence, truthfulness, non-stealing, control of sexual energy and non-attachment. One should follow a daily lifestyle of purity, contentment, austerity, Self-study and surrender to the Divine. These are the preliminary practices of Yoga (Yamas and Niyamas) as defined in the Yoga Sutras, the classic text on Yoga. Naturally, one cannot succeed in these perfectly in the beginning but they should be the guiding principles to improve our behaviour.

We should live a life of integrity, with emotional balance, right relationships and a vocation that is helpful to others. Sitting in a comfortable posture (asana), calmness of the breath (pranayama), withdrawing the mind from sensory distractions (pratyahara), and concentrated attention (dharana) are the yogic practices that allow deep meditation to unfold within us. We must cultivate these regularly.

What is the Power of Meditation?

Meditation may appear to some to be a useless act. It doesn't produce anything tangible or help anyone in an overt manner. To understand its great efficacy, we must recognise the role of the mind. The mind is our instrument for perceiving truth. It is like the mirror in a telescope. If that mirror is tarnished or uneven, we cannot perceive things correctly. If that mirror is clear and even, then we can perceive things as they are, which is to see the Divine presence in all.

Meditation brings clarity to the mind to allow us to perceive the truth, which aids in right judgement in all that we do. Once we know the truth, we can act in harmony with it. The very knowledge of truth is the greatest of all powers. Hence meditation is the most important practice that we can engage in for happiness, well-being and inner growth. It can gain all the worlds and all time, which we discover within us. Meditation is the main form of worship in Sanatana Dharma, which is to honour the Self within. It is the highest dharmic action of our consciousness that attunes us with all. Without daily meditation it is difficult to develop the insight to deal with our ever-changing and complicated world.

What is Self-Inquiry?

Self-inquiry (Atma-vicar) is the most important meditation practice of the Yoga of Knowledge (Jnana Yoga). It consists of tracing the I-thought back to its origin in pure consciousness within us. One casts aside the object portion of one's thoughts, the this or that with which the I has been identified, especially the I-am-the-body idea, and strives to discover the pure I-in-itself devoid of all objectivity. This means to try to find out who we truly are in our eternal Being as apart from the transient becoming in our outer lives.

Self-inquiry system is perhaps best explained in the modern world in the teachings of Ramana Maharshi, though it is the essence of Vedanta as found in the Upanishads and Bhagavad Gita. It is the royal path to non-duality (Advaita). The teachings of Shankaracharya also explain it in detail.

Unless we first know ourselves we cannot truly know anything. Yet because of our attachment to body and mind, we fail to contact our inner being and get caught in our transient, becoming in the material world, as our true nature. Through Self-inquiry we come to know our true nature as pure consciousness for which the body and mind are mere instruments, not who we really are, which is all-pervasive Being-Consciousness-Bliss (Sat-Chit-Ananda).

What is Samadhi?
Yoga culminates in the state of samadhi perhaps best described as unity consciousness, a state of absorption in pure awareness beyond the body and mind, in which one is immersed in bliss or Ananda. In fact, Yoga in the *Yoga Sutras* is traditionally defined as samadhi, which is also the goal of Yoga. Yet there are lower and higher states of samadhi, with the highest samadhi of the Atman or Purusha as the state of Self-realization and liberation from birth, death and karma, along with transcendence of time and space.

Samadhi as the goal of Yoga is the ultimate goal of Hindu Dharma and the basis of all direct spiritual experience. Hinduism exists to guide each individual to a state of samadhi as his or her natural state of awareness. Hindu Dharma aims to uplift us to the highest light of consciousness, in which we learn to see the entire universe and all creatures within us. Such samadhi is a state of higher intelligence and deeper perception that we must approach with discernment and understand with a deeper wisdom. It is not some strange trance, illusion, mindlessness or possession, as its detractors would like to portray.

All the other joys that we seek in life are but reflections of the highest samadhi that is our true nature. This is Hinduism's message of supreme happiness for everyone and for the entire universe. Please feel free to share it with all!

What is the Yoga of Devotion (Bhakti Yoga)?

The Yoga of Devotion is devotion to Ishvara or the Cosmic Lord as a spiritual path. It is not mere devotion to a religious leader or holy book, but devotion to the Divine Being as the inner reality behind the entire universe and the ground of our own being.

The Yoga of Devotion involves repeating Divine names, chanting, singing, rituals and a deep meditation in which we come into proximity to the Divine within us and are able to merge into it. Devotion (Bhakti) usually relies upon a form, which may be that of a particular deity, avatar or teacher, though formless devotion exists as well and is often combined with meditation on form. Devotion usually establishes a relationship with God as father, mother or beloved. Devotional practices, however, are not simply formalities or technicalities but a spontaneous unfoldment of the heart in its love of God.

Devotion is the most basic and easiest of all spiritual paths because love of the Divine is inherent in the soul. It forms the most common aspect of Hindu Dharma. Even if we cannot think of knowing God, we can uncover this spontaneous love of the Creator, Preserver and Dissolver of the universe. Devotion is also the basis of wisdom because only if we love truth can we really learn what it is. All of our human problems occur from seeking love apart from the Divine. Seeking love in the Divine, which is to recognise the Divine love in all creation and at the core of our hearts, is the end to all suffering.

What is the Importance of Surrender?

Surrender to the divine within is the primary approach of the Yoga of Devotion (Bhakti Yoga). It consists in offering oneself completely to the Divine or inner truth. This requires consecrating our thoughts and feelings, wishes and desires to the Divine to work with, according to the Divine Will.

Surrender is the deepest capacity of the individual soul or Jivatman. It arises naturally when we give up personal seeking in the outer world as our main focus in life. By surrendering to the Divine presence in all things, we gain the grace inherent in everything. Surrender then is an acknowledgement of the universal truth and a perception of the universal Being in all beings.

We suffer in life from unwillingness to surrender our ego. We try to impose our limited personal will upon the unlimited universe, which leads to frustration. We think that the burdens of the world belong to us and that we must try to save everyone. Surrender, which is recognizing the Divine rulership over all, means letting go of this personal will, which will then bring real peace and happiness. We cannot change life, nor do we need to try to. The Divine power or Ishvara-Shakti is ever at work, accomplishing all that is necessary to do. If we look within and surrender, we will find that all the imperfections of the world lose their significance.

Why Should One Repeat Mantras?
Mantra is perhaps the key and most characteristic practice of all the forms of Hindu Yoga and sadhana. Sound makes up the mind. It determines the field of awareness in which we think, feel and perceive. You can observe this for yourself. Note the kinds of sounds you repeat and take in during the day and see how these affect you from physical to psychological levels. A harmonious sound pattern in the mind facilitates a deeper awareness. A disturbed sound pattern in the mind prevents our awareness from going deeper.

Mantras are yogically energised sound patterns designed to link us up to the Divine Word or cosmic creative vibration. They help purify and silence the mind to allow for deep meditation and samadhi. Mantras set up a different kind of energy in the mind, an intentional energization of the mind toward spiritual practice and realization. Simplest and most important are single syllable *bija* mantras like OM or 'Hreem'.

Mantras are simple and easy to do, as they only require that we recite a word audibly or mentally. Mantras can be done anywhere or anytime as they do not depend upon any external substances. Mantra is thereby the most practical tool of the spiritual life. All of us should do regular mantras to connect with the Divine. Then we will no longer have to struggle to meditate. Mantra should become the ground of our minds, then nothing that comes from the realm of the senses can imbalance us.

What is the Yoga of Service (Karma Yoga)?

True service is to serve the Divine to help a higher consciousness unfold in the world. This requires devotion and surrender within. True service is not merely promoting one religious creed against another or fostering conversion to a belief. True selfless service is only possible when our actions are not based upon ulterior motives, when we are not seeking special results for ourselves in what we do.

Service to others may involve all manner of help whether charity, medical aid, teaching, or establishing schools and hospitals. It may include helping animals and caring for the Earth itself. It may involve political action but approached with care, sensitivity and selflessness. Whether these outer actions are spiritually beneficial and constitute true Karma Yoga depends upon on whether we are working with respect to the Divine presence in all.

Whatever we do in life should be an offering to the Divine, not done for our personal benefit only. If it is not then our action is deficient and will not bring what we truly aspire for. Our spiritual practice itself, including meditation done properly, is the highest service in which we bring the Divine power directly into our own minds and the entire world with which we are connected. In serving others there is no lesser person that we need to save. It is a matter of helping each person discover his or her own Divine Self and essence.

What is the Place of Compassion in Hinduism?

Hindu Dharma emphasises compassion as the main attitude we should have towards other creatures, and charity or giving as the main duty that we need to perform in life. Compassion consists of offering prayers, blessings and good wishes for all beings, including animals, plants, departed ancestors and inhabitants of subtle worlds, such as we find in Hindu prayers for universal peace. Charity consists of actions done to benefit other people and the world, not merely material aid but service of all types, including teaching and caring for others.

Yet charity is part of the outer dimension of the compassion. In the oneness of reality there is really no one to give and no one to receive. True compassion must rest upon Self-knowledge or it becomes a separative act. True compassion is not helping those we consider to be weak, poor or deprived, but respecting and nurturing the Divine Self in all creatures.

Compassion toward others should be balanced with devotion to the Divine. True compassion comes from the Divine and flows through us by the strength of our devotion. True compassion has no secret motive to gain, or to receive recognition as being a compassionate person. It is part of the movement of Oneness in which we do not see any real difference between the Self and other.

What is the Place of Prayer in Hindu Thought?

Since the ancient Vedas, Hindu teachings contain prayers, praises and propitiations to the Divine reality in its different aspects. Prayers may be offered at various levels. The lower level consists of praying to the Divine for ordinary goals of life like health, wealth, and personal happiness to benefit us personally in our outer lives. The higher level is to pray to the Divine for spiritual knowledge and Divine love. This helps bring us into the spiritual life, our Yoga and meditation practices. There is a third form in which we pray to the Divine for the benefit of others, such as prayers for universal peace and understanding, which is essential for social harmony and well being.

There is a science of prayer through which we can connect with the Divine energies in the universe to bring about the fulfilment of the desires of the soul. For this purpose, the use of the appropriate mantras and rituals is very important. Prayer, like mantra, can also be misapplied and used for non-spiritual ends. If our prayer is motivated by the wish to control or hurt others, for example, it is impure or tamasic. Prayer to convert others to a belief is another lower form of prayer that is tinged with egoism and violence.

Prayer is preliminary to meditation through which alone we can discover a direct knowledge of the Divine. Real communion with the Divine comes through the silent mind, the mind that is not seeking anything for itself but is open to the bliss of pure existence. The receptive mind is the highest state of prayer, in which no thought occurs.

Why Should One Perform Rituals?

Whatever action we do repeatedly over time becomes a kind of ritual that shapes our behaviour. If we jog every day or watch a certain programme every week then these actions gain a certain momentum in our lives. Any routine or discipline is a kind of ritual. Religious rituals are special actions or sacraments performed with a spiritual intent to set in motion a higher power in our lives. Hindu Dharma contains many such rituals that employ all the essences of nature—flowers, fragrances, fruits, incense, lamps, and artistic forms—to help bring higher vibrations into the world. This is the basis of Hindu pujas and temple worship.

Dharma requires the application of consciousness in sacred action, which is a kind of ritual. Dharmic rituals purify the mind and draw benefic forces into society. They change our psychic field so that our minds become receptive to higher forces. All rituals should be properly empowered with mantras to truly be efficacious. We should remember that the most important ritual or regular action we can do is meditation, which is the great ritual of awareness, offering the seen into the seer for the beauty of unitary reality.

Why Are There So Many Hindu Rituals?

Hindus recognise a Divine presence or Gods and Goddesses everywhere, in people, plants, animals, and different places in nature. They may perform ritual worship to consecrate inanimate objects like books, automobiles or computers and bring a sacred energy into how we use them. While this may appear as a superstition to those of us who have lost our sense of the sacred, there is an important and universal meaning behind it.

To worship something in the Hindu sense means to recognise the Divine presence within it and to be open to its grace. We need the favour, communication and understanding of all that we are connected with in life; and nothing is really without consciousness or apart from the Divine.

Hindu ritual worship (puja) is both an art and science for accomplishing this. We need to honour the Divine in everything, particularly in the most simple and intimate things of our lives. If we only honour the Divine in the distance, we remain ignorant of its all-pervasive being, and our own ordinary actions will be ungodly. To have a strong and yet diverse culture of ritual aids in the development of the human spirit and our harmonious interaction with the rhythms of the universe, including unfolding our own creativity.

What is the Importance of Temples?

Temples are sacred places where the power of collective spiritual aspiration is developed and focused. We could say that temples are like power stations for generating a higher consciousness in the world. They are communication centres to contact the Divine and the cosmic powers and allow them to descend. Temples serve to bring in spiritual energies and purify our collective psyche of negative karmas. A real temple is a place of inner worship, not just outer ceremonies. It is not a church where preaching goes on, but a place of peace in which meditation and devotional worship occurs to open our minds and hearts directly to the Divine.

For the Hindu mind, spirituality and life are not separate, just as God and nature are one. A Hindu temple includes life and people, along with deities and gurus. It is not a monument to a uniform belief, but an expression of life in all of its richness and abundance.

A Hindu temple includes artwork, paintings and sculptures of various types. It includes music and dance, and the temple itself is a place where regular festivals are celebrated. It has a place for animals like elephants, monkeys, cows or peacocks. It has incense, ghee lamps, flowers and generally a water tank for ritual bathing. Even food and sweets are there. It is a place not only for adults but also for children to play. It is a place not just for prayer at a particular time of the day but a place one can come at any time. The Hindu temple is a miniature universe. It includes everything and therefore it does not stand apart from anything, therefore drawing us into the cosmic reality.

What is the Importance of Pilgrimage (Yatra)?

Pilgrimage consists of visiting sacred sites for worship and meditation. These sacred places may be manmade structures like temples or powerful locations in nature like mountains or rivers, such as the Himalayas or the Ganga. Such places in nature may be made more holy by the practices that various sages and yogis have performed there. Hindus recognise innumerable holy places and find them wherever they live. There are numerous temples and tirthas that Hindus have recognised throughout the sacred geography of India.

Each place has its own energy based in the location and actions performed there. Certain places have a greater spiritual energy than others, which we can benefit from by visiting them with receptivity. Yet the pilgrimage to external holy places should include an inner pilgrimage or spiritual quest, which is mantra and meditation. Actually our entire life is a pilgrimage and all places are sacred sites if we know how to look. This is what we learn through going to holy places. All of us should perform regular pilgrimages, particularly when we want to change our lives in a higher direction, honouring nature and the cosmic temple within us.

Hindus regularly perform the largest pilgrimages in the world from the Kumbha Melas that tens of million attend, to many local shrines and temples that in total draw in even more visitors. From Mt Kailash in Tibet to Kanyakumari at the southernmost tip of India, there are regular pilgrimages engaging Hindu devotees, and most Hindus are proud of participating in many of these.

What is the Place of Monasticism in Hindu Dharma?
Most religions have monastic orders, which occur as an integral part of human spiritual aspiration. Such orders, properly formulated, allow individuals to devote themselves exclusively to spiritual practices by not placing outer social demands upon them through work and family.

The Hindu tradition has numerous monastic traditions of sadhus and swamis, with the largest number of monks of any religion in the world today, numbering probably more than two million in various orders. Yet, Hindu monks do not always live or reside together at particular monastic institutions. They may wander, taking food from donors, stopping temporarily at different ashrams, or take hermitage in the mountains or wilderness. They may create their own centres or ashrams, where they teach or develop small communities. They devote their lives to Yoga and meditation and often become great teachers.

True monasticism, however, should not be confused with missionaries, whose aim is converting others to a belief. If one is not performing spiritual practices, monasticism may be no more than service to a dogma or institution. Certain militant or political monastic orders have done great damage in the world fanatically promoting their beliefs. Nor does the value of monasticism exclude the value of the married or householder life. While the monastic path can be more direct, the householder life is generally more practical for most people and can, in time, lead to the same goal.

What is the Importance of Non-Violence?

Non-violence or ahimsa is perhaps the cardinal virtue recognised in dharmic traditions. Non-violence is the supreme Dharma, the great law of honouring life, to the extent that if we commit non-violence, we cease to be truly religious and lose our connection with the Divine.

Dharma means natural law and the most basic natural law is to remain in harmony with our fellow creatures. No creature likes to suffer. To attune ourselves with the nature of all beings, we should not seek suffering for any being. Non-violence, therefore, is the foundation of all true ethics of truthfulness, honesty and non-stealing. Non-violence in Hinduism is the universal great vow. Only if we have an attitude of non-violence toward all beings can we have true universality. Ahimsa purifies our own mind and hearts.

True ahimsa means not to wish harm for any being in thought, word and deed. It is not merely a matter of refraining from physical violence, which even a coward can do. It means non-violence in our own homes and families as well. Nor is it limited to human beings. It means to not be violent towards plants, animals or the Earth itself.

Non-violence is essential to Self-realization because if we see the Self in all beings and all beings in the Self, we cannot possibly wish harm to anyone. Violence is the denial of the spiritual life that is based upon inner peace. To use violence to promote a religion is to deny the real spirit of religion. To try to make a religion spread through the use of force is not to spread religion but to encourage plunder and destruction.

What is the Role of Prayers for Peace in Hindu Dharma?

Hinduism abounds with beautiful prayers, chants and mantras for peace, happiness and well-being for all people, all creatures and for the entire world. The Vedas contain special mantras to draw universal peace into our human lives through the heavens, the atmosphere, the Earth, the waters, the forests and the whole of life. We reside in a universe pervaded by peace as the very ground of existence or Brahman. If we open up to that power of peace in our environment, it can enter into all that we do. Nature's ecosystem is one of universal peace but we as human beings have forgotten and ignored this in our preoccupation with our separative life and mind.

According to Vedic thought, peace is not a manmade truce or compromise, not a compact between different people to suspend or end human conflicts. Any peace that is made between human beings can be broken. To establish enduring peace, we must make ourselves receptive to the peace that is the true nature of the cosmos and our own inner Self. This requires surrendering our ego, our personal emotions and our selfish desires.

We can best define the Divine as immutable peace or Shanti. Boundless peace is the essence of the Eternal Being that is not limited by the waves of time. Embracing that peace, we can let go of all the bonds of sorrow.

Om Shanti! Shanti! Shanti!

Does Non-Violence Exclude Self-Defence?

True non-violence recognises the right of people to defend themselves, their lives and their property, including family, community and country, from unprovoked attack. However, monks and yogis who have renounced the world no longer have any attachments. They are not required to defend anything, though it is not wrong for them to defend themselves or others if they choose to do so.

It is important that non-violence does not become an excuse for not defending the truth or saving lives. Non-violence does not mean to passively and fearfully allow the forces of untruth to push forward unquestioned. It does not mean to bow down to bullies and tyrants and let them wreak havoc.

True non-violence is not cowardice that flees from confrontation but courage that faces all confrontations without running away or resorting to unnecessary force. Yet even if we have to resort to physical violence to protect ourselves or others, which may be necessary at times in this cruel world, it should be a last resort, and we should do so without hatred in our hearts.

Why is There Violence in Some Hindu Stories?

The main violence that we observe in Hindu mythology is the destruction of various demons by deities, avatars or great sages, as in the story of Lord Rama and Ravana in the Ramayana. These stories are symbolic of the victory truth over falsehood and are far from ordinary depictions of human violence, much less a glorification of it. Even in the Mahabharata War, violence was taken up by Arjuna and the Pandavas as the last measure after all else has failed, as part of a defensive battle. There is nowhere in Hinduism a glorification of violence to promote religion or as part of wars of conversion.

There are violent and corrupt elements in human society that promote crime and conflict that must be kept in check. The best way is through the proper education that prevents negative behavioural patterns from developing. Yet if these negative actions do arise, it may be necessary to restrain those who perpetrate them, sometimes by force, just as a tumour must sometimes be surgically removed to save the health of the body.

For this purpose of restraint, Hinduism honours the role of the warrior class, which includes occupations like the police and the military. Such spiritual warriors should aim at preventing harm in the world and actively stopping it from occurring. For them, knowing how to avoid violence is as important as knowing how to respond with force if necessary. Rama, Krishna, Arjuna and

Yudhishthira are some of the great warrior heroes of Hindu culture who demonstrate such restraint, Self-discipline and courage. If Dharma is attacked, Dharma must be defended, not with brutality but with justice.

What is the Place of Art in Hindu Dharma?

The Western world has suffered from a split between the sacred and the profane going back nearly two thousand years. Into the realm of the profane was placed most of art, science and philosophy. The sacred was limited to the realm of religious law and theology, in which creative expression was denigrated along with the idea that the world is evil and God has no image. This denial of images naturally stifles art, including of a sacred nature. When images were allowed, as in Catholic Christianity, their forms were restricted according to religious doctrines. Similarly, music was sometimes banned as unholy or limited in its forms or usage. When art did escape the shackles of religion, which began in Europe with the Renaissance, it developed apart from religion and became a personal expression, not a way of connecting with the cosmic mind as in Hindu thought.

In India this split between art and religion did not occur, though Hindus do discriminate the outer or mundane realms from inner spirituality. In the Hindu view, art can be a way of yogic knowledge. It is a question of attitude and approach. Art can be a natural expression of devotion or love of the Divine.

Hindu Dharma abounds with poetry, drama, sculpture, painting, music and dance as an integral part of worship, as part of the temple life and its regular activities. The forms of Hindu art embrace all the beauty and variety of life and nature. Hindu music is not sombre or rarefied but full of vitality. Hindu sculpture can be voluptuous. It is often hard for people to tell the difference between Hindu religious art on one hand, and art of a folk or personal nature on the other. The two were never separate to the Hindu mind, which offers all art forms to the Divine within as act of devotion.

Art is one of the doors to the spiritual life. Creativity is a step toward Divinity. Such art, however, should be done to honour the sacred as a path of Yoga, in which case it can embrace all the beauty of nature and wisdom of awareness. Art produced out of selfish or commercial motives, or which comes from the intellect only, cannot take us to the fountainhead of creativity that lies within. Today we need a creative renaissance, in which art in all of its forms is once more taken up as an integral part of the spiritual life and yogic quest. Art should be a form of worship, filled with devotion, and carrying the power of the cosmic being.

What is the Value of Vedic Astrology?

Astrology is one of the most important cosmic sciences because it shows how the subtle forces of the universe affect our destiny, both individual and collective. A comprehensive system of astrology, astronomy and cosmology is necessary for a complete understanding of the workings of universe and the workings of the law of karma.

Vedic or Hindu astrology (Jyotish) is a complex and intricate system of inner knowledge imbued with the wisdom of innumerable sages and Selfrealised yogis. It is a profound science with many layers, reflecting the multidimensional harmony of the universe. It can help us understand the inner energy patterns behind our health, career, relationships and the development of our spiritual life. It provides the keys to the unfoldment of our life on all levels, in its different cycles and seasons. Jyotish is said to be the very eye of the Vedas, providing us the vision for right action inwardly and outwardly, guiding the soul forward.

Such a science of astrology should not be confused with crude fortune telling. It is not a matter of wishful thinking but of a detailed study of how the stars, planets and natural time cycles affect us according to certain cosmic laws and sacred mathematics. The true astrologer is the ultimate psychologist and sociologist who can help us build the foundation for a yogic life. He or she unfolds the inner meaning behind our changing life events so that we can take the appropriate action at the appropriate time and fully use our soul's potential in this human incarnation.

What is the Healing Power of Ayurvedic Medicine?

Health is the foundation of all that we do. Without adequate health and well-being of the body, we will not have the energy to pursue any of the goals of life. Yet true health is not merely physical strength and stamina but purity of body and mind, which is also necessary for sustaining any spiritual practice. As a yogic form of healing, Ayurveda directs us to Self-understanding as the ultimate means of harmony and happiness. It does not stop short with feeling good physically but shows us how to use the healthy body to pursue a higher life of creativity and awareness.

Ayurveda, the science (veda) of life (ayur), is the medical aspect of the universal tradition of Sanatana Dharma, Vedic medicine for body and mind. It shows us how the great forces of nature work within us to sustain our body-mind functioning and how they can be consciously used to enhance the energy and capacity of our entire being. Ayurveda promotes positive health through the use of right diet, herbs, specially prepared mineral formulations, special massage methods, and profound therapies of detoxification and rejuvenation. It recommends a lifestyle based upon the ascertainment of our unique psychophysical constitution according to the balance of the elements and biological humours of Vata, Pitta and Kapha within us. By doing so it helps bring all the healing powers of nature into our own daily activity.

Ayurveda is the medicine of nature, the medicine of life that connects us to the healing forces of the greater universe of consciousness. Until we restore the healing forces of nature in society, our planet must remain in crisis and our medical systems based upon chemical drugs will be more of a curse than a blessing for our greater well-being. Ayurvedic medicine is, therefore, of crucial importance for healing ourselves and healing our world. It is the foundation of any true Vedic or yogic life.

Why Should One Learn Sanskrit?

An essential part of any spiritual tradition is a language and terminology of higher consciousness. Such a universal mantric language exists within Sanatana Dharma as Sanskrit, which arises from the inner vision of the ancient yogis and seers. Sanskrit is the oldest of the Indo-European languages and has been looked upon as the mother of all languages. There is no language of such antiquity that has been preserved in such depth and with such extensive teachings.

Language is based upon sound and meaning. The meaning is most important but the sound should be appropriate to it. This is why poetry, which blends sound and meaning, has so much power. Each sound has a certain energetic quality that can be useful for conveying certain meanings. Sanskrit is a purely vibrational language in which sound and meaning are united in the right way to teach the inner truth beyond the visible world. Sanskrit reflects the laws and powers of cosmic intelligence and structures human speech according to universal law. That is why Sanskrit is often called the language of the Gods.

As such, Sanskrit is an extremely precise language for working with spiritual experiences and higher consciousness that are otherwise hard to describe. Not surprisingly, we have had to import many Sanskrit words into English—like guru, mantra, prana, Shakti, and Kundalini—to help us understand the deeper realms that our ordinary language and mentality is not familiar with.

Learning Sanskrit can be an important tool for developing the mind, controlling thought, sharpening perception and increasing creativity. It also provides access to the largest literature of Self-knowledge and Yoga in the world: Hindu, Buddhist and Jain teachings going back for many thousands of years. However, we should not merely learn to read Sanskrit or approach it as a dead language.

The power of Sanskrit resides in its sound. We should learn to speak and chant it, eventually even to think in terms of it. Sanskrit is the basis of the most powerful Hindu and Buddhist mantras. The very letters of the Sanskrit alphabet form a garland of mantras that holds the key to many cosmic forces.

Classical Sanskrit was codified by the great grammarian Panini (c. 500 BC), whose classic the *Ashtadhyaya* is still studied for a proper understanding of the language. His model of language was recently found to be the most scientific for use with computers. Sanskrit is thus both the language of the past and the future. Through it we can communicate with all time.

Most of the distortions about Hinduism have arisen from mistranslating or even ignoring the Sanskrit terms that explain the teachings. If one approaches Hinduism through Sanskrit, one will find no problems in understanding its true meaning as Sanatana Dharma. All the distortions born of trying to recast Hinduism in the mould of Abrahamic traditions will disappear. If you study Hinduism in Sanskrit texts, you will be able to understand its true teachings.

The almighty power of the Supreme Divinities is only One.
Rigveda III.55.1

Endless vast paths encircle Heaven and Earth.
Rigveda V.45.2

May Heaven and the Atmosphere grant us peace. May the Earth give us peace along with the Waters. May the herbs and the forests be peaceful to us. May all the cosmic powers grant us peace.

May the Divine Being grant us peace. May the entire universe be at peace. May there be the peace of peace. May that peace dwell within me.
Shukla Yajurveda XXXVI.17

Questions on Hinduism 2: Hindu Dharma and the World Today

In this section we will examine the important issues of culture, religion, and spirituality from the standpoint of Hindu thought to see not only what is relevant today, but what is truly universal and meaningful. We will find much that remains significant not only in Hindu spirituality but also in its cultural forms, regardless of whether we live in India or in other countries.

A. Religion, Spirituality and Humanity

Should We Follow Any Religion at All?

If we look at what religions have done to humanity throughout history, it appears that it might be better not to be religious at all. It would save us from many wars, hostilities and misunderstandings, such as history is mired with. On the other hand, the record of materialist ideologies like communism, socialism and capitalism has not been better, and has similarly resulted in exploitation and violence on a large scale. Most importantly, none of us appears to be content thinking that this is our only life to live and all of us wish to live forever.

Spirituality in the true sense is a means of discovering the Divine or eternal reality within us, not a dogma defining what God is outside of ourselves. Such spirituality is not an organised belief system but a set of spiritual and yogic practices to be adapted on an individual basis. These practices include the full range of human approaches to the Divine, the paths of Knowledge (Jnana Yoga), Devotion (Bhakti Yoga), Service (Karma Yoga) and Meditation Techniques (Raja Yoga). While we should discard religion in the outer sense as organised dogma and social conditioning, we should embrace spirituality in the inner sense as Yoga and meditation. Otherwise our lives will have no enduring meaning and we will take nothing with us at death but frustration and sorrow.

What is the Real Purpose of Religion?

Religion, particularly as the term has been formulated in the Western world, contains two aspects. First, religions teach certain moral and ethical principles. Religion tells us not to be selfish, not to harm others, not to lie, steal, or cheat, but to do good, to be helpful, compassionate, and thoughtful. These are universal human values that all societies require to function. While the details of such principles vary in different religions, all religions contain these to some degree.

Second, religions contain an aspect of dogma. They brand certain actions wrong not because they violate any universal ethics but because they go against a particular belief. For example, if a religion tells us that it is wrong to call upon the Divine by another name than the one sanctioned by the it, or that it is heretical to think that God is not limited to a certain prophet or incarnation, these are not statements of universal truth but dogmas that reflect only the opinion of a particular group. Such dogmas end up promoting actions that violate universal ethics, causing us to mistrust and mistreat those who do not subscribe to them, such as believers and non-believers.

The first aspect of religion, universal ethics, is preliminary to the spiritual path and the foundation for it if complete in its formulation. The second side, theological dogma, can be harmful to the spiritual path and contradict the first side of religion. It is spiritually unethical to insist that one sins by questioning religious dogma, or that by not following the prescriptions of a particular religious belief one has done an act of the same negative nature as harming another person.

Organised religion combines the nectar of universal ethics with the poison of exclusive belief. Unless we can sift the nectar from the poison, such religion will likely harm our spiritual potential. Following universal ethics completely, like the principles of truthfulness and non-violence, we have the basis for a deeper spiritual path.

What is the Difference Between Religion and Inner Spirituality?

Religion and spirituality are not the same thing as many of us have discovered. Religion at best serves to provide ethical principles and outer ways of worship through rituals and prayers. True spirituality consists of internal attitudes and practices that lead to a real change of consciousness, like the many paths of Yoga. Today the world needs not a new religious belief but a new experiential spirituality at an individual level; such as abound in Hindu Dharma.

To achieve the true goal of life we should follow an enlightenment path, founded by enlightened sages that leads to Self-realization. All that is called religion does not do this and may remain caught in emotion, opinion or arrogance. Some religious groups oppose any inner spirituality or mysticism because it removes the individual from the control of religious authorities. Hindu Dharma honours individual spiritual practice or sadhana as the basis of its practices and encourages each one to engage in these.

Why Should We Follow Any Tradition at All?

Outer religious traditions often set up various unquestionable authorities and conditioning patterns that stifle individual intelligence and creativity. They form vested interests that war with one other to control the minds of people. However, if we look deeply, we see that such criticisms do not apply to the idea of an inner spiritual tradition, which is continuity in a field of inner knowledge.

It is not possible to avoid tradition in anything we do. We must develop teachings that grow and continue with every generation. This development, over time itself, becomes tradition. As soon as a teaching endures beyond the lifetime of a teacher it becomes a tradition. Or, as soon as it expands beyond the teachings of one person, it becomes a tradition.

One person in isolation cannot accomplish much in any field. Without a tradition of science to work from, what can one person do in the name of science, for example? Just as we need continuity, which is tradition, in other branches of learning, so we must have it in the spiritual realm. Otherwise each person is compelled to start from the beginning.

Culture and intelligence are collectively developed, the product of many people working together over a long period of time. Tradition is important in all that we do. Language, for example, cannot be developed by one person alone. It is part of a great collective effort and historical tradition going back over centuries. A comprehensive and open spiritual tradition is the need of our times. Tradition provides a guideline of experience to help us grow. Yet tradition must be kept open and alive and not become rigid or authoritarian. For this, tradition must base itself not on fixed forms but on living spiritual experience, such as great gurus can provide. Tradition should be a field of resources for all to benefit from, not a set of dogmas no one is allowed to question.

Are All Religions the Same?

Because there are many common points in the religious experience, which takes us in the direction of unity consciousness, some people have come to the conclusion that all religions are basically the same—that it doesn't matter if one goes to a temple, church or mosque, or whether one prays, fasts or meditates. They believe that as long as one is doing something that can be called religious, one will likely gain the same spiritual goal only along a different route.

Let us compare this with the field of art to show the weakness of this line of thought. Because there is a unity of the human creative experience behind all art does not mean that all art is the same, and it certainly does not mean that all that is called art is good art. Similarly, that there is a unity of scientific inquiry behind all scientific pursuits does not mean that all science is the same, that all scientific theories are correct and lead to the same conclusions, or that it does not matter what experimental procedures we employ.

There is a tremendous gap between organised religion, which divides people by belief, and the inner religious or spiritual experience, which unites them. And the religious experience itself has different stages, levels and variations. All religious experiences are not merely equal or the same. There are many gradations between ordinary human consciousness and the highest Self-realization, which should not all be lumped together. Religious experiences can occur in an impure or untrained mind and be mixed with egoism and illusion. In addition, different spiritual practices, like the Yogas of Knowledge and Devotion, proceed by different lines and have their own characteristic experiences that may be impersonal or personal. While we should recognise the general unity of spiritual experiences, we should also acknowledge their diversity and different levels.

That all religions are one is a statement similar to that all water is one. This does not mean that all water is fit to drink. There are religious doctrines and practices, which are outward, limited or of preliminary value, and those that are inappropriate or even wrong altogether, just as is the case for human behaviour in all spheres of life. To discover the inner truth in any field requires a great deal of discrimination, a discerning of the essence, not merely a superficial equation all things as equal.

Are All Religions Alternative Approaches to the Same Truth?

One may recognise that differences exist between religions but consider these to be merely various alternatives, just as different roads may lead ultimately to the same goal. This is true of spiritual teachings that have practices of contemplation and meditation, but differ in outer factors of name and form, like different enlightenment or Self-realization traditions. We can consider these to be different approaches to the same truth. However, many religious teachings differ in fundamental values, goals and practices, not merely in outer names and forms. These cannot be merely alternative paths to the same reality.

For example, we can recognise that there are many different names for fire. Calling fire by a different name does not mean that one does not understand the nature of fire. But this is not to say that fire can differ in its essential nature and qualities, that for some people fire is hot and for other people it can be cold. While formal differences can be reconciled, substantial differences cannot. Truth must be the same. It cannot vary according to the varying beliefs and opinions of human beings.

When religious differences are merely a matter of words or forms, we can recognise a common truth behind them. If one person calls the ultimate reality love, another calls it truth, yet another calls it the infinite, and we can accept a common reality behind these different formulations. But when religious teachings have differences of a substantive nature, we cannot accept their varying views as equally true. For example, the law of karma and rebirth leading to bondage or liberation cannot be equally true as that of sin or salvation leading to heaven or hell because these two views are substantially different. One may try to reconcile them in various ways, but one view must end up as the final truth.

The goal of life is to discover the supreme truth, not merely to uphold religion as we know it, as truth. Religion at best is an expedient measure to aid us in the pursuit of higher consciousness. It should never be made an end-in-itself. If it is a question of religion or truth, we should always follow truth.

Can One Follow Many Spiritual Paths?

There are a number of spiritual paths that provide meditation practices which can, if applied with the proper background and guidance, lead to union with the Divine or the realization of our inner Self. In addition, it is always good to know something about the world's different spiritual and religious traditions, whether one resonates with them or not, in order to broaden one's mental horizon, just as it is good to know something about the different cultures and customs of various lands and peoples.

However, human life does not provide the time for us to follow out the practices of a variety of spiritual traditions, which require a certain period of application in order to work properly, except perhaps as a preliminary exploration. For one's actual practice one has to choose a certain approach and a connection with specific teachers, generally within the same tradition, and follow this with long-term dedication.

We can compare this with any field of learning. One can recognise the validity of various artistic approaches, but one cannot practice all techniques of art. One cannot be simultaneously a sculptor, painter, musician and dancer, in ancient, medieval and modern styles, though of course some versatility is possible or even desirable. In one's actual practice one will have to make a choice and follow it out. Moreover, the aim of a spiritual practice is not merely to learn about various traditions but to know oneself, and for this the teaching is a guideline, not the goal. To be a true artist one does not need to study all forms of art, which will more like produce an art scholar, but only to discover one's own inner creativity. If we spend our time exploring different teachings and traditions, rather than performing our own meditation practices, we have missed the point. The important thing is to reach the goal, not to wander between the paths.

What Do All Hindus Believe?

Hindu Dharma does not emphasise a particular code of beliefs that divides humanity into believers and non-believers. It does not begin with the assertion 'I believe in God' but with the recognition 'The Divine or universal truth and my inner nature are one'. It does not state that only those of our faith can find God or truth but that the nature of all beings is Divine and unlimited. Hindu Dharma does not propose simplistic articles of faith, like the belief in various miracles or special revelations, but directs us to experience the supreme truth as clearly as we can see the sun rise in the morning.

Hinduism is not centred around a particular name or form but on the truth that lies within and behind all names and forms. It emphasises knowing the seer, not simply the seen. It is an open tradition that encourages a diversity of approaches, not a monolithic religion consisting of a standard creed.

The principles that Hindus accept are not articles of faith but Dharmas or natural laws. Such are the law of karma, rebirth, the existence of a cosmic Lord (Ishvara) and guiding intelligence, the beneficence of the world of nature, a multileveled universe from the material world to the highest consciousness, and Self-realization as the ultimate goal of life. Hindus similarly share common practices like ritual, prayer, pilgrimage, charity, Yoga and meditation but there is no prescribed system of activities that all Hindus must follow. There are common Hindu values and attitudes like non-violence, truthfulness, and Self-discipline, which are behind these practices.

Hindu practices are employed as ways of finding truth, not as dogmas that tell us what that truth is supposed to be. Hindu Dharma tells us that it is more important to give people the means to find truth themselves, rather than to tell them what truth is supposed to be. As truth is our own nature, the best way to let it come forth is to no longer impose any external influences upon it.

Many people who may not formally regard themselves as Hindus may have a Hindu view of reality. This is because the Hindu view is not a sectarian view but that of the whole, the totality, which is that One Self is all. Hinduism includes not only the religions of this world but also those of the different planes of consciousness up to the Absolute. It is not only the religion of one incarnation but of all our births, whether in this world or another.

Isn't a Scientific Approach to Spirituality Required?

Without a rational and scientific approach to the spiritual life, the spiritual life easily becomes dogma or superstition. Yet, to scientifically approach the spiritual life is a different procedure than to scientifically approach the outer world. The Divine as the infinite and eternal cannot be observed in a laboratory, dissected on a table, or seen in a telescope or a microscope. It requires an inner scientific approach to discover, which means directly observing the workings of our own minds to discern the consciousness behind them. It rests on the ability to discriminate between the eternal and the transient and to focus one's awareness on the eternal.

The beauty of dharmic traditions is that they have maintained a rational approach to the spiritual life that can be used by everyone. Yet the spiritual life is not merely a science, it is also an art, and must be approached with sensitivity and creativity. The spiritual aspect of life is most subtle and requires an appropriate refinement of mind to discern. It cannot, like an object on the table, be obvious to our outer vision. The science of Yoga presents such a rational approach to spirituality that we must develop on a global basis.

We do this by taking up the practices and seeing how they really work within us and in our own lives.

What is the Cultural Relevance of Self-knowledge?

We need spiritual teachings appropriate for our changing circumstances, whatever these may be. For this it is essential to follow a living spiritual tradition, not a dead and stereotyped belief. Yet as the goal of the spiritual life is the eternal, the teaching must be grounded in timeless reality and not merely be a fad of the moment. The forms we follow should be based on the eternal truth but adjusted according to the needs of the times.

The universal teaching is a science of Self-realization. To know ourselves is the most important consideration, whatever our cultural or geographical background. That inner Self transcends time, space and objectivity. Yet it is important to connect with a living tradition of Self-knowledge, so that we can find a teacher and teaching suitable for our temperament.

Moreover, Self-knowledge creates a certain culture and way of life. It creates an awareness of our posture, from which the science of asana or yogic postures arose. It creates an awareness of breath, from which the science of pranayama arose. It creates an awareness of speech, from which the Sanskrit language and Mantra Yoga arose. It creates a science of health, from which Ayurveda arose. It creates an understanding of symbol and ritual, from which the science of puja (Hindu ritual) arose. A culture of Self-knowledge is useful and this is the essence of Sanatana Dharma. Naturally it has to be continually adjusted individually and collectively.

What the world needs is a living tradition of higher consciousness in every country, which goes back to enlightened and Self-realised teachers. Since the West has not preserved such a tradition in its culture, it must connect up with traditions where it is still vibrant. Hindu Dharma, offering such enlightened teaching, without insisting upon the adaptation of an exclusive religious identity, is an excellent foundation for this.

What is the Importance of a Yogic Tradition?

Spiritual traditions exist to various degrees and for various purposes. What is necessary is a comprehensive spiritual tradition that contains a complete and practical science of Self-realization. Fragmentary, broken or incomplete spiritual and occult traditions have some benefit but are usually not sufficient for full realization.

A comprehensive spiritual tradition must contain all the different paths of knowledge, devotion, action and service and in the proper orientation. It should recognise the importance of posture, breath, mantra, concentration and meditation. It should allow the use of ritual, form and image, as well as direct, formless and imageless approaches. It must be based upon an understanding of the law of karma and the process of rebirth. Yet it must be free of fixation upon any particular personality, book, name or idea. And it must be connected to teachers who have realised this truth. The Yoga tradition is such a complete spiritual tradition applied to all human temperaments and through thousands of years of experience and carries the depth and breadth of Sanatana Dharma behind it.

Can I Keep My Existing Belief and Still Practise Yoga?

Yogic practices are designed to lead us to the universal truth, which is pure consciousness. However, to do so they must cause us to question dogmas and limited beliefs of all kinds. This means that if the goal of one's religion is Self-realization than one can freely follow that religion along with yogic paths to Self-realization. If the goal of one's religion is less than that, then one's religion is at best a preliminary step and may have to be modified or given up over time.

To know one's Self one must go beyond all theories, names and forms, all the movements of the conditioned mind. We do not need to depend upon any belief. Rather we should learn to believe in ourselves, in our nature as pure consciousness that does not require any external support. Only then can we abide in our true nature. Usually one has to give up one's outer religious belief to find the inner truth, or at least make it into something secondary. All religions belong to the Self, but the Self cannot be limited to any religious identity.

That being said, if one's concern is with the outer aspects of Yoga primarily, as exercise, fitness and wellness, then one can do so from any number of backgrounds, even atheism. But that is not what the true Yoga tradition is about, at best a preliminary step into the yogic view of life.

Is Yoga Hindu?

Yoga originally is the science of meditation that appears in Vedic teachings as the essence of its spiritual practices. Yoga is not merely postures but includes pranayama, mantra and meditation, even embracing ritual in many Yoga traditions. Yoga is an integral part of Sanatana Dharma or the eternal tradition, its very way of action. We could say that Yoga is the practice and Veda is the knowledge.

Yet whether we regard Yoga as Hindu or not also depends upon what we consider Hinduism to be. If we follow the superficial and stereotyped view that Hinduism is an ethnic religion, then Yoga, which is a universal science, goes far beyond Hinduism. However, if we understand Hinduism relative to Sanatana Dharma as a universal tradition, then we see that Yoga and Sanatana Dharma must always go together.

Yoga as a union with universal consciousness, is the primary practice of Sanatana Dharma as the universal path. Just as Sanatana Dharma leads us to universality, so does Yoga. Sanatana Dharma is the greater science and culture of Yoga, its application to all aspects of life. The universality we find in Yoga is a reflection of that inherent in the Hindu tradition that Yoga is rooted in.

Is Yoga Not Enough? Why Should We Talk of Hinduism?

Yoga and Vedanta, which are the ways of spiritual practice and Self-knowledge, are the most important aspects of Sanatana

Dharma, forming its inner dimension. Yet the outer dimension of Hinduism is still relevant because it presents a way of life and an understanding of the universe in harmony with this inner knowledge.

Ayurveda, Vedic astrology, Vastu, Sanskrit, Vedic and Tantric rituals, and Hindu music and dance are important factors in building a spiritual and yogic culture. Many Yoga gurus have followed and taught these subjects as well. These reflect an understanding of yogic principles in all aspects of life, so, what we do individually and collectively supports a deeper spiritual quest. It is not enough for us merely to perform spiritual practices. We need a culture and way of life that allows them to flourish. Hindu Dharma provides that in abundance. We cannot understand Yoga or Vedanta without acknowledging their broader connections in the Hindu tradition.

Shouldn't Western People Follow a Western Religion?

Some people in the Western world believe that Eastern religions, like Hinduism and Buddhism, have no place in the West, which should follow Western religions like Christianity and Islam. Such people do not understand that Eastern dharmic traditions are not religious belief systems but universal ways of spiritual knowledge.

We note a curious cultural prejudice here. Those born in the West do not mind if peoples in Eastern countries are converted to Western religious beliefs. Many of them donate to such conversion activities that often have government support or sanction. Westerners are not asking Christian missionaries to be recalled from Asia because the Western Christian religion is not appropriate for Eastern people. Westerners do not think that it is wrong for Western religion or for Western art and culture to go to the East, regarding them to be of universal value. Yet they often call their systems 'Western' and want to maintain their geographical purity when so-called 'Eastern' teachings gain recognition in the so-called West.

If Western religions are going to be exported to the Eastern world, Eastern religions can also be imported to the West, just as the movement of trade must go in both directions. What is important is to take the best in human culture whatever its origin. We don't refuse a peach because it comes from what was originally a Chinese tree. So too, we should not refuse meditation teachings because other cultures have developed them better than our culture has.

And why should it be a problem for us if anyone finds spiritual benefit from a teaching that arises outside of their given cultural context? After all spiritual knowledge transcends limitations of time and space. Western culture has not historically given emphasis to spiritual knowledge as has occurred in the East. That many Westerners have found benefit from Eastern dharmic teachings is a fact to be honoured and cultural chauvinism to deny it.

True religion, whether it predominates in the Eastern or Western parts of the globe, is not a matter of geography. All the religions of the world are followed in areas far beyond the geographical locale of their origin. Religion speaks of the ultimate issues of life and death and should orient us to the eternal and the universal. In this respect, Hindu Dharma with its universal view has a greater relevance for all human beings than any belief system that divides humanity into believers and non-believers.

Is Hinduism Relevant to Westerners?

Many people in the Western world are fed up with organised religions, churches and dogmas. What attracts them to Eastern traditions is that these are not organised religions emphasizing dogma, sin or salvation, but offer individualised spiritual practices outside of fixed belief systems. However, though Westerners may be happy to adapt aspects of Hindu Dharma like various systems of Yoga and meditation, they may feel no need to become Hindus in the religious sense, which they may equate with the same religious problems that they are seeking to get beyond.

Western spiritual seekers should realise that Hinduism is not religious tradition like those of the West but a dharmic tradition, in fact the foundation of the dharmic traditions of Asia. It is not aiming to narrow down our sense of who we are or what we can do. It provides a set of spiritual resources, carefully gathered since the most ancient times, which is available, like a wonderful set of tools, to help us build our own inner life. It also provides the gurus and guidance to apply these.

Hindu Dharma shows how spirituality can be integrated into our whole life. As such, it can have great value for reformulating a global spiritual culture today. Just as those born in the East must recognise the validity of modern science for all humanity, so Westerners may have to recognise the validity or Yoga or a science of consciousness.

What is the Ancient Western Vedic Heritage?

The Western world, particularly Europe, has had many connections with dharmic traditions throughout history. At an early ancient period, we see a commonality of language, culture and religion between the European and the Vedic. For example, there are many terms in common between English and Sanskrit: mother-matar, father-pitar, brother-bhratar, and sister-svasar. There are many European and Vedic equivalent names for the Divine: Divine-Deva, Zeus-Dyaus, Jupiter-Dyaus Pitar, or Uranus-Varuna.

The Greek and Roman reverence for the Gods and Goddesses through temple worship is of the same order as the worship that goes on in temples in India today. Ancient Celtic traditions are close to the Vedic in their forms and practices, particularly in the mysticism of the Druids and their sacred groves. The Germanic, Baltic and Slavic traditions have many Vedic affinities as well. At the original core of pre-Christian European culture is a Vedic affinity or perhaps even a Vedic identity, particularly the worship of Agni or the sacred fire.

Westerners need not regard the Vedic heritage as simply eastern; it is universal and also part of an older European heritage that can again be reclaimed today. The hold of the exclusive religions of the Middle Ages—which suppressed older European spiritual traditions along with their dharmic connections—is coming to an end. The study of this ancient Western Vedic heritage is one of the most important areas of historical research today and is crucial for reclaiming the spiritual and yogic foundations of Western culture. Yet we also find similar Vedic and dharmic heritages in the cultures of Central and West Asia, Southeast Asia and East Asia, along with the global influence of Hinduism.

Aren't There Many Things Wrong with Modern Hinduism?

There are naturally many problems in a vast and highly populated country like India, including social inequities, but these are a distortion of the Hindu Dharma, which teaches that society should function as a single organism for the benefit of all. To recognise the value of Hindu Dharma, we need not blind ourselves to any social, moral or spiritual failings. On the contrary, it becomes the responsibility of one who recognises dharma to promote it in all possible ways, not only in oneself but also in society.

However, to reject the spiritual side of the Hindu tradition because of outer problems associated with Indian society today is a great mistake. One should regard the great gurus of Hindu Dharma as role models, not the current society of India that is the product of many trends, of which a real application of Hindu Dharma is not as central as most people think. Modern India has been dominated by social, political and economic trends from the Western world, primarily Socialism like that of Eastern Europe, with Capitalism now coming back into prominence.

It is not the yogic science of Self-realization that has caused the social problems in India but the same materialism and corruption that has created problems in every country. In fact, all the countries in the world today are facing tremendous problems, not just from lack of economic development but also from excess affluence and consumerism in the countries that are already developed.

Should One Formally Become a Hindu?

As a universal approach, the teachings of the Hindu tradition do not require a particular outer religious affiliation to benefit from them but only that we live a truthful life. One does not have to formally become a Hindu in order to receive the inner teachings of Yoga and meditation. All that we need is a sincere aspiration to discover the Divine or our true nature.

However, it can be very helpful to formally become a Hindu because it provides one a stronger connection to the world's oldest, continually existing enlightenment tradition. It brings one into the family of the rishis and yogis and aligns us with their grace and guidance. It is more than just being part of a Yoga lineage; it is being part of an entire network of such lineages.

We grow in life relative to the associations we make, particularly at the level of the heart. To enter into an association with the sages is the best thing, particularly with a tradition that embraces spiritual knowledge of all types. But we must put these teachings into practice for this association to be truly meaningful.

Won't A Person Lose their Identity by Becoming a Hindu?

We are human beings first of all and the legacy of all humanity belongs to us. Identity is something that we are going to lose anyway in the course of time. Identity is what blocks our understanding of the eternal. Our true identity is in consciousness, not in any cultural association, even of a religious nature.

We should adopt whatever furthers our spiritual life, not just meditation practices but also all forms of culture, knowledge and behaviour, from wherever we may find it. Whatever we assume through this attitude is not a divisive identity but a way of action in harmony with the universe. Should people recognise their connection with Sanatana Dharma and its great stream of teachers and teachings, it can only be good. It will strengthen our true identity in the Self and not cause us to lose anything that really belongs to us.

B. Civilizational and Social Issues

What is the Hindu View of Civilization?

According to Hindu Dharma and its great gurus, civilization should consist of the progressive unfoldment of consciousness toward the ultimate goal of Self-realization. The soul through the evolution of body and mind gradually develops the powers of the senses, emotion, and intelligence until it can discover its true nature as pure consciousness. The entire universe is a development of the civilization and culture of consciousness that is the supreme reality.

Plants and animals have their societies and forms of communication. Civilization or culture is not unique to human beings or to this planet but occurs everywhere in the universe that abounds with intelligent life. Yet human civilization has its particular role in the evolution of life. Human civilization should be based on a culture of spiritual aspiration through which we can embody the universal consciousness in our own creaturely existence. This is neither the culture of religious belief nor that of materialistic science. It requires seeking the infinite in a rational, sensitive and experiential manner, not the promotion of an institution, ideology or type of behaviour as final.

True culture begins with the spiritual life and is based upon honouring the sages who have realised their true nature, who are the most important and inspiring figures for us to study and to emulate. Our modern civilization should look beyond matter, energy and information to cosmic intelligence and transcendent awareness. That is the true development of human life, inner transformation, not just a more sophisticated technology.

How Does Hinduism View Western Civilization Today?

Western civilization is a comparatively recent phenomenon compared to older spiritual cultures like the Hindu that go back over five thousand years. Prior to what we know of as history,

Sanatana Dharma recognises previous world ages or *yugas* going back long into what our culture would regard as the prehistoric era. For Hindus the modern era began with the Buddha some 2500 years ago, about when the ancient Vedic era ended. Similarly, Hindus view Christianity and Islam as new religions, which have yet to entirely develop the depth and tolerance that experience teaches.

According to Hindu thinkers, Western civilization is immature and at an early phase in which personal pleasure and sensory indulgence are the most important values, what are called Kama or desire in Hindu thought. Even Western religions are caught in a physical view of reality and look to some heavenly world as their goal, which is often little more than a glorified physical world.

Western civilization has produced some genuine mystics over the centuries, but no enduring tradition of Self-realization and yogic practice. Western science has so far failed to produce a science of consciousness, though it is taking a turn in this direction. Western art has commonly become a mere personal expression, not connecting us with the cosmic powers.

The problem is that Western civilization and its commercial values are destroying the planet and its deeper cultural traditions and need to be adjusted. There are positive trends in Western civilization, to be sure, with a gradual casting off the boundaries of medieval religions and modern nation states towards a new planetary view of existence. Western civilization has a freedom of inquiry and curiosity about the world that can lead to a deeper knowledge over time. This may take decades to develop and can be hastened by a greater receptivity to the Himalayan sages. Western thinkers should remain humble and not get trapped in the arrogance of the intellect, but should look to a higher awareness. We must become cosmic beings in our consciousness, not just planetary in our technology.

How Can We Integrate the East and West?

We must bring together what is best in both East and West and not merely throw them randomly. The better part of the Eastern world, particularly India, is its inner spirituality of Yoga and meditation. The better part of the Western world is its science and humanitarianism.

The Western world has made many gains in the outer world through science and technology, extending into the global information era. The Eastern world, particularly India, has made similar gains in the inner world, developing a science and ethics of consciousness. For a complete human development both the inner and the outer sides of our nature must be considered. As long as the outer side of the human being is not developed—as long as we are living in poverty, disease and ignorance of the forces of nature—the inner side of the human being as the cultivation of higher awareness must be limited. On the other hand, as long as the inner side of the human being is not developed—as long as we have no ability to look within and explore the universe of the mind—the outer side of the human being, however well developed through science and technology, cannot give us true happiness.

This does not mean there has been nothing of spiritual value in the Western world or nothing of scientific value in the East. It is a matter of proportion. The greatest integration will occur when we recognise that East and West are just the two sides of our own nature that require their proper places.

Why is India Socially Backward?

As Hinduism has been the main religion of India for thousands of years, there is a tendency to identify the backward social conditions that we still find in parts of India with Hinduism. However, we should note that modern India has not formulated itself according to the principles of Sanatana Dharma, but in its original constitution declared itself to be a secular, Socialist state. Not surprisingly, India is suffering from many of the same problems of other Socialist and Communist states and their stifling bureaucracies.

Though the majority of people in India are Hindus and its recent political leaders have been primarily of Hindu ancestry, there has been little of the Hindu religion and its spiritual values in the political or educational systems, particularly since Mahatma Gandhi. Only recently, Prime Minister Narendra Modi, since 2014, has been willing to appear publicly on a regular basis as a proud Hindu.

Poverty and related evils occur in Christian, Islamic and Buddhist, as well as Hindu countries. Yet because India is the only Hindu-majority country (with the exception of Nepal), there is a greater tendency to identify its problems with the religion. We don't identify the poverty in the Philippines, for example, with its Catholic religion. Nor do we identify the success of Japan with its Buddhist-Shinto tradition.

We should address the real causes of poverty throughout the world, which are largely educational and economic, but not confuse them with the spiritual life, whose aim is not merely to improve society materially but to bring us into contact with the immeasurable. As India is now liberalizing its economy, it is becoming a more prosperous country without changing its religion. Meanwhile Hindu immigrants in Western countries, notably, the United States of America, the United Kingdom and Canada are among the most affluent and educated of religious groups, while maintaining their religious identity.

What is the Hindu View of Economics?

Hindu Dharma teaches independence (svatantra) in all domains of life and acknowledges the validity of the commercial (vaishya) class and its freedom to pursue prosperity as a valid goal of life. Hinduism teaches the individual to be Self-sufficient and confident of his or her own Divinity. It does not make the individual subordinate to the state. Similarly, it does not make the individual subordinate to big business but encourages an organic development of economic resources affording all people dignity of work, and maintaining maximum economic independence for all communities.

The Hindu concept of Dharma contains an understanding of the proper role and limitation of the merchant class that should serve society, not rule over it, following the guidance of sages and yogis. Commercial development is necessary but must be based upon respect for the Earth, charity for all people, and respect for the spiritual life. This is the traditional Hindu economics of Lakshmi or abundance, which is why India dominated world trade for centuries and spirituality along with it.

How Should Hindus Relate to Western Culture?

The Western culture is primarily secular and commercial. Its main benefit is its practical efficiency and outer freedom. Its main limitation is its attachment to sensation and entertainment, which keep us bound to the material world.

Western culture, though it has religion, is not a religious culture. On one hand, this frees Western culture from religious dogma, intolerance and bigotry that makes life difficult in countries dominated by a single religious belief. On the other hand, it leaves Western culture in a spiritual vacuum, which may deprive people of a deeper connection with the Divine or any pursuit of higher awareness.

Hindu culture is not a religious culture in the sense of dominant Western faiths and has a universal and open-minded approach that similarly grants much personal freedom. Yet it is not a materialistic culture. It is based upon yogic values and practices, a tradition of sadhana or spiritual practice. Therefore, Hinduism does not have to reject what is beneficial in Western culture but can add a spiritual and yogic dimension to it. Hindus should take what is helpful from Western culture in improving our outer lives, but offer in return a deeper culture of consciousness. The true quality in life we must develop is our quality of awareness and peace of mind.

What is the Hindu View of Modern Science?

Hindu Dharma does not require that we reject science or follow regressive superstitions. For example, Hinduism does not require that we believe that the world was created six thousand years ago, nor is it opposed to the theory of evolution, which it formulated long ago in a spiritual way as an evolution not merely of form but also of consciousness.

Hindu Dharma recognises the validity of all forms of knowledge yet it says that knowledge is of two types. The lower knowledge—based on name, form and number—can only help us understand the outer world. It cannot reveal our true nature or help us discover the Eternal.

1) This lower knowledge is the realm of science, based upon measurement and observation of the external world. It allows us to understand and control the forces of nature.

2) The higher knowledge, which is yogic spirituality, is based upon meditation and direct perception of the workings of the mind. This alone brings liberation and the attainment of immortality, through which one can transcend time, space and karma.

Though science has its place, it has limitations, and where material science ends, the spiritual science of consciousness, which is Yoga, begins. To be truly scientific or objective, we must recognise both levels of truth and afford each its respective place. The dialogue between these two forms of science is crucial for the future development of humanity and for developing a real and comprehensive understanding of the universe.

How Does Hindu Dharma View Information Technology?

We live in a new social era dominated by information technology. The amount of information that the ordinary person has access to today far exceeds what people had in pervious centuries or even a decade ago. Our sophisticated technology has freed us from the outer drudgery of life and greatly improved transportation, commerce and communication.

Yet information, which is an activity of the outer mind, is not true knowledge, which is beyond name and form as a higher state of awareness. Such information can help us in practical matters but it cannot answer the deeper questions of life such as what is our true nature, why we are born, and what in us may transcend time and death.

Technology meanwhile provides us with many advances in the equipment and instruments that we have, making our outer life easier. But we cannot use technology to directly access the inner world of consciousness. That requires turning to the senses within and silence of mind. It means connecting with cosmic intelligence, not simply a human energy or information grid.

If we can add Yoga and meditation, the prime practices of Hindu Dharma, to our high tech way of life we can compensate for its side effects and increase it benefits. We should both begin and end our day with meditation so we are rooted in our inner awareness, not simply dependent upon outer stimulation. Then we can access the outer world through our new technology as needed, rather than letting it dominate our lives and disturb our nervous systems, as is too often the case today.

How Does Hindu Dharma View Artificial Intelligence?

In Hindu thought going back to the Vedas, the entire universe is regarded as a single consciousness or cosmic being called the Purusha. The Purusha is the inner Self, also called Atman, behind and within all creatures. Its nature is pure intelligence or Prajna and it is the source of life or Prana. The Purusha is Self-existent and independent of all the forces and limitations of the external world.

The intelligence of the Purusha is not artificial, man-made or dependent upon any machine. It is pure, immutable, Self-aware and all pervasive. Obviously, there can be no artificial intelligence devised in our material world that can equal or replace the supreme intelligence behind the universe. Artificial intelligence is still mechanical and programmed, not spontaneous and Self-existent. It is a construct, not something inherent in the nature of existence.

True intelligence is not artificial but organic, ecological and synthetic. We need to awaken our own inner intelligence through Yoga and meditation. Otherwise artificial intelligence may also turn us into mere machines. The mind tends to imitate its environment. If we surround ourselves with artificial intelligence, we will become more artificial ourselves. If we open to our inner intelligence, our entire lives will be filled with creativity and insight.

How Does Hindu Dharma View the Social Media?
Up to recently the mainstream media became the dominant force in the global mind and world communication. Yet, it remained dominated by vested interests in terms of business, politics or religion, not objective or unbiased in its functioning. It has acted to limit and scale down our access to information outwardly and it undermines the credence once given to the pursuit of higher knowledge inwardly.

The new social media adds a democratic element to global communication and can give a voice to groups who have been intentionally kept out of the mainstream media because of their different views, which has unfortunately been the case for Hindus since the colonial era, with rare exceptions. The new Hindu social media is of great importance and adds a dynamic force to the new Hindu renaissance. It should be encouraged and supported as part of the new Hindu media and educational approaches.

Yet we must remember that social media should not be a substitute for sadhana or detract us from spending time in meditation. Meditation provides the insight to share on the social media. We must remember that the world is Maya or an appearance that requires deeper scrutiny to know the truth behind it. The media is the Maya of the Maya, filtering that illusion further according to the nature and bias of the media. We must not get taken in by the Maya of the media but learn to skilfully use the media to promote a deeper awareness on the inner truth of existence, which is the reality of consciousness over material forms.

Will Science and Yogic Spirituality be Reconciled?

While modern science has yet to recognise a higher yogic science, it has begun to slowly move in that direction. The mechanistic or Newtonian view of the universe is now dead. The idea of the universe as energy, the Einsteinian view, is also coming into question in favour of a universe structured by information, which ultimately implies intelligence. The idea of the universe as a formation of consciousness is now being seriously considered at least by a few. It is only a matter of time, which could be a little as a few decades, for this idea to be validated in scientific experiments. Once this occurs, modern scientists will have to seriously examine the knowledge of Yoga and Vedanta relative to the inner levels of the mind.

Yogic spirituality requires freedom of inquiry, which science has also developed on a mundane level. Such freedom of examination must be brought into the workings of the mind and psyche, so that by questioning our very ego we can discover our true Self beyond all sorrow. This level of introspection of course affects us personally and requires a new way of life. It cannot simply be taken up as another profession. Self-realization is the ultimate scientific achievement for all people. It requires the development of a spiritual psychology, including understanding higher states of awareness, which alone can bridge the gap between science and religion.

How Does Hinduism View the Women's Movement?

The women's movement or feminism, is primarily a political and intellectual movement to provide women with the same social and economic rights, education and expression that have long been afforded to men. It is part of several political movements that have occurred in the world for providing social justice to groups that have been historically oppressed, marginalised or discriminated against.

Hindu Dharma has presented the world with a well-developed tradition of Goddess or Devi worship, honouring of Shakti or the feminine power, in innumerable forms like Durga, Kali, Sarasvati, Lakshmi and Parvati. It has many great women gurus and yoginis, which is a tradition that is still flourishing today. Many Hindu women gurus, often called Ma or Mother, travel and teach throughout the world, like Mata Amritandamayi and her numerous followers. This Goddess or Shakti tradition is based on a direct experience of the Divine Mother and her cosmic powers. It arises from the devotion of the inner heart, though it does have its profound philosophies and cosmologies to articulate it.

However, women have been kept subordinate in many Hindu communities and not allowed to develop their life and expression as freely as men. This is a fall from Sanatana Dharma, which teaches us to honour the feminine principle, and should be rectified. Hindu Dharma's spiritual honouring of the Goddess should translate into honouring the feminine principle outwardly in human society as well.

The modern feminist movement has been helpful in upholding the material and intellectual rights of women. Yet it is also important is to reclaim a true women's spirituality or path of Self-realization, which Western political and materialistic values have yet to comprehend. Fortunately, many women today are looking in a yogic direction and taking interest in the experiential forms of spirituality, such as Hinduism, in which the Goddess still lives and communicates to us directly. The encounter of the women's movement with the living Goddess through Hinduism has the capacity to transform humanity.

What is the Hindu View of the Earth?

Hindus worship the Earth as a Goddess and manifestation of the Divine World Mother. They recognise that the Earth is not just a material formation, but a cosmic power pervaded with a

Divine Presence and following a Divine purpose. Hindus honour all creatures on Earth, her plants and animals, and the various beauties of the planet, the mountains, rivers, forests and oceans, which contain many sacred places and afford us may special cosmic connections.

This Hindu worship of the Earth is not a primitive pantheism but part of a greater awareness that recognises the Divine not only in Heaven, but in the very ground on which we stand. Such recognition of the Divine essence in the Earth is essential today when we are destroying the planet and marginalizing its species by our exploitation of nature.

If we view the Earth as a Goddess and as our Mother we will certainly use her resources correctly, kindly and with discretion. If we fail to do this, we will abuse not only the Earth but also all creatures on it, eventually destroying the ground on which we live, and devastating our home in nature. Honouring our Earth Mother is essential for the future well being of the planet.

How Does Hinduism View the Ecological Movement?

The current ecological movement represents one of the most idealistic sides of the modern psyche. It encourages us to respect the sacred nature of all life and acknowledge the unity of existence. It helps foster new attitudes and new technologies that can help us live at peace with our fellow human beings and all the creatures around us. Given the extreme ecological crisis on the planet, an ecological perspective is necessary in all that we do.

For Hindus, ecology is not merely a social movement but part of a living spirituality. Hinduism is inherently an ecological dharma. It finds a Divine presence everywhere in nature and allows us to link up to the cosmic life. It honours and worships the Earth as pervaded with consciousness. Hindu rituals present a scientific and spiritual means of connecting to the powers of nature, through which we can restore our ecological balance. Yoga itself is based on a philosophy of integration, which is the very movement of life seeking greater wholeness. It demands an ecological approach to all that we do.

However, many modern Hindus do not follow an ecological view of life, or understand the ecological dimension of Hindu thought. For this reason, there has been a degradation even of Hindu sacred sites in India, notably in the Himalayas. Hindus need it to reclaim the ecological background of their own tradition and use to restore their natural environments, to make the world a suitable temple for the Divine awareness that pervades nature's beauty and bounty. Such a yogic approach to ecology is the need of the time and it is important that we take it up with determination and dedication.

Why Do Hindus Revere Cows?

It is curious how we approach the religions of other cultures by reacting to what, for us, appears to be the lowest or most objectionable side of what they do. Dominant Western religions have conditioned people not to respect the so-called lower forms of life and to think that those who do so are somehow primitive or superstitious.

The cow is a symbol of Divine love and grace. With no thought of itself, but out of love, it produces milk that nourishes other creatures. Respect for the cow is meant to instil the virtues of gentleness and receptivity into the human mind. Hindus do not literally worship cows. The cow to them is a great symbol of cosmic beneficence and the Divine Mother.

We can judge how a culture values the spiritual life by how it treats its cows. By this standard modern culture, which not only eats cows but raises them under artificial and cruel circumstances, is quite deficient in any deeper sensitivity. We should not only revere cows but respect all life, particularly those creatures weaker than ourselves.

What is the Importance of Vegetarianism in Hinduism?

Most religions strive to reduce the consumption of meat or to turn it into a sacred ritual to be done with care. Some religions turn the eating of meat into a sacrifice, a ritual that requires special preparation, a practice found in many native traditions like those of the American Indians. They make sure to use all parts of the animal and ask for forgiveness for their action of harming the creature. Only meat that is appropriately sanctified is considered proper for eating. Such meat consumption is very different than our modern commercial culture, in which animals are raised in a brutal and mechanical way for the meat industry.

Hindu Dharma promotes vegetarianism particularly for monks and for those who aspire to devote themselves to the spiritual life. Eating of meat is not allowed in Hindu temples and religious institutions and is restricted during Hindu holidays. However, Hinduism does not reject those who eat meat from being Hindus. It recognises meat eating as part of certain human temperaments, such as those of the warrior type or Kshatriyas, but recommends that they keep this practice within limits or make it into a sacrifice. Hinduism accepts it as part of certain cultures like those in mountain regions where vegetarian food is not always easy to get. Hindus, in particular, avoid eating of beef, to which many add avoiding the consumption of any red meat.

A meat diet can cause many diseases. Modern studies show that cancer, heart disease, arthritis and other major ailments occur more frequently in heavy meat eaters, and that vegetarians have generally a better longevity. In addition, we must consider the ecological crisis on the planet today, in which meat consumption is one of the prime causes of pollution and devastation of the natural environment. So even if we eat meat, we should strive to keep it a small part of our diet.

Does Hindu Thought Envision a New Spiritual Age for Humanity?

Many people today are looking for the dawning of a new age for humanity, perhaps ushered in by various cataclysms or natural disasters. Various cycles of civilization and different ages of humanity have come and gone through the great movement of time. Our current civilization is neither the first nor the last, nor the highest. Hinduism has witnessed the rise and fall of many great civilizations of the world since ancient Egypt and Sumeria. It has an awareness of previous world ages, thousands of years before the present cycle of civilization that began at the end of the last Ice Age. Hindu thought understands these cyclical changes and recognises the eternal truths that transcend them.

A new thinking in spirituality, religion, and healing has emerged worldwide over the past few decades. It includes a number of strands with Eastern enlightenment traditions, Western occult approaches and new trends in health, psychology, sociology and ecology. Its approach is synthetic as well as visionary. It contains a strong influence from Yoga, Buddhism, Vedanta, Ayurveda and Hindu thought.

While we should endeavour to create a new age of consciousness, it should be based upon the eternal, not upon transient desires or ungrounded speculations. It should not be a science fiction fantasy but a yogic reality. We should not overlook the older proven Self-knowledge teachings of humanity in an attempt to be modern and to find quick and easy ways of achieving our goals. A real new age for humanity should be based upon reclaiming our planetary heritage and our connection with the greater universe of consciousness, such as older wisdom traditions can lead us towards.

What Will the Future of Humanity Be Like?

For our planet to prosper we must shift to a clean form of technology, relying on solar and other renewable resources, and discarding oil and other 'dirty' forms of power that damage and pollute the Earth and atmosphere. We must gradually reintegrate our cities into nature by reducing their size and creating more parks and a greater open space between buildings. We must restore the quality of our food, air and water by reducing our reliance on chemicals and fostering organic methods of agriculture. We must place larger regions of the planet into nature reserves where plants and animals can live without human interference and exploitation. We must reduce our consumption of meat and establish a more vegetarian diet.

We must return to natural forms of healing using herbs, diet and bodywork such as found in Ayurveda and other traditional systems of medicine. We must develop a new psychology that considers the yogic knowledge of the higher levels of the mind and the role of karma. We must move in the direction of a global mantric language, for which Sanskrit is the best prototype. We must create an educational approach that encourages creativity and deep inquiry, rather than the mere memorizing of information or gaining of mechanical skills.

We must move away from sectarian and exclusivist religions and return to universal ethical values of non-violence and human unity. We must develop internal approaches to the spiritual life through yogic practices and meditation. We must promote Self-discipline, Self-control and the building of character in order to create real leaders, giving up the culture of sensation, entertainment and instant gratification. We must restore the family system and community life, not as a rigid formation promoting narrow beliefs, but as an organic unfoldment of human and universal interconnectedness. If we do not do these things voluntarily, nature may bring us shocks to impel us in this direction. We must learn to serve life, not to exploit it or take it.

Truth, knowledge, infinite Brahman - He who knows That hidden in the supreme ether of the heart attains all desires.

Taittiriya Upanishad II.1

Bliss is the supreme reality. From bliss all beings are born, by bliss they live, into bliss they return.

Taittiriya Upanishad III.6

Surrender is powerful. In surrender I take refuge. Surrender upholds Heaven and Earth. Surrender to the Gods, surrender is their ruler. Through surrender even great sins we have committed are removed.

Rigveda VI.51.8

Questions on Hinduism 3:
Explaining Hinduism to Others

What does a modern Hindu say, particularly when questioned by those who may know little about the Hindu tradition, to explain what Hinduism really is and what its prime teachings are? The following section has been devised to deal with these problems of expressing Hinduism in the modern age, which requires affirming its vast universality without losing its distinctive character. It also includes some important material on Vedic teachings their foundation, structure and different aspects.

A. What is Hindu Dharma?

How Does Hinduism Define Itself?

Hinduism defines itself in terms of Sanatana Dharma, which means the 'universal tradition'. Such a comprehensive teaching is evident in the many-sided yogic and meditational practices of Hinduism, the vast culture of Hinduism including art, medicine and science, and in the Hindu recognition of the importance of all systems of knowledge, material and spiritual. The social customs of Hinduism, with their emphasis on spiritual values, are also based upon such a broad view, though some of these have departed from it through the long course of time.

It is important to redefine Hinduism in terms of Sanatana Dharma, to see its true relevance. Yet, it is also important to redefine Sanatana Dharma or the universal tradition in terms of Hinduism because Hinduism has maintained a living tradition of open spiritual knowledge through the millennia, which the rest of the world has largely lost or been deprived of. Above all, Hindus should define their tradition through their own practices, their own sadhanas, and not through the criteria of other religious systems of very different natures.

Should the Term Sanatana Dharma Replace Hinduism?

The term Hinduism is subject to many misunderstandings, while Sanatana Dharma better communicates the real meaning of the tradition. If Hindus use this term more frequently, they will promote a greater understanding of the real tradition they follow and better allow those of other backgrounds to appreciate it. To gain recognition for the term Sanatana Dharma, we must first understand the meaning of Dharma as natural law and as one's deeper nature, which is radically different from the idea of religion as a code of beliefs. Dharma is not religion, though it is sometimes translated as such but refers to the inherent laws of life and consciousness, especially the law of karma.

Yet owing to familiarity and convenience of usage, we cannot simply dismiss the term Hinduism or Hindu Dharma as inappropriate. We must define it properly, which is as Sanatana Dharma, not as the religion of a particular country or ethnicity. Hinduism should come to connote Sanatana Dharma. This requires looking at Hinduism with new eyes.

How Have the Great Teachers of Hinduism Related to Religion?
The many great sages of India—the ancient Vedic seers from Manu to Krishna, the teachers of classical India like Shankara or Ramanuja, and modern yogis like Vivekananda, Ramana Maharshi, Sri Aurobindo or Anandamayi Ma to mention a few—speak of themselves as part of a great universal tradition of truth relevant to all beings. They have not represented themselves as Hindus as opposed to some other religious group, nor have they failed to honour the Hindu tradition in its depth and diversity. They have placed themselves in the same great stream of rishi and yoga traditions and lineages going back to the *Vedas.*

If we want to see what Hinduism is really like, we should look to the lives and teachings of the great sages, men and women, who have arisen from its background. In such extraordinary individuals, we can discern the essence of universal spirituality, fully developed in form and expression through a particular lineage and manifold teachings, but without limiting boundaries. These great gurus provide a model for the entire world to follow. And this model derives from the Hindu tradition itself. It is not something these individuals have produced apart from their cultural background or traditions.

What are the Main Deity Lines of Hindu Dharma?
Hinduism is based upon Deity worship, both using forms and formless. Each Hindu deity represents the Supreme Deity and ultimately of one's higher Self. The worship of Hindu deities reflects practices of Yoga and meditation, not just outer rituals, prayers and

beliefs. It is mainly part of Bhakti Yoga or the Yoga of Devotion but reflects other yogic paths as well. Hinduism traditionally is divided into five main deity lines, such as Adi Shankara taught:

1) *Vaishnava* or worshippers of Vishnu
2) *Shaiva* or worshippers of Shiva
3) *Shakta* or worshippers of the Goddess (Devi or Shakti)
4) *Ganapata* or worshippers of Ganapati (Ganesha)
5) *Saura* or worshippers of the Sun (Surya)

Sometimes worship of Lord Skanda (Kartikkeya or Muruga) is counted as another branch. Sometimes Buddha or Buddhism or Jainism are also added other lines. Under the Surya (sun) branch is sometimes included the Vedic teaching in general, which is largely a worship of the sun as the symbol of the supreme light of awareness. While the Shakta or Goddess tradition is a separate line, each branch of Hindu deities also has its forms of the Goddess or Devi. Sometimes, Vedanta as the Smarta tradition is regarding as integrating or transcending these five divisions. At other times, the older Vedic tradition forms another Vedic line. Such variations arise as the Hindu tradition is thousands of years old and has developed in many different ways.

However, these divisions overlap in their common Hindu background. Many other groups and subgroups exist, including recent and modern movements like Arya Samaj, Ramakrishna-Vedanta or the Swaminarayan movement.

How Do Shaivas and Vaishnavas Differ?

Shaivas and Vaishnavas, followers of Shiva and Vishnu, differ mainly in name and form, not fundamental teachings. They share the same principles, like karma and rebirth, and the same practices like puja (ritual), mantra and meditation. Shiva is considered to be the best devotee of Lord Vishnu and Vishnu is considered to be the best devotee of Lord Shiva.

Generally speaking, Vishnu represents the benign and approachable form of the Deity, who is worshipped more in the cities and plains of India. Shiva portrays the transcendent and transformative form of the Divine worshipped more in the mountains and villages. Dualistic and non-dualistic forms of philosophy can be found among both groups, as well as every type of yogic practice. Both Shaivite and Vaishnava traditions have vast literatures, special temples and holy places, and their own orders of monks and swamis.

Sometimes the five Hindu deity lines coalesce into two, the Vaishnava and Shaiva. As Shakti is usually the consort of Shiva, her worship can be included with his, while her Lakshmi form can be included under Vishnu. As Ganesha is the son of Shiva and Shakti, his worship usually goes along with his parents. As Surya, the Sun, is generally related to Vishnu, his worship usually goes along with that of Vishnu. This is why Hindus are commonly divided into Shaivites and Vaishnavas.

What are the Main Hindu Forms of the Goddess or Divine Mother?

Hinduism contains many feminine forms of the Divine Mother like Ma Kali, and Ma Durga, Ma Lakshmi and Ma Sarasvati, including forms like Jagadamba and Jaganmata, the Mother of the Universe! These represent different feminine qualities and functions of the Divine. For example, Ma Kali portrays transformative energy, Ma Lakshmi nourishing and sustaining powers, and Ma Sarasvati creative and stimulating forces, while Durga is the Divine Mother in her protective role. Tripura Sundari is the form of the Goddess as representing beauty, bliss and transcendence. These are but a few of the many aspects of the Devi.

Besides the trinity of Sarasvati, Lakshmi and Kali, Hinduism has nine forms of Durga (Navadurga), ten Mahavidyas or Great Goddess forms of Knowledge, seven Cosmic Mothers or Matrikas and sixty-four Yoginis. No other spiritual tradition has this wealth of feminine form nor honours the Goddess as the Mother of all.

Hinduism has many dual male-female forms like Radha-Krishna, Sita-Rama, Uma-Mahesh and Lakshmi-Narayan in which the female form is usually addressed first. The different masculine forms of the Divine in Hinduism all have their feminine counterparts or consorts.

Without giving proper honour to the feminine, a religion must be incomplete and one-sided, which must result in its teachings having negative consequences. Without recognizing the feminine aspect of Divinity, one cannot claim to know the truth. Honouring the feminine is necessary to restore wholeness, completeness and universality. Yet the Divine feminine is not just feminine qualities of an abstract Godhead but the Cosmic Mother and the supreme power of Consciousness, Chit-Shakti.

What are the Vedas and Their Importance?

The Vedas are the largest and oldest literature that remains from the ancient world. They are also the oldest books in any Indo-European language and the oldest scriptures of the Hindu tradition or Sanatana Dharma. There are four Vedas that form the foundation of Hindu thought:

1) *Rigveda* or Veda of mantra, consisting of a thousand mantric hymns.
2) *Samaveda* or Veda of chant or song, mainly a selection of hymns from the *Rigveda*.
3) *Yajurveda* or Veda of ritual, both outer and inner.
4) *Atharva Veda* or Veda of additional mantras, prayers and propitiations.

Yajurveda followers are the largest Vedic group in India and are divided into two main subgroups, the Shukla or White Yajurveda School which prevails in the north of India, and the Krishna or

Black Yajurveda School which prevails in the south. Each of these four Vedic branches is in turn divided into four parts:

1) *Samhita* or mantra portion
2) *Brahmana* or prose ritualistic portion
3) *Aranyaka* or contemplative section
4) Upanishad or Self-knowledge portion

The Samhita is the main and most important section and the oldest. Brahmanas, Aranyakas and Upanishads are closely connected as different levels of interpretation of the Samhita. Brahmanas mainly interpret the Samhita in terms of ritual, Upanishads in terms of knowledge, with Aranyakas combining both. Some Upanishads occur in Aranyakas, others in Brahmanas, yet others by themselves. The Brahmanas are the longest of this group.

The Vedas are composed in an ancient mantric language that requires a special insight in order to truly comprehend. For this reason, the Vedas are usually approached through the Upanishads and the Bhagavad Gita, which are composed in an easier to understand terminology.

The importance of the Vedas today is mainly for setting forth the main rituals and mantras of Hindu practice. Vedic rituals like Agnihotra and Vedic mantras like Gayatri are performed by many Hindus to the present day. The Upanishads are most important for establishing the main philosophy and meditation approaches of Hinduism. Yet there are many later texts called Upanishads which stand outside this division of the dozen or so Vedic Upanishads.

Vedic mantras contain the seeds of these yogic higher practices, if one can penetrate through the veil of their symbols, as has been explained by such modern teachers as Dayananda Sarasvati, Sri Aurobindo, Ganapati Muni, Kapali Shastri, Sri Anirvan, Brahmarshi Daivarat and Maharishi Mahesh Yogi.

Who are the Vedic Rishis?

The Vedic rishis were the seers of the Vedic mantras. They consist of certain exalted individuals as well as their extended families or *gotras*, whose communities continue throughout India today. Vedic rishis are regarded as seers of the Cosmic Word, the primal sound vibration behind the universe represented by OM. They are portrayed as great yogis who have accessed higher states of consciousness and planes of existence far beyond the human. The rishis sometimes form a class of higher beings involved in the creation of various worlds. They are honoured as great spiritual gurus and makers of culture. Such teachings as Yoga, Vedanta and Ayurveda are traced back to various ancient rishis, as well as other aspects of ancient Hindu culture, art, music, mathematics and science.

Renowned rishis include the Rishi Vasishta, who has the largest number of hymns in the *Rigveda*, including the Mrityunjaya mantra to Lord Shiva. Traditions of Yoga and Vedanta are traced back to him that he received through Hiranyagarbha, a Vedic solar deity form. Rishi Vishvamitra is the seer of the Gayatri mantra, which remains the primary prayer or chant of Hindus today. Vishvamitra was a royal sage, or Rajarshi, with whom martial arts and Hatha Yoga traditions are connected. Another important rishi was Agastya, called a brother of Vasishta, who is highly honoured in South India and connected to the origins of the Tamil language and Tamil cultures.

Other famous Vedic rishis include Angiras, Bhrigu, Atharva, Brihaspati, Shukra, Bharadvaja, Atri, Kanwa, Gotama and Vamadeva. Many rishi families and traditions are connected to these. The ancient Persians mention the Atharvas and the Bhrigus. Some modern gurus like Sri Aurobindo are called modern rishis. The rishi model is of a spiritual humanity behind our historical civilization, a background guidance of enlightened seers, sages and yogis that we can still access within our own deeper consciousness.

The main rishis are often said to be seven in number, Sapta Rishi, a concept we find in the seven sages of many ancient mystical traditions. The seven are sometimes identified with the seven stars of the Big Dipper constellation or the seven planets (Sun, Moon and five visible planets), or even the seven chakras or seven planes of existence. They are part of a vast cosmic symbolism like everything Vedic.

What are the Main Vedic Deities and Their Significance?

Vedic deities reflect the higher light of consciousness, which are reflected as the main powers of light in the world of nature. The four main Vedic deities or prime aspects of the Godhead (Brahman) are Agni, Indra, Soma and Surya.

1) Agni is not only fire as a cosmic force, but the power of speech and mantra, and the Divine light embodied in the material world, including the energy of our own soul.

2) Indra is light as a cosmic force, particularly in the form of lightning or electrical energy. At an inner level, Indra is the power of Prana and the yogic practice of pranayama.

3) Soma is the reflective aspect of light at a cosmic level, reflected in the Moon, water and magnetic energy. At an inner level, Soma is the mind and the power of meditation.

4) Surya is the Sun or pure illumination as a cosmic force. At an inner level, Surya represents the Purusha, or light of awareness, that pervades the universe.

These are only general indications as the four deities overlap in various ways in terms of both form and function, each containing the others, as all represent various facets of the Divine light. Relative to Yoga practice:

1) Agni represents the Kundalini fire in the root or earth chakra that ascends to open the chakras and manifest all the higher powers of consciousness.

2) Indra represents the power of perception in the third eye and meditative insight in general.

3) Soma represents the bliss of meditation and samadhi through the crown or head chakra, which descends as nectar of bliss feeding the Kundalini fire.

4) Surya represents the inner light of awareness in the spiritual heart, the presence of the Supreme Self behind all processes.

Awakening and balancing these four forces is the essence of the Vedic Yoga, and occurs on several languages and according to several aspects.

What are the Six *Vedangas*?

There are six *Vedangas*, literally limbs of the Vedas.

1) *Kalpa* or ritual
2) *Shiksha* or pronunciation
3) *Chhandas* or metre
4) *Vyakarana* or grammar
5) *Nirukta* or etymology
6) *Jyotisha* or astrology and timing

The *Vedangas* allow us to properly pronounce, understand and employ the Vedic mantras, along with their associated rituals and meditations. Vedic astrology and astronomy helps us understand the rhythms of time and karma, for right timing of Vedic practices. Yet ritual here is not just a religious ceremony but life in harmony with the rhythms of the universe.

What are the Four *Upavedas*?

Upavedas are secondary Vedic texts to expand our application of the Vedic mantras. These four are *Ayurveda, Gandharva Veda, Sthapatya Veda* and *Dhanur Veda*.

1) Ayurveda is the Vedic system of medicine for promoting overall well-being and for treating diseases of body and mind. Ayurvedic medicine is one of the main medical systems in India today and is spreading worldwide for its efficacy treating

disease and promoting wellness and longevity. It is the yogic system of medicine.

2) Gandharva Veda is Vedic music and dance and the traditions that have arisen out of the Vedas and is the basis of Hindu music. Traditional Indian dance also derives from it.

3) Sthapatya Veda is Vedic architecture and directional sciences also called *Vastu*. It is still used for construction of houses, public buildings and temples in India, and being taken up for architectural purposes worldwide. Vastu also teaches us the proper directions for meditation and how to access the healing power of various directional influences into our lives.

4) Dhanur Veda, which means the Veda of the bow, refers to the Vedic martial arts. These include various forms of fighting with the hands or with weapons. It is most popular in South India today.

What is the Hindu View of Philosophy?

India has witnessed the greatest development of spiritual philosophies in history, which form an essential component of the Yoga of knowledge. Hinduism has produced among the world's most important philosophies, particularly the various schools of Vedanta. Yet its view of philosophy its very different than that of the West. The correct Hindu word for philosophy is darshana, which means 'a way of perception'. Each of the philosophies of Hinduism is a spiritual approach that requires following a certain life-style, ethic disciplines and practicing various yogic methods to arrive at this perception. Hindu philosophies are meant to help us realise the truth beyond the world of the senses. They aim to transcend the ordinary mind-body complex.

According to a Vedantic view, there is little real philosophy in the Western world. Western philosophical thinking has largely declined since the time of Plato and the early Greek philosophers, abandoning spiritual experience and a transcendent view of life for rational, speculative, and utilitarian considerations. It has fallen increasingly under the domination of the senses, and is now often an apologetic for a scientific-materialistic view that is unaware of higher dimensions of consciousness. Even Western religious philosophy, as in the case of Christian and Islamic theology, has little of the experiential spirituality and exploration of higher states of consciousness and samadhi found in Hindu and Buddhist systems.

Philosophy in India continues to be a living and experiential endeavour. Modern India has not only maintained its ancient philosophical traditions but has produced great new philosophers like Sri Aurobindo, who were also master yogis, and have brought in many new important insights for the future evolution of humanity.

What are the Six Systems of Vedic Philosophy or Vedic Darshanas?

There are six systems of Vedic philosophy deriving from ancient time, which accept the authority of the Vedas and try to organise Vedic thought in a systematic manner. Some groups call these the six schools of Indian philosophy, which is incorrect, as Indian philosophy has non-Vedic and post-Vedic schools as well.

School	Topic	Founder	Main Text
Nyaya	School of Logic	Gautama	*Nyaya Sutras* of Gautama
Vaisheshika	Categories	Kannada	*Vaisheshika Sutras*
Samkhya	Cosmic Principles	Kapila	*Samkhya Karika* of Ishvara Krishna

School	Topic	Founder	Main Text
Yoga	Yoga Practice	Hiranyagarbha	*Yoga Sutras* of Patanjali
Purva Mimamsa	Ritual and Dharma	Jaimini	*Jaimini Sutras*
Vedanta or Uttara Mimamsa	Metaphysics and Self-realization	Badarayana	*Brahma Sutras* of Badarayana

Each of the six darshana-schools has its founder and primary text, which is sometimes that of its founder, sometimes a later compilation. These darshana texts are called sutras and consist of short statements or phrases. They require upon extensive commentaries, of which there are several in traditional Hindu thought, some with variant opinions.

These six schools usually come in groups of two. Nyaya and Vaisheshika philosophies deal with logic, the means of knowledge and how to categorise our experiences, which is the foundation of all clear thinking and systematic inquiry.

Samkhya sets forth the main principles of cosmic existence up to the Purusha or Supreme Self. Yoga sets forth the practical means to realise the Purusha based upon Samkhya and the Vedas. Yet, note that the term Yoga, here, is used in a specific sense relative to Yoga Darshana, not for all the branches of Yoga as Knowledge (Jnana), Devotion (Bhakti), Karma (Action) and so on.

Purva Mimamsa reflects a ritualistic interpretation of Vedic texts designed to allow us to achieve better karmic results in this life and the next. It sets forth the science of ritual and Karma Yoga. Uttara Mimamsa or Vedanta deals with the theology and philosophy of God and the Absolute and how to realise them. There are many different systems of Vedantic thought in India, including Tantric systems. Most systems of Jnana and Bhakti Yoga, the Yogas of Knowledge and Devotion are of this type.

All six systems have many points in common and can be regarded as complementary sides of Vedic thought. They can all be called Vedantic as all accept the authority of the Bhagavad Gita and Upanishads, the Vedantic portion of the Vedas. They all have some sort of Yoga or inner practice to go along with them, particularly meditation, which all honour.

Of the darshana texts, the most important is the Brahma Sutras of Badarayana, the main text of the Vedanta Darshana. Most different schools and sects of Hinduism rest upon an interpretation of the Brahma Sutras by its founder or main teacher. This is particularly true of the Vedantic schools that predominate in India today.

What are the Main Schools of Vedanta?
The different schools of Vedanta vary mainly in whether they consider the Divine Reality of Being-Consciousness-Bliss (Brahman) to be a pure unity, or whether there is some degree of duality between the soul and the Divine. All Vedantic philosophies emphasise Brahman as the supreme reality. Advaita Vedanta or non-dualistic Vedanta, whose most important traditional teacher is Shankaracharya, teaches that the soul and God are absolutely one. Visishtadvaita, or qualified non-duality, based on the works of Ramanuja, teaches that the soul and God are one in essence but different in manifestation. Dvaita, or dualistic Vedanta of Madhva, teaches that God and the soul though deeply related are different, like lover and beloved. Lord Chaitanya's school of Achintyabhedabheda accepts both difference and non-difference and says Truth is indescribable. There are several other schools as well.

All Vedantic systems, whether they call the world real or unreal, accept the law of karma, ethical disciplines like non-violence, and the practice of various yogic and meditational methods. Even dualistic Vedanta is not dualistic in the sense of Western monotheistic religions, which require the resurrection of the physical body and the soul living in that body in Heaven worshipping God in the distance. Dualistic Vedanta conceives the difference between God and the soul to be very subtle at a level of deep awareness.

All systems of Vedanta regard the true relationship between God and the soul to occur only in samadhi or a state of deep spiritual absorption that goes far beyond the ordinary mind and senses, in which the physical body is all but forgotten. They teach that we can experience the Divine within ourselves much more vividly than anything else we have ever known.

What is the Importance of Vedic Science?

Vedic science is a complete cosmic science of consciousness starting with the Vedas, Upanishads and the Bhagavad Gita, combining the six *Vedangas*, the four *Upavedas*, the six Vedic Darshanas and related systems of thought, inquiry and practice. Its most important aspects are Yoga, Vedanta, the Science of Ritual, Ayurveda, Vedic astrology and Vastu. It rests upon the Vedic mantras but shows their broad relevance and utility on all these different levels of experience and practice.

Vedic science is not only the oldest science in the world; it is also the most futuristic. It teaches us how to understand the power of consciousness behind the universe and unfold that within us. It unlocks the mystic keys to the physiology of the body, the dynamics of the mind, the laws of physics, and all the Divine powers at work in the world. For the ultimate well-being and development of higher awareness in humanity, we need a new group of Vedic scientists from all over the world. Vedic knowledge now has global respect and such new Vedic thinkers may already be with us. Vedic knowledge systems are at the forefront of the knowledge revolution on the planet.

What is the Antiquity of the Vedas?

The Vedas are said to represent eternal teachings and mantras of Sanatana Dharma. Therefore, in essence they have no date and are ever inherent in the cosmic mind. However, the current compilation of the

Vedas that exists is said to have been completed around the time of the Mahabharata War by Veda Vyasa Krishna Dvaipayana, under the inspiration of Sri Krishna. The Puranas regard it as the twenty-eighth compilation of the Vedas in our current cycle of worldages. Veda Vyasa based his compilation on much earlier material, mentioning kings and dynasties that ruled many generations before the time of Krishna. The *Rigveda* is the oldest core of the Vedas and was of great antiquity even at the time of Veda Vyasa.

When the Greeks came to India after Alexander, in the third century BC, one of their historians, Megasthenes, records that the Hindus had a tradition of one hundred and fifty three kings going back over six thousand and four hundred years to around six thousand and seven hundred BC. Vedic astronomical references, stellar positions of solstices and equinoxes also go back well before two thousand BC, when stars like Aldeberan (Vedic star Rohini) in Taurus marked the vernal equinox. This means that the core of the Vedic teachings may be as much as ten thousand years old with its last added material around four thousand years ago. The Vedas reflect the time when the Sarasvati River was the main center of habitation in India, which dried up around four thousand years ago.

Are Hindus Aryans?

Aryan is a common Sanskrit term for nobility, respect and honour that occur throughout Sanskrit literature going back to the oldest *Rigveda*. It was never used in the sense of race, ethnicity or skin colour, which was a misuse and misinterpretation of the term introduced by colonial European thinkers in recent centuries who used the race concept to justify their domination of non-European peoples.

Hindus, Buddhists and Jains use the term Aryan to describe their tradition and its great leaders. Buddhists' four noble truths are Aryan truths, as the actual term translated as noble is Aryan. When Arjuna initially refused to fight on the Kurukshetra battlefield, Krishna said that he was doing something un-Aryan, or not noble.

The distortion of the term Aryan reflects how much European thought has distorted Hindu Dharma. It tells us that we must re-examine many such terms and the entire modern European interpretation of the history of India, which remains highly Eurocentric.

Is the Aryan Invasion or Migration Theory Disproved?

The Aryan Invasion theory is a nineteenth century European historical conjecture, reflecting a trend of the time to define cultures mainly in terms of ethnicity, language families and their proposed migrations and invasions. In recent decades, the Aryan Invasion theory has been discredited because no archaeological evidence or any other type of hard data for it has ever been found for it. Such evidence that has been proposed like the archaeologist Wheeler, who suggested a massacre at Mohenjodaro, have not stood the test of time.

The archaeological record, on the contrary, shows an organic and indigenous development of culture and civilization in the Indian subcontinent going back to at least seven thousand BC (the Mehrgarh site for example), with little input from outside regions and no records of significant movements of people into India or destroyed cities in India from such Aryan invaders. No one has ever been able to locate any intrusive Aryans in this historical record at all.

This decline of the Aryan Invasion theory has led to two main camps. The first camp holds that instead of an invasion there was a small migration that brought in the language and culture of the Vedas into India after one thousand five hundred BC. This, they hold on linguistic grounds only as so far they have not produced any non-linguistic evidence for it.

The second camp holds that there was no invasion or migration but that the Vedic people were indigenous to India, as one of the main inhabitants of the region. For this they point out several reasons. The Vedic culture emphasises the Sarasvati River, flowing between the Yamuna and the Shutudri (Sutlej). Such a great river existed in ancient India and was the main site of human habitation and urban development up to its drying up that occurred shortly after two thousand BC according to current geological studies. Both the Archeological Survey of India (ASI) and the Geological Survey of India (GSI) have proved this identity of Vedic, Harappan and Sarasvati civilization through numerous research papers and excavations.

The lack of archaeological evidence for any such proposed invasion or migration discredits the theory altogether. The proposed Aryans could not have changed the languages of the subcontinent back to their roots without leaving any trace in the archaeological record. So far there are no ruins, artefacts, encampments, skeletons, destroyed cities or anything else that has been identified as belonging to the incoming Aryans. Unless we have solid evidence for the so-called Aryans coming from the outside, we cannot uphold it on linguistic speculation only. The Indo-European languages could just as well have diffused from India, as it had a large urban culture to promote it.

Why Do Hindus Worship Swastikas?

The Swastika incites terror in the minds of people today owing to its brutal usage by the Nazis in Germany during the last century, and its continued usage by some racist groups.

The Swastika is an ancient Indian symbol of good fortune and the wheel of dharma that one finds in Hindu, Buddhist and Jain depictions. It is one of the most common symbols found in the ancient Indus-Sarasvati or Harappan civilization in India going back five thousand years. It is commonly used with the deity Ganesha in Hindu thought and Diwali as a festival of light. Yet, the Swastika is a common artistic motif found in many cultures, not only in ancient India, but also the Middle East and Europe, even having some Native American depictions. To read modern European politics into this widely used ancient symbols shows a lack of examination and a distorted Eurocentric view of humanity.

The world should honour the Swastika as a design and art form extensively used through history and very common to India. The association of Hindus with Nazi ideas because of their use of the Swastika for thousands of years shows how superficial our views of India have been. Sadly, certain leftist and communist groups, particularly in India, have deceptively used the traditional Hindu use of the Swastika to condemn all Hindus as Nazi like in their views and practices, if not Nazi sympathisers.

What is the Importance of the Mahabharata?

The Mahabharata is one of the longest books in the world. It is often called the fifth Veda as it presents Vedic teachings in stories and in a more common language. The most important portion of the Mahabharata is the Bhagavad Gita of Sri Krishna, which is probably the most important text for all Hindus. But the Mahabharata contains many other deeper spiritual and yogic teachings as in the Moksha Dharma Parva and Anu Gita. The philosophy of the Mahabharata synthesises and expands the teachings of the Upanishads. It goes into detail about the practice of Yoga and related teachings.

The Hindu religion, as it appears today, remains largely the religion portrayed in the Mahabharata, in which the main deities of Hinduism like Shiva, Vishnu, Durga, Ganesha and Skanda are explained and honoured, including avatars like Rama and Krishna. The Mahabharata presents a synthesis of Hindu philosophies including Samkhya, Yoga, Vedanta, Vaishnavism and Shaivism. It contains many other popular teachings like the Thousand Names of Vishnu and the Thousand Names of Shiva. All those who wish to understand Hindu Dharma should study the Mahabharata, not just for its wonderful story but for its profound teachings.

What is the Importance of the Ramayana?

The Ramayana is the oldest of Hinduism's great epics and the most ancient poetic (kavya) work. Its story centres on the figure of Lord Rama, regarded as an incarnation of Vishnu, and an ideal person and king. The Ramayana contains many notable figures like Sita, Rama's wife, Hanuman, the monkey warrior, and Lakshman, the brother of Rama. The Ramayana sets forth the principles of dharmic action in human life, providing living examples for these.

The Ramayana is probably the greatest epic of all Asia. It is found not only in India but in Thailand, Indochina and Indonesia, among Buddhist as well as Hindu groups. There are several versions of this beautiful text of which the most ancient is the Sanskrit of Valmiki. The most popular, recent version is the Hindi of Tulsidas from the sixteenth century that is commonly chanted and sung throughout North India. Ramayana depictions figure strongly in India and South Asian art. The name of Rama is also one of the most important of all mantras.

What are the Many Puranas and Their Significance?

The Puranas are ancient and medieval Hindu texts that contain a broad range of encyclopaedic teachings about all aspects of life including religion, science, medicine, history, geography, social customs, Yoga, mantra, worship and meditation. There are many different Puranas, which gradually added new material over a very long period of time. They were said to have begun at the time of the Mahabharata War but continued to develop as a branch of literature of their own until recent times.

The Puranas generally relate to primary Hindu deities like Shiva, Vishnu and the Goddess, but usually mention the other main deities as well. There are eighteen major Puranas and several minor Puranas. Puranas usually are based on and expand somewhat the themes and teachings of the Mahabharata. Most notable are the *Vishnu Purana, Vayu Purana, Agni Purana, Garuda Purana, Srimad Bhagavatam* and *Devi Purana*. The Puranas are one of the most important branches of Hindu thought and perhaps the most neglected, though they are long, intricate and cover many subjects. They require profound study and research. All Hindus should look into them.

Don't Hindu Texts Like the Manu Samhita Degrade the Role of Women?

Hindu thought contains many texts on various subjects, not all scriptural in nature. Manu Samhita is one of many Dharma Sutra texts, which were the basis of Hindu code of conduct in eras long past. As a particular text, Manu Samhita is around two thousand years old and is mainly concerned with the social situation of that time period. Within the Dharma Sutra, literature a variety of opinions are given on various topics.

Manu Samhita contains a great regard for Yoga, meditation and asceticism. However, we cannot compare it to social law codes today in respects of social liberalism. It does, overall, subordinate women and regard them as requiring protection. Manu Samhita is not a scriptural text that all Hindus must follow, but just one of many ancient law codes, which has undergone considerable changes over time.

Compared to law codes of its time, like the Book of Leviticus in the Bible, which many Christians accept as the Word of God, the law code of Manu is very liberal and spiritual. It is more progressive overall than the Islamic Sharia that is still the basis of Islamic law in the great majority of Islamic countries in the world today. Yet it is certainly dated in a number of aspects.

We must remember that even in the United States, slavery was legal until 1863, as it was in many Christian countries. If we are going to judge Hinduism today by one of its very ancient law codes, then we should do the same for other religions. Hindus today have created new social customs in line with changing times, as have different Hindu groups and thinkers. In Hindu thought, the spiritual path of Self-realization is eternal, but social customs must change with time.

What is Tantra?

Tantra is a set of medieval Hindu teachings providing rituals and Yoga practices to achieve the various goals of life, including liberation. Buddhist and Jain Tantras of a similar nature also exist.

The highest Tantras are spiritual texts teaching the worship of deities, mantras, and meditation to achieve union with the Divine and Self-realization. They are great yogic teachings and imbued with the higher truths of Vedanta, like Kashmir Shaivism. Hatha Yoga and Siddha Yoga are also higher Tantric teachings. Tantras of an intermediate level use rituals and mantras to gain personal goals like health, prosperity, marital happiness or children. Inferior Tantras use similar methods to gain control over the minds of other people or even inflict harm. Inferior Tantras are a kind of black magic that no spiritual person can really approve of.

In the Western world today, Tantra is mainly known through various sexual Tantric practices. In fact, to most Westerners Tantra means sex. Such sexual Tantras were sometimes part of the intermediate or inferior Tantras, not the higher Tantras. They constitute a small portion of Tantric teachings and should not be made to represent Tantra as a whole.

Tantra emphasises the use of mantra to gain the goals of life. As the Goddess represents the Divine Word and the forces of nature, and most Tantric approaches are based on worshipping her and Lord Shiva. She controls all energies and gives mastery over all techniques. The Goddess is the power of Yoga, the Yoga Shakti that leads us to our true Self. True Tantra shows us how to worship the Goddess and realise her power within ourselves.

Why Are Hindu Deities Portrayed in Wrathful Forms?

Hindu Gods and Goddesses can have fierce forms, including wearing garlands of skulls, being adorned with snakes, and other frightening appearances. Even deities that are benefic may carry powerful weapons, like swords, bows and arrows, or axes. This may disturb people, particularly those who do not understand symbolic language.

The Divine transcends our ordinary sensory perception of the world. It dwarfs our mind and ego. It includes death and goes beyond it. It consumes everything. Experiencing this infinite reality is very humbling, even frightening to those who are trapped in the world of limitation, as it takes away our ordinary identity and makes the world appear to be unreal. Spiritual realization is like death because it is the dissolution of our ego, or the sense of a separate Self. Such apparently terrible deities show these experiences of transcendence, in which even evil, death and suffering are integrated into a truth beyond all duality.

There is another way in which the Divine is frightening. It destroys all the forces of ignorance, illusion and negativity. It eliminates all the demons of false thinking that dwell in our minds. As such, a destroyer of negativity, it may appear fierce or as a warrior, but it is only something that those trapped in negativity need fear.

It is easy to see the Divine in the beautiful and beneficent, but to enter into the Oneness we must also see the Divine in the terrible and transformative, like a power of lightning. Without recognizing the Divine even in death we cannot go beyond death. Because of this, Hindu and Buddhist traditions have always recognised the importance of wrathful Deities and their ability to protect us at a psychic level. They have never encouraged that we become wrathful and harm other people in the name of our God.

Why Are Hindu Deities Portrayed in Erotic Forms?

Hindu deities and temple sculpture often appears erotic or voluptuous, so that Western missionaries thought these images were only a glorification of sexuality even though they were part of a tradition that has always valued asceticism.

The Divine is the ultimate bliss and delight, Ananda. Union with the Divine is the supreme love, in which the male and female sides of our nature and the masculine and feminine aspects of consciousness must unite. To show this inner unification, Hindu artists have traditionally employed graphic images. Such images are symbolic like Radha and Krishna, who represent the soul and its love of God. To the Hindu mind, our passions should be directed to the Divine. For this reason, it has not hesitated to portray them as part of a spiritual symbolism. But to confuse these with a glorification of sexuality is to completely misinterpret them.

The love between Radha and Krishna is also a symbol of Divine love, but many Western scholars would similarly like to reduce it to human passion only. The Hindu mind has a cosmic connection and draws out the cosmic meaning of symbols. That is why, for it, all of nature is a book of Divine wisdom, forces and powers. Mystics in all traditions, including Sufis and Christian mystics have employed such symbolism at a poetic level, but avoided presenting them as artistic depictions.

Isn't the Shiva Linga a Sexual Symbol?

The Shiva Linga is the symbol of Shiva or the cosmic masculine force. Forms of Shiva Lingas include the Sun and Moon, mountains, fire, certain trees, conical rocks and crystals, and also the sexual organs of male creatures. All these demonstrate an ascending energy in nature, aiming at a state of transcendence.

However, it is wrong to think that the Shiva Linga is limited to a symbol of sexuality. It is a symbol of cosmic power, stability, eternity and bliss. Unfortunately, the Western mind has a sexual obsession and cannot see beyond the sexual aspects of any symbolism. Shiva and Shakti forces are not simply biological energies but the prime duality of cosmic forces that arise from Pure Consciousness, the Shiva principle, and its power, the Shakti principle. These underlie all the dualities of natural forces, and create the web of electromagnetic energies, gravitational forces, and powers of light through which the universe exists and functions. To reduce them to merely a sexual symbolism is not a sign of any higher awareness.

What is the Basis of the Caste System?

Caste is the most criticised part of Hinduism and the most difficult to explain to the modern mind. It appears as a religiously reinforced form of social oppression. Yet caste is not something unique to Hindus, nor is caste as it exists in India today, truly reflective of the older teachings of Hinduism as to how society should be structured.

Caste arose as part of an ancient division of society into priests, nobility (warriors), merchants (and farmers), and servants, such as occurred throughout the ancient world and up into recent centuries existed even in Europe.

Behind the caste system was originally a great idea that became distorted. The Hindu social system (Varnashrama Dharma), which degenerated into caste, gave people who developed their minds pre-eminence in society over the warrior and merchant classes. Unfortunately, people were judged by their family of birth rather than by the real qualities of their character, which turned this helpful idea into a misleading appearance.

Such caste by birth has persisted more in India because of conservative social attitudes. Yet it is no more essential to Hinduism today than it has been to other religions that were once represented by the same types of social systems. Many modern Hindu religious leaders have spoken against caste limitations and many older teachers did so as well. Traditional Hindu texts like the Vedas or Mahabharata portray a much more open society than what the caste system became over time. Modern Hindu sects like Arya Samaj do not recognise caste at all. So it is wrong to think that caste, particularly by birth, represents the original Hindu social order or is required for all Hindus.

Hindu Dharma as a way of spiritual knowledge may be associated with any number of social systems. Yet, it does state that society should found itself on dharma or spiritual values to be really harmonious. Hinduism teaches that there is an organic structure to society, that certain types of people exist to fulfil the different functions of the social being, like the arms, feet or brain of the body. Through this organic structure, it regards all humanity, in fact the entire universe, as one great Being. Each one of us is not only part of that universal Being, each one of us is that universal Being in its totality. This is the real meaning of our social interconnectedness.

In the modern civilization, the merchant (commercial) class rules the world. The warrior class (those with the most guns or best weapons) also has much power. Spiritual people today, the true Brahmins, have little regard or power in society. We should not think that our modern social order is the best but should look to a dharmic ordering of society that emphasises the pursuit of higher consciousness as the true goal of life.

Hindus should work hard to eradicate oppressive caste divisions within Hindu society that remain. Caste is a stain on the real spirit and unity teaching of Sanatana Dharma, which inhibits its beneficial teachings from spreading worldwide. Yet at the same time, Hindus should work to maintain a social order based upon dharmic values, in which Yoga and meditation are emphasised. Hindus need not give up their strong family and community connections, which serve to protect and support the individual, but must remember the greater Vedic teaching that the entire world is one family (vasudhaiva kutumbakam).

Who is a True Brahmin?

A true Brahmin is a person of spiritual knowledge grounded in cosmic intelligence, who understands the universal order and works to further it in the world. To become a true Brahmin means to remain in a state of learning, ever seeking to open up to the Divine Reality. It requires a life of seeking truth and upholding firm ethical and spiritual principles like non-violence, non-attachment, humility and truthfulness. Such a true Brahmin cannot be created by mere birth alone but requires daily spiritual practice or sadhana.

Such aware individuals become the teachers of society and should be respected, not for their position, but for their connection with cosmic reality that they bring to all. All cultures have their wise and learned people whom they revere, people who could be called their Brahmins. They should be people of Self-realization for society to truly flourish. We should train at least a portion of society from birth to pursue the spiritual life. Otherwise our society's spiritual potential cannot truly flower. This is the basis of a real Brahmin class but it is a condition gained by temperament, merit and behaviour. The individuals who belong to it must live the appropriate lifestyle, which requires humility and regard for the welfare of all creatures.

What is the Best Single Book to Learn about Hindu Dharma?

While Hinduism has many great books and scriptures, probably the most accessible and comprehensive of these is the Bhagavad Gita of Sri Krishna. The Gita is not only honoured by followers of Krishna and Vishnu, but is sacred to all Hindus. It clearly sets forth the prime Vedantic teachings of karma, rebirth, liberation and the immortality of the soul in the higher Self.

The Gita is also probably the most important text on Yoga in the true sense of a way of Self-realization. Each chapter forms a particular Yoga teaching. Krishna is said to be the Yogavatara, the avatar or Divine incarnation of Yoga. The Gita explains in detail the Yoga paths of knowledge, devotion and service and makes clear many other yogic terms and practices only addressed briefly in the Yoga Sutras. It has tremendous knowledge on human psychology and the workings of the cosmos, the human mind and the three gunas as well. One should start the study of Hindu philosophy and Yoga with the Bhagavad Gita.

B. Hindu Dharma and Other Religions

What is Hindu Religious Pluralism?

Hindus believe that there are many spiritual and religious paths to higher consciousness both inside the main religions of the world and outside of them. The Hindu view is one of pluralism. It recognises a unity of truth, but many ways to approach it—some direct and some indirect. Yet it also recognises that not all paths lead to truth; there are paths that lead to illusion as well.

Contrary to this Hindu view are religious traditions that believe that they alone have the truth or the only real relationship with the Divine or eternal must come through them. We can call these 'exclusive religious traditions'. They are generally exclusive in their actions and try to convert the entire world to their beliefs.

It is not enough today for religious leaders to come together on a political front and affirm world peace and the unity of humanity. As long as religions are dividing humanity into hostile camps of believers and the non-believers—those favoured by God and those condemned by God—they are still promoting violence and vision. It is crucial that all religious leaders affirm that no religious group owns the truth but, rather, that there are many paths to the Divine or ultimate reality, which has many names. We need a global declaration of religious pluralism in order to truly promote world peace. Otherwise our talk of peace cannot be taken seriously.

We need not agree on which path is best for us or even which path might be best for humanity overall. But we should affirm pluralism in religion just as we affirm pluralism in politics and other spheres of life. Just as in democracies, we affirm the rights of others to vote differently than we do, so too in religion, we should affirm the rights of others to follow other spiritual paths than our own. The Hindu approach of Sanatana Dharma, taking a universal view, can be a good aid so that our society can move from religious exclusivism to religious pluralism, which is as important for society as its rejection of racism.

What is Hindu Theism?

As a universal tradition, Hinduism includes recognition of a Cosmic Lord and Creator called Ishvara, the supreme power. However, it does not regard theism as the only approach to the spiritual life, nor does it have only one formulation of theism for everyone to follow. Hindu theism takes many names and forms like those of Brahma, Vishnu or Shiva, who stand for the Divine in its roles of creating, preserving and dissolving the universe. It may emphasise the Divine as feminine in attributes, like Sarasvati, Lakshmi and Kali.

Hindu theism is an experiential system, not a code of belief. It is not enough to believe in God; we must come to experience the Divine within us through yogic practices. Hindu Dharma emphasises our inner relationship to the Divine, not a mere outer formal identity. This is the path of Bhakti Yoga, the Yoga of Devotion.

Hindu theism can include monism or the view that the individual soul and the Divine are one. This view recognises that God as a personal reality rests upon the Divine as the principle of existence or the Absolute, Brahma. Or Hindu theism may take a dualistic approach regarding the individual soul as communing or partaking of the supreme deity but not becoming entirely one with it.

Like other systems of dharmic thought, Hindu theism recognises the law karma and rebirth, and the practice of Yoga as the way to experience the Divine. According to Hindu theism, the Divine has not created us to reward or punish us, but to know Him/Her and to become part of His/Her eternal and infinite delight, which is the ultimate destiny of all souls.

What is the Hindu View of Western Theology?

Western religions are theologically and philosophically weak, emphasizing emotional beliefs over any meditative inquiry. They rest on limited ideas of only one life for the soul. They turn God into a tyrant, meting eternal rewards and punishments for the deeds or beliefs of a single life of the souls he has created. Only if theism is tied to the acceptance of karma and rebirth—that individual souls undergo a cycle of repeated births until they realise the Divine connection within themselves—is it a truly rational and spiritual system. For this, Western theism should look to Hindu theism.

True theology should set forth an understanding of the cosmos, the principles of cosmic creation, and the way for the soul to return to its unity with the Divine. Theology should link us up with the Divine Father/Mother of the universe through all its forms and functions on the various levels of this manifold universe inwardly and outwardly. Theology should not be a system of dogmas to follow without question, or ideas to limit our thoughts to but should direct us inwardly to realization of the Divine within us.

Most Western monotheism is of a sharply dualistic nature, making God, the soul and the world of nature different, often making heaven into a glorified physical world where creaturely forms continue. It is based on principles of faith, which are not to be questioned however arbitrary. It often appears more as a rationalization of a belief rather than a deep inquiry into universal Truth.

Western theology mainly follows the Greek philosopher Aristotle, who curiously was a pagan, not a Christian, slanting his ideas into a Biblical direction of faith. Western theology does not recognise the ultimate reality of the Self or Atman, which it does not mention, and rejects important cosmic laws like that of karma. Western theology has much to learn from Hindu theology. Hindus should seek to dialogue with Western theology to help raise the level of theological thinking in the world. In this way, theology can be used to direct us to the spiritual path to experience the Divine through Bhakti Yoga.

Do Hindus Have Prophets and Messiahs?
Hinduism does not look to prophets or messiahs who have a special relationship with God that other people cannot have

and whom we must use as intermediaries, which is the usual view of Christianity and Islam. Hinduism looks to great gurus and spiritual guides who set forth paths to Self-realization to be adapted on an individual basis. From the Hindu view, which has seen the coming and going of many religious systems, great teachers and Divine incarnations manifest periodically in order to guide human beings relative to changing circumstances. There is no beginning or end to such great teachers, though we may prefer to follow one or another.

Hindu history records hundreds of such sages from ancient to modern times that we should honour, not restricting ourselves to only one, as if knowledge of the Divine, which is infinite, was the property of one person or line of people. More important than any prophet or saviour is a true guru who can teach us how to contact the truth within our own nature. Self-realization is what liberates us from ignorance and karma, not any prophet, and for this even the guru is only an aid.

What are Avatars?

Sanatana Dharma recognises a perennial stream of great teachers and sages; some whose spiritual qualities are so pure that they could be called veritable incarnations of the Divine. These special incarnations can be called avatars, literally 'Divine descents'. Today the term avatar is often used loosely for various great teachers.

In the traditional Hindu sense, avatars appear to uphold and renovate Sanatana Dharma or the eternal teaching. They represent the manifestation of Lord Vishnu, the Divine power that preserves and protects the universe. In this regard there are usually ten avatars of Vishnu, but sometimes as many as twenty-six. Such great avatars of Vishnu were Rama and Krishna and, by some accounts, the Buddha.

The lives of avatars, which often contain various miraculous and legendary elements, are grand symbols of the spiritual search and go far beyond anything merely human. Their lives and characters become models for others to study and emulate. The worship of avatars is an important part of Hindu devotional practices and the subject of many teachings, but has deeper yogic implications as well.

Are Christ and Mohammed Avatars?

Some Hindu groups have used the term avatar in a broad sense for anyone who has founded a major world religion, in which case Christ and Mohammed could be called avatars. However, this is not the original meaning of the term, which has nothing to do with organised religion but is part of a yogic and cosmic symbolism.

Christ and Mohammed are not part of the traditional Hindu scheme of the ten avatars of Vishnu nor, we might add, are all the great sages of Hinduism. The avatar order reflects a certain teaching, which is one line of approach and is not meant to be inclusive of all the great teachers of humanity. These ten are Matsya (Fish), Kurma (Tortoise), Varaha (Boar), Vamana (Dwarf), Narasimha (Man-lion), Rama, Krishna, Buddha and Kalki.

According to orthodox Islam, Mohammed is not an avatar but a prophet of God, a messenger, not a Divine incarnation. According to orthodox Christianity, Christ was not another avatar or incarnation of God but the only Son of God. While Hindus can redefine these teachers in light of their own views, they should recognise that the great majority of the members and teachers of these religions would find that to be a misrepresentation their faith as they practice it to call their founders avatars or include them among a Hindu list of avatar figures.

Some Muslim groups like to identify Mohammed with Kalki as the last avatar as an aid to converting Hindus to Islam. However, they are unwilling to accept the teachings of karma and rebirth, or the practices of Yoga and meditation, and the idea of Self-realization, the Sanatana Dharma that all avatars take birth to uphold in the Hindu tradition.

Was Jesus Christ a Yogi?

Some gurus from India have taught that Christ was a yogi, connected to the teachings of Sri Krishna and died in India. They point out Yoga based teachings in the sayings attributed to Jesus, as well as the non-violent approach followed by him. They claim that Church later obscured and then eradicated the yogic roots of original Christianity.

Other writers have pointed out that Yoga and Vedanta influences in the Greco-Roman world existed from the time of Alexander, if not before, to the fall of the Roman Empire many centuries after Christ. They note an extensive trade and communication network between India and the Near East going back to the time of the Egyptian pharaohs. They suggest a yogic influence not simply on early Christianity but upon older Essene Judaism, Gnosticism, Greek philosophy and other pagan movements, including teachers like Plotinus and Apollonius of Tyana.

Other Hindu thinkers consider that yogic and mystical elements combined with early Christianity from the surrounding Greco-Roman culture but were not original to it. Yet other Hindu thinkers find that the New Testament contains the seeds of intolerance and exclusivism not appropriate to the Yoga tradition.

Overall, there is no single Hindu view on Jesus, with aspects of both honouring him and criticising the dogmas of Christianity. However, no great gurus from India accept the idea of Jesus as the only Son of God or heaven and hell as the ultimate goal of life. In short, Hindu gurus may accept a yogic influence on Jesus, or a mystical basis to his teaching, but they do not accept the predominant theologies or beliefs of mainstream Christianity.

Unfortunately, the image of Jesus as a Yogi is used by Christian missionaries in India today to soften Hindus up for conversion, and even though these missionaries do not practice Yoga, encourage their members to do so, or honour the great gurus of Hindu Yoga traditions, ancient and modern. Their Jesus as a Yogi propaganda is just a conversion ploy.

What is the Relationship Between Sufism and Yoga?

Sufi is a term for Islamic mystics and thinkers, orthodox and unorthodox, peaceful and militant. There are many groups of Sufis with different views from respecting all religions to exclusively promoting Islam. Many Islamic empires from the Caliphate of Turkey to the Mughal Empire had prominent Sufi influences. Some Islamic armies had Sufis marching along with them. Some Indian Sufis have adopted Yoga practices like pranayama, mantra and meditation, but these do not represent all or even perhaps the majority of Sufis through history.

There are many possible correlations between Sufi and Vedantic philosophies that are worthy of examination, but significant points of divergence as well. While Yoga and Sufism both speak of spiritual realization and unity consciousness, Sufis do not accept karma and rebirth, and as practicing Muslims do not use images in their forms of worship. Hindus should examine what Sufis actually teach and find out what their real factors in common are, noting their differences as well. Sufis cannot be looked upon as one type only. Yet great individual Sufis like Rumi should certainly be honoured.

Why Does Hinduism Portray Subtle Beings beyond the Human?

There are many different worlds, levels and layers of the universe beyond the physical, each with its corresponding types of creatures or entities. Many of these beings are more advanced than humans. Hindus call them Gods or Devas, though there are different levels of such entities, with the highest Gods being powers of spiritual knowledge. There are also various classes of sages and seers who exist at different levels of consciousness and their particular worlds and possess various cosmic powers.

Devas serve to guide or help human beings and aid in their evolution. Yet these beings may not always be enlightened, though their intelligence may be far beyond what is ordinarily human. They may have powers of creativity or perception like the ability to see the future or know the past, which they can relay to human beings to various degrees. However, contact with them is no substitute for our own Yoga practices and the guidance of great gurus.

Divine forces assume various appearances relative to the condition of the human mind. Coming into contact with an influx of spiritual energy, the human mind may imagine that it is contacting an angel or some higher entity. All such Gods, angels and devils dwell within us as various formations of the power of consciousness. We should understand the nature of consciousness, which is the supreme reality, beyond all external appearances.

Do Hindus Believe in Revelation?

Hinduism is a timeless religion, a formulation of Sanatana Dharma, the eternal tradition, is not based upon any particular historical revelation—the message given to a particular person at a particular time and place, nor is it looking toward some end of the world. It recognises the eternity of creation and the immortality of the soul. Its revelation is that of the eternal in the here and now, in each individual, which is a matter of direct perception, a message received from another.

According to Sanatana Dharma the revelation that we all need is Self-revelation, not that of an external deity. Self-revelation is enlightenment or Self-illumination that arises when the mind is silent. This revelation transcends all words and all religious authorities and takes us beyond time. Great sages may bring important messages to humanity at different times or places but these are not the ultimate revelation that only comes through our own inner practices. Though we should honour the messages of all the great sages, we should use these to understand the eternal, not to trap ourselves in any temporal event, which must be limiting and eventually come to an end.

What is the Hindu View of Scriptures?

Scripture in the Western religious sense means the Word of God as revealed in a particular book like the Bible or Koran. Scripture can also stand for an inspired book or source teaching that a particular religion honours as important. The primary books of various religions, like the Bhagavad Gita of Hinduism or the Tao Teh Ching of Taoism, may be called scriptures even though their followers may not call them the Word of God. In this vast universe, any number of scriptures or inspired spiritual books are possible. Hindus have many sacred texts like the Vedas, Upanishads, Agamas and Puranas.

However, the true Divine Word is a cosmic sound vibration that can never be put in human language, which is inherently limited by time, place and culture. The Divine Word is a state of consciousness, best revealed in silence of mind in which no concept prevails. It is not a mere book that can be pulled off a shelf and quoted. It is formed not in any ordinary language but in the language of mantra, particularly the mantra OM, which is the essence of the Vedas.

Different spiritual and religious teachings develop relative to the level and temperaments of people according to time, place, and culture. This is the same as differences in food and clothing, which reflect universal human needs for food and shelter. Some so-called scriptures have much higher truths in them, others may have very little. We cannot simply equate all books called scriptures and make them true, though each may have some value. The idea that only one scripture is true is like saying that only one type of food is good. The idea that all scriptures are true is like saying that all food is equally good. The highest truth is to contact the Divine Word and presence within our own hearts. This takes us beyond the need for external scriptures, and reveals to us the Divine essence that all higher teachings are pointing to.

What is the Hindu View of Sin?

Hinduism does not believe that human beings suffer from any original sin or inherent fault in their nature that must be corrected by an external influence or special grace. On the contrary, Sanatana

Dharma teaches that our original nature is pure goodness, Being-Consciousness-Bliss, and that we are all inherently one with the Divine.

The Hindu concept of sin or papa is one of uncleanliness, the accumulation of something extraneous that must be removed for us to return to our inherent purity. For example, the body naturally gets dirty and one has to clean it. Such dirt is not a sin, though it is unhealthy not to keep oneself clean. There are similar emotional and mental impurities. In our natural activity we may pick up wrong impressions, attitudes, and experiences. We should cleanse our minds regularly of these through ritual, mantra and meditation. Such mental impurities, if allowed to accumulate, can cause emotional imbalances and lead to wrong actions that may result in harm.

The Hindu view of sin is free of the ideas of guilt, fear and punishment. From its point of view, the greatest sin is to call a person a sinner. There is not and never will be such an entity as a sinner. The same Divine Self exists in all beings that through ignorance alone commit wrong actions. To call a person a sinner is to deny their Divine essence and make them identify with the sin, which reinforces its hold on them.

Whatever we think, that we become. If we think that we are fallen, wretched and mere sinners, that we become. If we think that we are God, we become God. We should not debase ourselves with thoughts that are not great. There are no sinners, though there are wrong actions. We should not condemn a person as a sinner but should try to understand to awaken their inner being. Right action is acting with respect for the sacred nature of all beings.

What is the Hindu View of Salvation?
Hinduism does not teach that we are sinners in need of salvation but that we are the Divine itself, needing to awaken to our true nature. We are suffering from ignorance and the cure for this is knowledge. We have forgotten our true Self, which is eternal,

and are caught in the outer world, which is transient. The Hindu concept is one of liberation or Moksha, which is very different than the idea of salvation and should not be equated with it. Liberation is not from sin but from ignorance, which is the misconception that we are other than the Divine. Even those who perform good deeds according to the prescriptions of a particular religion remain bound by ignorance and not liberated if they do not know their true Self.

Hinduism does not look to salvation or to a saviour on the outside but asks us to look within. It aims at mergence in the Divine, who is the true being of all. The only way to reach this is through right meditation that clears the mind of the impressions (samskaras) that bind it to the external world. Liberation takes us beyond the cycle of rebirth, while salvation is just an emotional or mental state, which may bring some temporary peace or happiness, but no final release. Even those who think that they are saved must be born again until they have worked out their karmas and come to understand their true nature.

Is There any Day of the Final Judgement in Hinduism?

Hinduism is not a religion of judgement but of acceptance. It is not based upon the condemnation of anyone but upon the recognition of the sole reality of the Divine. There is no final, absolute or irrevocable judgement about anything in life. As all actions are limited and relative, bound to the realm of time and space, their results must have an end. Can there be a final judgement about the sun, the wind or the rain? So too, human beings, who are replicas of the entire universe, can never be judged in any conclusive manner. In essence we are consciousness, which is one with God as our true Self. We can never be removed from it. However long we may appear to stay away from it, we must eventually return to it as our real home.

Actions have specific results that we must experience as long as we are bound to the realm of desire. However, action itself does not bind the soul but only the concept 'I-am-the-doer'. The ego or doer-sense causes us to identify personally with what we do, to seek gain externally and leads us to do wrong, Self-aggrandizing actions.

In reality there is no doer because consciousness transcends all material forms. If there is no doer, who is there to be judged? The soul is inherently free of action and its results, just as it transcends body and mind that are its instruments. Once we realise this truth we go beyond cause and effect. But as long as we are attached to action, we cannot experience inner freedom and must be karmically accountable for what we have done.

God does not judge anyone, nor does a wise person judge others. The other person is God, who are we to judge God? Our actions speak for themselves and bring about their specific results. God does not punish a person for harming another. The very action of harm has its effect on the person who projects it. The only final judgement for all creatures is: 'You are the Self of all. Live according to your nature and be happy'.

Is There Hindu Fundamentalism?

Fundamentalism in religion generally consists of literally believing in a single religion, prophet or saviour, a particular scripture as literally the word of God and the insistence that all human beings accept it. Fundamentalism does not exist in Hinduism as it does in belief-oriented religions because Hinduism does not insist upon such singularist formulations, nor does it claim that it alone has the truth. There is no exclusivism in Hinduism that can sustain such religious fundamentalism. No true Hindu would say that only the Hindu teachings are true and all others are false. No true Hindu would say that only Hindus can find God or the Divine and non-Hindus must go to hell.

There are traditional Hindus who wish to preserve Hindu values and a Hindu way of life, which is a culture of devotion and meditation. There are also socially backward Hindus who may be trying to preserve regressive Hindu social customs. This is the closest thing to any rigid Hindu fundamentalism but however wrong it may be, to associate it with a monolithic religious fundamentalism seeking to convert the world is misleading. Such socially regressive forms of Hinduism are best countered by teaching real Sanatana Dharma, which honours the unique contribution of each person to the cosmic order and ask us to see the same Self in all beings.

Is There Militancy in Hinduism?

Militancy has not existed in Hinduism to the extent that it has in belief-oriented religions. This is owing to the tolerant spirit of Hindu Dharma and its emphasis on non-violence. Hindus have never invaded any country and tried to convert its people through force, propaganda, or economic pressure, the way Christian and Islamic countries have done through history. There is no Hindu history of holy wars, crusades, or foreign conquests, and no Hindu church militant or Hindu global Jihad.

According to the Hindu view, it is against Dharma or true religion to invade another country and try to convert it, to impose religious taxes on those of other beliefs, to promote missions that aim at conversion by misrepresenting other religions, or to denigrate the cultures of other people.

Most of what has been called Hindu militancy is a reaction against Islamic or Christian fundamentalism and militancy that has long made India its target. Hindus have been under siege by missionary groups for centuries, with the usage of money, deception and violence to convert them. That Hindus might overreact to such aggression at times may be regrettable but should be put in the proper context. Probably none of the other major religions of the world has responded with such lack of violence to the conversion efforts directed against them.

Yet Hindus do have a warrior tradition or Kshatriya Dharma whose purpose and place in society is to protect the dharmic teachings and traditions. That kind of Hindu militancy is important, though today more a struggle in the media realm than simply on the battlefield.

What is the Hindu View of Conversion?

There is only one true religion, the universal tradition of truth. The different religions of the world are different formulations or perhaps distortions of that One Truth. Recognizing this, Hindus do not see the need to convert people to a particular belief. They recognise the Divine presence that exists already in everyone. If the other is God or the same Self, what are we going to convert people to and why? What is important is to recognise the internal Divinity in all, not to make other people copy our idea of religion.

Different spiritual approaches may be better for different people but this is to choose an angle of approach to the One Truth. Such different teachings are not distinct religions but complementary formulations of the one religion of truth. Sanatana Dharma recognises that many such approaches are possible and a diversity of them should be encouraged, but the underlying universality of truth should never be forgotten.

To get people to think that they have a particular religious identity and it should be replaced with another, is to confuse the Self with the body and is a sign of ignorance. The Divine is our essential nature, our inner being. Actually, we don't have any religious identity at all. Our true religious identity or sacred nature is of the Self of all. Hindu Dharma honours this natural, eternal and universal religion of life.

Can One Be Converted to Hinduism?

Hinduism holds that we are all born in universal truth. As immortal souls we can never be apart from it. We are inherently part of Sanatana Dharma. Even if we assume a contrary religious identity, we can never really leave Hinduism. Can one ever be apart from the Divine, whatever one's religious affiliation may be? Whatever our religious affiliation may be, the laws of the universe do not change for us, nor does our responsibility for our actions.

However, Hindus do share their teachings and welcome others to study these, not because they are seeking converts in order to dominate the world, but because they recognise that all human beings are of one family. Such sharing is not trying to save others but trying to connect all human beings to the cosmic being.

One can formally become a Hindu by undergoing a ceremony called Shuddhi (purification), a short ritual lasting about two hours. Various Hindu groups provide this service, which may also connect people to a specific Hindu sect or sampradaya or the teaching of a specific guru.

Yet becoming a Hindu does not mean converting to a belief that limits our freedom of inquiry. It does not require accepting a specific prophet, Son of God, scripture or church. It gives full freedom to follow whatever leads to the highest reality. One can be a Hindu and still follow truth wherever one finds it. Joining Hindu Dharma in the true sense is an inclusive, not exclusive process that eventually allows us to embrace the entire universe. It is a recognition of Sanatana Dharma, which requires us to respect all dharmic traditions and principles, whatever their source. It is not a mere change of label that is required to become a true Hindu but that we begin a life of spiritual practice or sadhana.

Should Members of Other Religions Become Hindus?
The true purpose of religion is to know the Divine, which is to know one's Self. The Hindu tradition contains the full range of meditation practices leading to Self-realization, which are not clearly understood or available in all religious traditions and are entirely absent in a number of them. If one is serious about the real purpose of life, which is the inner quest, Hindu teachings can be of great importance.

Hinduism, directing us to Self-realization, can be of immense benefit to those of any religious or non-religious background. It offers to us an intricate system of higher knowledge that integrates religion into an inner spiritual view and higher consciousness. Hindu Dharma teaches cosmic laws like karma and rebirth that everyone should know. It emphasises universal ethical practices like non-violence and principles of dharmic living like honouring the sacred nature of all life, which are essential to world peace. It contains a complete science of Yoga and meditation, which all people can practice to experience their true nature and highest potentials.

Many mystics subscribe to views and practices similar to Hinduism, including karma, rebirth, mantra, and meditation, even though the more orthodox religions around them may not accept these. The advantage of Hindu Dharma is that it is a tradition, which does not have a gulf between the mystics and the orthodox and provides spiritual practices for individuals of all levels of development. In this regard, if one wants to follow a yogic spiritual tradition, Hinduism has a great deal to offer, in fact, an immeasurable value.

Can It Benefit a Hindu to Join Other Religions?
A true Hindu recognises the portion of universal truth that is manifest everywhere. Great teachings and good values can be found among individuals of various backgrounds that should be honoured. However, this does not require that Hindus formally join a particular church, particularly those that promote exclusive beliefs and divide humanity into hostile camps.

A true Hindu can never take upon one exclusive religious identity as opposed to another, which is a denial of the Divine Self within. Hindu Dharma recognises the truth of unity consciousness, and attempts to maintain that in an open tradition. It says that we should recognise all true spiritual teachings as different approaches to the universal Dharma, which honours the sacred nature and immortality of all beings. Usually it is a spiritual loss if a Hindu joins another religion because they are leaving a tradition that emphasises spiritual practices leading to Self-realization for one that considers mere faith or belief to be sufficient.

Must One Be Born a Hindu?

Some say that a person must be born a Hindu in order to be a Hindu, implying that there is no way for Westerners or other non-Hindus to actually become Hindus. A clear examination of how Hinduism has spread historically shows this not to be true.

Hindus today include all the peoples of the subcontinent of India, including the Nepalese and Assamese, who are of the Tibeto-Burman group of peoples. Hinduism was long dominant in Indonesia and Indochina among the various groups living there, going back perhaps two thousand years. The island of Bali is still Hindu. Clearly Hinduism could not have spread so far if it was restricted to those born as Hindus. We read of ancient Greeks in India becoming Hindus, and also Hindu teachings spreading into Central Asia. Yet after centuries of foreign attacks Hindus have been suspicious of non-Hindus and become hesitant to accept them into their tradition.

The vast spread of Hinduism from Central Asia to as far as the Philippines, with Hindu kingdoms like the Vietnamese Champak Shaivites shows that Hinduism has had no boundaries by land or sea. It is time for Hindus to embrace this expansive nature of their inherent culture, which the gurus of India are already following by taking Yoga, Vedanta and Ayurveda to the entire world.

Should One Follow One's Religion of Birth?

We are born into many things, some which are beneficial, others that may form obstacles or limitations. The religion of our family of birth may be a help or a hindrance to our inner being, depending both upon what it is and how we apply it. The individual is not born with a religious identity stamped on their body or mind.

Religion, properly understood, should be an aid to Self-realization and not an end-in-itself. One should follow whatever religious teachings most aid in this realization, regardless of their origin. If the religion one is born into has a living Self-realization tradition that one can follow, one should certainly adapt it. If the religion of one's birth does not have such a tradition, then one should look to teachings that do. We must learn to use religion to further our inner understanding and cease letting religion use us to further the vested interests, usually of a worldly nature, that sustain it. We do not belong to any particular religion; rather all religions belong to us.

In the global age that is dawning, we no longer are restricted to the culture of our area of birth but have access to that of all humanity. We should strive to benefit from the spiritual legacy of the human race, just as we are learning to benefit from the scientific knowledge of all areas of the world.

Is Hinduism a Cult?

Cults are temporary religious movements in which some charismatic leader uses for mere personal benefit. Cults are usually centred on one person and isolate people from ordinary functioning in society.

A religion like Hinduism that has existed for thousands of years is not centred on any particular personality, and has produced many great people in all walks of life, is not a cult. There are Hindus who are successful in all fields both in the East and the West as scientists, doctors, lawyers, artists and so on. In fact, Hindus in America have a much higher standard of education and income than the average American.

Unfortunately, some people, including some countries in the world, do not accept Hinduism as a valid religion and portray it as cult or superstition only. Sometimes they call Yoga a cult as well. Such people are caught in religious prejudices.

From the Vedantic view, any teaching which states that God is outside of ourselves is a cult because it confuses our internal reality, which is pure consciousness, with something external.

Actually, whatever separate identity we assert apart from universal truth becomes a cult. Whatever limits truth, which is infinite and eternal, to a particular manifestation is a cult or false presentation of reality.

Why Do Christians and Muslims Seek to Convert Hindus?

Over the centuries, Christians and Muslims have sent out not only missionaries but also armies to convert Hindus. Today they are probably spending more money than at any point in history to achieve this aim, with multinational businesses and petrodollars. Obviously one does not seek to convert someone whose views one truly respects. Clearly such groups do not appreciate Hinduism, its many rishis, sages, yoga practices or philosophies of consciousness. If they appreciated this higher knowledge, they would be come to Hindu gurus to learn or to share, as many people have, not to preach or condemn.

This conversion-promoting mentality reflects an outward view of life, in which religion becomes a social and political institution whose main goal is to increase in numbers. It inhibits the internal dimension of religion or the spiritual quest, which it is often opposed to, and which the very groups that it seeks to convert usually know more about than the missionaries themselves.

Such missionaries are to be pitied. Though they may have idealism and passion, much like politicians, they have not understood the real purpose of spirituality, which is not to convince other people to follow your belief but to awaken the Divine Self in all. They need to be taught that the true sharing spirit in religion is not the missionary spirit of conversion but the yogic spirit of perceiving the same Self in all beings.

What is the Hindu Model of Religious Coexistence?

Hindus have throughout the centuries both coexisted and provided a refuge for many other religious groups including Jews, Christians, Zoroastrians, certain Muslim sects and Bahais. There is a greater religious diversity in India today than perhaps any other country in Asia or even the entire world and there has been for many centuries.

Yet in spite of this Hindu tolerance of other religions, Hindus still endure massive efforts to convert them, combined with deliberate media and academic distortions. While Hindus have respected other religions, other religions have seldom respected Hindu Dharma in return—and has rarely taken any action to counter wrong ideas about what Hinduism truly teaches. This is particularly sad because Hinduism contains the deeper spiritual and yogic teachings that the world desperately needs.

Religion should first teach us coexistence, live and let live, honouring a diversity of spiritual and cultural paths, even if we do not agree with them. To accomplish this each religion must recognise that truth is a universal principle and cannot be owned by any faith or belief. Otherwise, religion is not fulfilling its purpose of connecting us to the universal truth but consigning us to narrow human prejudices, which has unfortunately been the main historical record to present times.

Questions on Hinduism 4:
Towards an Awakened Hinduism
and Resurgent Sanatana Dharma

There are many groups who do not want Hindus to maintain their traditions or expand their influence in the world. Hindu is still under attack in the postcolonial era by the same materialistic and sectarian forces. This section addresses the issues of resurgent Hinduism and how to make Sanatana Dharma both an outer and an inner inspiration for all people.

Can One Be a Hindu in the Modern World?

Sanatana Dharma, not being limited to a point in time or space, can be adapted to any time, place or person. As a perpetual or perennial tradition, it demands names and forms appropriate to changing circumstances. Yet to follow such an eternal tradition is not to be superficially modern—a creature of the moment, pursuing the latest social trends—but to live at the heart of creation.

To be modern and progressive today, one is inclined to abandon tradition and embrace the current popular culture of entertainment and sensation, or to take up modern intellectual culture and politics which shuns spirituality. Our contemporary global culture fails to answer the deeper purpose of life. The ultimate issue is not to be in harmony with the transient times in which we live but to discover what transcends time. Then we can become citizens of the universe and of all time, not just creatures of one historical age or another.

Hindu Dharma teaches us to both understand the current period we live in and aspire to the eternal. As such, it is always relevant to everyone and to every generation. This requires that we adapt its teachings to our own lives and aspiration.

Should Hindus Be Proud of Their Tradition?

Hindus should be proud of their spiritual tradition, which remains the oldest and most comprehensive in the world. They should be proud of the many great rishis, sages and yogis it has consistently produced over the centuries, in both periods of material abundance and those of poverty and foreign domination.

Hindus should be proud of their great modern gurus who show that the experience of God is not the birth right of every human being. What other religion of recent times has produced such figures as Ramana Maharshi, Sri Aurobindo, Paramahansa Ramakrishna, Anandamayi Ma, Mata Amritanandamayi, and Paramahansa Yogananda, to name but a very few?

Above all, Hindus should be proud of Hinduism's basis in Sanatana Dharma as a universal tradition and its refusal to cast itself into the mould of exclusive, particularised, and divisive religious identities. But to do this Hindus must also manifest the universality of their tradition by how they live and by sharing it with the world at large, including at education and media levels.

The pride of the ego, which is separative, is always divisive, as it insists that only its point of view is correct. Yet the soul or our inner being has another pride, which is recognition of the value of the inner Self over material appearances. One should be proud in a spiritual sense about the universal element in oneself and in one's Dharma. We are the Divine itself in manifestation. We are not mere creatures but the universal Self in its own manifestation. All time and space is but our shadows. The mentality of a slave or a sinner does not suit our infinite Being. The individual soul should be proud of the eternal truth of its nature, which states that 'I am the entire universe'.

We need not bow down to any external religious authority. We need only recognise the Divine presence within ourselves. This is Sanatana Dharma, the enduring truth of all that is. Such dignity of our true nature can take us beyond all division and sorrow.

Why Are Hindus Apologetic About Being Hindus?

Hinduism is not an aggressive system and encourages humility and respect for all. It promotes itself through teaching and sharing, not through preaching and condemnation. In the current commercial world, which has little of deeper spirituality, many Hindus find that their ancient tradition appears out of place. This has caused them to feel apologetic about their practices as part of attempts to accommodate or please others. Yet most importantly, Hindus have to deal with missionary and Marxist propaganda against their religion and so may feel defensive, not knowing how to communicate what Hinduism really is.

To counter this apologetic presentation, Hindus need to learn the essence of Sanatana Dharma and share it with others. This can begin with learning the Bhagavad Gita and the basics of Vedanta. Only Hindus who don't understand the real meaning of their tradition and the centrality of its yogic approaches to world spirituality can be dominated by negative views of who they are. In fact, Hinduism, through Vedanta or the science of Self-realization, is the teaching of lion-hearted souls. It is for the fearless and independent, for those willing to transcend the external view of reality.

Yet not all Hindus are apologetic about being Hindus. The apologetic Hindu may soon be a thing of the past, as the great value of Yoga, Vedanta, Ayurveda, Vedic knowledge and Sanatana Dharma spreads throughout the world. The main thing is for Hindus to share their teachings with others so that all can benefit from its deep wisdom and profound practices.

Should Hindus Be More Aggressive?

Hindus suffer from passivity and disunity, as many have said. These are probably their main enemies, not just external opposition. Hindus are generally hesitant, if they assert themselves at all. A more positive, expansive Self-confident spirit in their tradition is essential, both for their own personal practice and the collective well-being.

This does not require that Hindus become violent, but it does require that they wake up and become proactive in their policies. Perhaps in this process some Hindus may become temporarily over assertive but even this may be better than remaining overly passive. The present crisis in the world today, and in India, demands action both inwardly and outwardly. Let all aware individuals rise to the occasion and bring the light of truth and Self-realization into the world from whatever angle they can. We must promote Dharma in both our outer and inner lives. Without bringing Sanatana Dharma back into the world, our society will continue to drift in confusion.

What is Hindu Activism?

Hindu activism is the work of Hindu groups and individuals to remove distortions and denigrations about Hindus that remain common in the world today. Given all the other forms of activism going on in the world today, it is important that Hindus also develop a social presence to preserve their culture, values, traditions and deep spiritual knowledge relative to trends of a contrary nature. If a culture cannot stand up for itself in the global arena, it is likely to be misrepresented or become the target of disinformation by other groups seeking power and control.

In addition, Hindu activism should stand up for all of humanity's experiential spiritual traditions, especially native traditions that lack the resources to defend themselves. It should stand up for the Earth, the plants and animals, and the sacred value of all nature. Hindu Dharma promotes a way of life based upon higher consciousness, not simply human beliefs and ideologies. It is not against material or scientific progress but holds that these should not occur at the expense of other creatures, our environment or our inner development.

Such Hindu activism is of great importance to bring a dharmic energy into the world. Unfortunately, much of what is called social activism today is a mask to promote the same old missionary, colonial, Marxist, commercial and materialistic agendas that have been trying to destroy traditional cultures for centuries. An alternative to this is crucial.

What is Hindu Nationalism?

Hindu nationalism is a derogatory term that we find in the Western media and among certain leftist political groups in India, including the Congress Party that are usually against any Hindu political voice.

Hindus are asking that discrimination against Hindus, which is common even in Hindu majority India, is removed. This is not any oppressive Hindu nationalism. It includes removing government control of Hindu temples and confiscation of their income, which is still happening on a vast scale, stopping court interference in Hindu religious practices, institutions and festivals, which is also common, and the restoration of Hindu sacred sites, which are neglected. In this regard, Hindus are only asking for the same rights that all other groups have. For example, state governments in India do not take over mosques or churches and seize their incomes for their own usage; similarly, courts do not interfere in Christian and Islamic practices.

In addition, Hindus are asking that the Hindu heritage of India be respected, as it is the dominant historical culture of the country to the present day and has a great history to be honoured. They are asking that anti-Hindu history books, products mainly of Congress Party endorsed by Marxist and Communist thinkers, designed to attack Hindu Dharma, are changed in light of new archaeological and geological evidence like that of the Sarasvati River.

The Hindu concept of state is not of a religious state enforcing a single church or belief on all, but of a country that honours the principles of dharma, which are universal ethical principles like non-violence and truthfulness. The Hindu view is to honour the Earth as our Mother and all life as sacred. This is not politics, but spirituality in action.

Has Hinduism Helped or Harmed India Economically?

India has largely been Hindu throughout its history and its economic problems are only of the last few centuries. These have largely been the product of foreign rule up to the independence of the country and then by the Socialist economic policies that modern India followed up to recent times. India's economic problems have not occurred because of the Hindu Dharma. India is now developing economically, not by giving up Hinduism, but by adopting sound economic policies.

Note that people are not asking poor Christian countries, of which there are still many in South America and Africa, to give up Christianity in order to get rid of their poverty. Nor did Japan become an economic superpower by giving up Buddhism and Shinto and becoming Christian. For economic development in Europe, people did not advocate a change of religion either but better economic policies. The same is true in regard to social problems. The West did not remove slavery by getting rid of Christianity, though many Christian groups sanctioned it. Inequality between the rich and poor in the world requires economic changes.

India can certainly solve its social and economic problems without a change of religion through Hindu Dharma itself. In fact, Hindu Dharma contains the yogic and meditative insight that can solve all human problems and unite us with our eternal essence in which nothing of enduring value will be lost.

Doesn't Hindu Activism Risk Making Hindus Violent?

There are many forms of activism among religious and political groups in the world, including those who follow views and beliefs historically more aggressive and violent than Hinduism. No one is telling these other religious groups to cease from activism because it might make them more violent. Of course, there is always the danger that activists can get caught in anger and possible violence, but that should not be used to discredit activism as a whole. Hindu activists will face the same challenges.

From the perspective of Sanatana Dharma, any true social activism should be rooted in dharma, which means promoting dharmic values and a way of life that honours the sacred nature of all existence. Outer activism should not be exclusive of inner spiritual practices or 'inner activism', but an expression of it. Even those working for the upliftment of society should take time for worship, mantra, and meditation.

A real Hindu activism will help reduce the amount of violence going on in the world. It will address the root causes of violence in religious exclusivism, in the exploitation of nature, and the blind promotion of material and commercial values as the most important goals of life. Hindu activism will encourage us to reconnect with the greater conscious universe and make our lives into a development of higher awareness. Hindu activism is necessary for India to reclaim its dharmic roots and share its broader yogic teachings.

Should Hindus Create Missionary Movements?
This would probably be better than for Hindus to idly sit by while less spiritual ideologies spread, with little scrutiny, all over the world and in India itself. Yet Hindus need not try to remake Hinduism according to the exclusivism and intolerance of missionary aggression. These groups may have better succeeded socially for a time but they have failed in the true spiritual quest for Self-realization, which is what is of ultimate importance.

Hindus should create educational movements promoting Yoga, Vedanta, Ayurveda, Vedic sciences, Sanskrit, Indian music and the greater culture of Sanatana Dharma. They should set up teaching centres, schools and universities, retreat centres and service organizations. While maintaining the diversity of Hinduism, Hindu groups should support each another and work with any group that accepts dharmic principles and is willing to live according to them. It is not just a question of emphasizing one name or label or another but of developing a higher consciousness in the world.

Hindu Dharma needs to enter into a new expansive phase of reaching out to the whole world and entire humanity to make the knowledge of the rishis into a shared global heritage. This does require conviction and determination, not apologetics and compromise.

Should Hindus Be More Political?

Hindus have probably been the least politically minded of all religious groups, whether as a majority in India or as minorities in other countries. The fact is that we live in a political world and votes do count and determine government policies. Political passivity does not bring any lasting benefits to a community, but allows it to be taken for granted.

There remains a great deal of prejudice and discrimination against Hindus at political, media and academic levels throughout the world. Many countries of the world do not even recognise Hinduism as a valid or legal religion. Yet Hindus seldom take action at a political level to address the inequities against them. They hope that such negative attitudes will magically disappear by ignoring them, which does not happen.

Hindus are not alone in being the victims of discrimination. Members of many racial and religious groups have suffered the same type of oppression and denigration. But most of these groups have taken action and corrected these problems. Hindus cannot expect the distortions against them to be removed unless they also take action at a political and social level to change these. In this regard, Hindus can follow politically the same type of strategies that other minorities have followed in the West to gain respect.

The situation in India has been such that Hindus rarely vote as a community, though Christian, Muslim and Marxist groups often vote en masse against them, and politicians divide the Hindu vote by caste. Only recently over the past few years has a Hindu vote arisen in India. We now find that political leaders are claiming to be Hindus, something that they did not do so in the past so as not to offend their minority vote banks. This new Hindu vote should be both careful and united and make sure to elect leaders that long term will work to remove the anti-Hindu policies that are common in India's political system.

Hindus should be aware of the political nature of the world in which we live and use the same type of political skills that other groups have mastered. Otherwise Hindus are bound to find themselves at a disadvantage, and much of the blame will rest upon their own shoulders. One must use the tools of the times in order to prosper, and today these involve the media, the internet and global communication.

The stunning new success of the Hindu movement on the social media is a good indication of progress in the Hindu movement. It has often caused anti-Hindu forces to become defensive or to retreat. Let Hindus speak out on all aspects of Dharma, both in society and in the spiritual life.

How Should Hindus Handle Academic Distortions of Hindu Dharma?

Hindus are among the least active groups in monitoring the academic presentations of their tradition and protesting against these when they are wrong, distorted or prejudiced. Several Hindu organizations are making efforts in this direction, so the situation is beginning to change, but much more work needs to be done.

Compare this condition to Islam that has spent many millions of dollars promoting a positive view of Islam in world education. We don't see the kind of negative presentations of Islam in American academia that we find about Hinduism in spite of Islamic terrorist attacks like 9/11 or the atrocities of the Islamic State (ISIS). This is owing to the greater effort that Muslims have made to correct them, even though such negative views of Muslims were common in the media until a few years ago. Much of this is owing to the power petrodollars but Hindus also have resources too than can be put to use to better communicate their profound teachings.

One of the reasons why Hindu study departments in schools and colleges have few Hindus teaching in them is that Hindus rarely choose to go into these fields. Hindu organizations should make sure that some of their members go into academia to correct these distortions wherever these arise. Hindu religious departments and India study classes worldwide are becoming dependent upon funding from the Hindu community. Hindus should not provide funding for academic studies departments that are negative about Hindu Dharma. This will have a great impact over time.

As important, Hindus should fund Hindu institutions, schools and training centres that produce well-trained teachers, priests and acharyas. All the other religions of the world have their own institutions and do not rely upon academia to train people in their religion. New Hindu and dharmic institutions should come up, including Vedic schools that promote all the Vedic arts, sciences and spiritual practices. For this purpose, a new generation of Hindu educators is necessary.

How Should Hindus Respond to the Challenges Posed by Christianity and Islam?

Hindus have long endured on-going Christian and Islamic efforts to convert them by various means, which are still quite extensive and well funded. Christian and Islamic groups have projected much criticism of Hinduism, most of it inaccurate. It is only proper that they hear a Hindu critique of their beliefs in response. This is not a matter of being critical but of maintaining fairness in debate and upholding the cause of truth.

Most Christian and Islamic groups do not recognise Hinduism as a valid religion. While there is some mutual acceptance of Abrahamic religions (Judaism, Christianity and Islam), there is a reluctance to accept religions outside this field. Most Christian and Muslim leaders criticise or reject Hindu-based Yoga and meditation practices. They do not accept God-realization or Self-realization at doctrinal levels and consider it to be arrogance or delusion.

These inimical views are connected to broader missionary agendas to subvert Hindu Dharma altogether. Hindus cannot sit quietly and let these distortions go without countering them. That would be Self-betrayal and cowardice, not real tolerance. As long as Christians and Muslims continue anti-Hindu propaganda, they should expect a critical Hindu response. Would they not do the same? Such a response is not simply to protect Hindu Dharma but to promote freedom of spiritual practices and the paths to Self-realizsation that Hinduism is based upon. Exclusive monotheism also must be reformed as it continues to destroy traditional cultures all over the world. Hindus should boldly speak out in defence of global spirituality over limiting dogmas.

How Can Hindus Better Promote Their Religion in Non-Hindu Countries?

Hindus must make known who they are and what they follow, so negative stereotypes about their tradition—which breed misunderstanding and intolerance—are countered in whatever country they may reside in or visit. They must organise themselves as a community with the common interest to promote a deeper spiritual knowledge in the world and seek allies in both religious and cultural spheres.

Hindus must recognise the value of Hindu Dharma for the entire world and its great treasures of yogic knowledge that are rare, if not unknown in other traditions. They should learn how to teach Hinduism, particularly Yoga and Vedanta, to non-Hindus, whether such people want to become Hindus or not. Like the ancient Vedic sages said, they should strive to make the entire world dharmic. Above all, they must be expansive, open-hearted, fearless, creative and compassionate, not in mere allegiance to a belief but out of contact with the Divine Self which is the basis of the whole of life. The conviction born of realization should be with them, supported by the devotions of the great gurus and yogis that Hindu Dharma has brought to the world in every generation.

How Should Hindu Children Be Raised?

To raise true Hindu children means following Hindu Dharma in the home and in the family. It means living the Dharma and having a culture of Dharma, which includes communities that maintain living traditions of ritual, Yoga and meditation.

Children are extremely impressionable about their environment. They want to be accepted and feel they are a part of the society in which they function. They are most influenced by sensation and their minds can easily be disturbed by wrong impressions. For this reason, children must be provided a field of learning in which they can flower inwardly. This requires the right atmosphere at home and the right relationship between the parents. Hindu parents must have an active interest in their traditions and pass them on to their children as living inspirations. They cannot expect from their children what they themselves do not do.

Along with the proper family life, the right educational system must be created that honours Dharma. Spiritual camps for children should be developed that immerse them in Hindu practices. Children must be brought into contact with real examples of the spiritual life, great gurus and teachers, so that they have a higher role model to follow. They must be brought into the world of nature to learn how to contact the immanent divinity around them. Without creating the proper environment and the right examples, it is not possible to motivate children to become spiritual, just as a plant will not grow without the proper water and light.

Hindu Dharma contains many stories that are helpful for teaching children, especially the Ramayana. Hindu children should be introduced to this wonderful literature, which can be quite entertaining, so that the seeds of spirituality can be planted in them. There are many child forms of the Divine like baby Krishna that they can be taught to emulate. Hindus should honour each child as a living Krishna.

What is the Importance of Hindu Dharma for the Youth?

The young people of the world, particularly in their late teens and twenties, possess an inherent idealism and urge to shape the future in a better way than the present. Hindu Dharma that is rooted in the Cosmic Mind has a futuristic vision connecting us to all time and space and beyond. Young people are not just interested in unquestioningly accepting a religious belief; they are interested in spiritual practices that they themselves can do. These include ritual, prayer, mantra, Yoga and meditation, so that they can experience the truth for themselves. They are looking to develop a higher state of awareness and contact their own true Self, not merely to follow others or believe what others may have said. They are seeking not just for an outer freedom to pursue material goals but an inner freedom to find lasting happiness in all that they do.

Hindu Dharma provides a rich culture for the youth that includes music, dance and art as part of a yogic vision. It shows us how to work with the secret powers of nature and the hidden potentials our own psyche, including an ecological view of life, a planetary vision, and Yoga and meditation paths for all. Hindu Dharma can fill the need for spiritual experience that young people have, which neither belief oriented religions nor scientific thought can provide.

What is the Importance of Hindu Dharma for the Elderly?

We live in a society in which the population is rapidly aging, a trend that is likely to continue for decades to come. Yet our current cultural values and activities are those for the youth, if not adolescents, emphasizing sensory enjoyment and pleasure as our primary pursuit in life. This leaves the elderly with little to do except try to act younger than their age, which only ends up causing depression.

Hindu Dharma teaches us that the spiritual stage of life—the period when our inner quest for Divinity becomes the strongest—does not come forth fully until after the age of fifty years. Of course, younger people should seek to develop a higher awareness. And rare individuals will seek it from birth.

This spiritual value for aging means that aging need not be a matter for worry or concern. Older age is a time for our inner being and eternal essence to come forth, a period of spiritual growth, expression and joy. Hindu Dharma provides a wealth of yogic teachings and practices for this culminating phase of life that allows our full potential to come forth. Its philosophies, mantras and meditations provide a depth of thought and wisdom for us to cultivate every moment. If one wants to age with dignity and grace, and to mature as a spiritual being, developing a consciousness that can transcend death, then one should take refuge in the teachings of Sanatana Dharma, the eternal tradition that carries us through and beyond all time.

Is Yours Not an Unrealistic View of Hinduism?

Very well, one could say, your view of Hinduism is universal, futuristic and beneficial for all to consider, but does the actual Hindu really think this way? Is not the average Hindu trapped in superstition and social backwardness? Are you not covering over this fact with a fantasy view of Hinduism?

The average Hindu may not be aware of the vastness of his or her own tradition. The person may not see beyond the particular sect he or she may belong to. But this is not to deny the underlying teaching. How many Westerners are aware of the beauty and profundity of European intellectual culture? Does this make Mozart or Shakespeare less important? How many of us today understand the formulas of modern physics? Does this mean that computers don't work for us?

There is always a gap between a spiritual teaching and its social application because our planet is not very spiritually evolved. We must raise people up to higher teachings, not reject higher teachings for ordinary pursuits that are easier to do. This is not just a question of Hinduism. We all have tremendous spiritual potential compared to which the other achievements of humanity—whether in art, science, business or religion—are at best adornments.

Let us not demean ourselves. All time and space are but your shadow. If we follow the paths of Yoga and the traditions of meditation, we can arrive at the universal Self. Many Hindus have done this and many other people can also if they follow similar practices and principles.

Do You Think Hinduism is a Superior Religion?

Hindu Dharma recognises the spiritual needs of all types and levels of people. There are no spiritual practices in any religion, whether it is the most simple nature worship or the most exalted meditational approach, without counterparts in Hinduism. Hinduism is probably the most comprehensive religion in the world. This is because it is not trapped in the seeking of superiority but recognises the same Divine Being and human aspiration everywhere.

We should seek out the highest truth, which is to know the Self, and this requires going beyond lesser truths. Recognizing the Self as the real goal of religion, Hinduism teaches us to seek this supreme reality and not rest content with lesser goals. That highest truth exists for all who look deeply into who they really are. No group can claim to own it, though only those who have realised it can guide us to it.

Yet should Hindus regard their tradition as superior, it need not bother anyone. Members of all religions tend to think that. Certainly Hindus have many good reasons to value their vast tradition, with its profound yogic and cultural practices. However, Hinduism teaches us that even if we regard our tradition as the best, we should remain open to the views of others and to discovering the truth through developing the higher states of consciousness within us. Any true spiritual tradition should encourage us to develop our own connection with the Divine, which is what is of ultimate value.

Our true superiority resides in Paramatman, the Supreme Self that is our true nature compared to which even the entire universe is but our shadow!

Can Everyone Benefit from Becoming Hindus?

It would be of tremendous benefit for the world if more people embraced Hindu Dharma, particularly if done with a real understanding of the Hindu tradition. The discovery of Sanatana Dharma, with its universal orientation, is like going home, rediscovering one's true Self. The greater the number of people who discover the meaning of Sanatana Dharma and its universal truths, the less the warring creeds will be able to divide people and the less materialism will be able lead people astray.

Today people even in India are not worried or offended if Hindus become Christians. Why should it bother them if the opposite occurs, particularly if more people embrace the deeper Hindu teachings of Yoga, Vedanta and Vedic knowledge? Yet sadly India's media is more worried about Hindu reconversion efforts in India, than the much larger targeting of Hindus for conversion by the multinational missionary and conversion business.

To become a Hindu in the real sense means recognizing that all the spiritual and religious practices of humanity from the most simple to the most exalted have their place. These should be honoured for the genuineness of aspiration behind them, not superficially judged according to their name and form. Such a synthetic view is what the world requires today.

Why should it bother us if people join a religious tradition as ancient and as spiritually vast as Hinduism, when it doesn't concern us if people join one exclusive belief or another? The main consideration is that we should follow a religious or spiritual teaching as a means of finding the Divine within us, which is our real Self. Otherwise whatever we join is only an illusion and a prejudice. The beauty of becoming a Hindu is that it provides many approaches to Self-knowledge and God-realization, and being better able to connect to the great gurus, rishis and yogis to guide us along the path.

Are You a Hindu?

I have studied the vast and various teachings originating in the Hindu tradition for fifty years including Yoga, Vedanta, Vedas, Ayurveda, and Vedic astrology and found an immense benefit in all of these. I have practiced these teachings and made them the basis of my life and work. Hindu Dharma was something I discovered through the unfoldment of my deeper aspirations and my search into the nature of consciousness. It was never imposed upon me from the outside. I did not become a Hindu so much as I discovered that I already was one, not as a sectarian belief but as an unbroken connection to the Cosmic Being.

I am happy to belong to this ancient and unending tradition of yogic knowledge, whose impressions upon the soul cannot be removed even by death. Hinduism has a boundless field of higher consciousness, like the lap of the Divine Mother, in which the soul can freely unfold its infinite capacities. To enter into this teaching is a great blessing to all.

Becoming a Hindu means learning how to discover the entire universe within us. It does not mean limiting oneself to one church or another but recognizing the universal energy that comes from the Self of all. It allows us to embrace all human aspiration towards the eternal, centred on a path of Self-realization for all.

However, I am sometimes sad that many Hindus still have insufficient appreciation or understanding of their own tradition, and non-Hindus are content to accept distortions about Hinduism without questioning these. It is a sign of ignorance to abandon such a profound spiritual system for modern political ideologies, like socialism and communism, to pursue material affluence, or to spiritually cripple oneself by following regressive religions and traditions devoid of any real practices for developing higher consciousness. Expressing the value of Hinduism as one born outside of India or the Hindu tradition, I hope I can encourage all Hindus to re-examine their roots, and all non-Hindus to examine this extraordinary tradition with a new vision.

Hindu Dharma: The Need of Our Times

What India and the world most needs is a vibrant, Self-confident and bold Hinduism, deeply spiritual, powerfully creative and dynamically working for global peace and understanding, promoting a discernment of higher values, principles and practices. Such a resurgent Hinduism will be at the forefront of a sustainable, scientific and economic development for the entire world but as integrated into a greater cosmic vision of unity with all.

In addition to a resurgent Hinduism, we need a planetary awakening of Sanatana Dharma through all native and dharmic traditions, including those of ancient Europe and the ancient Middle East, as well as through all aware individuals, groups and associations of whatever inclination, orientation or aspiration. Our greater spiritual heritage as a species must be honoured, not just our development in the material world. This is best held by the Vedas and their rishi lines that we can contact within ourselves whenever we are receptive to them.

May that Eternal Dharma arise again and reclaim its role in both the spiritual and social lives of all people!

Glossary

Agnihotra	- Vedic fire offerings
Ahamkara	- ego or Self-image
Ahimsa	- non-violence
Artha	- pursuit of wealth or prosperity
Arya	- noble or spiritual
Asana	- yogic postures
Atman	- the inner Self, pure consciousness
Atmavidya	- Self-knowledge
Atharva Veda	- most recent of four Vedas, also mantric text
Ayurveda	- Vedic natural healing and medical tradition
Bhagavad Gita	- scripture of Sri Krishna
Bhakti	- devotion
Brahma	- the Divine in its creative or teaching function
Brahmacharya	- control of sexual energy
Brahman	- God, the Absolute, the Supreme Being, the Uncreate
Brahmin	- member of the Brahmin class, responsible for religious teaching and the performance of rituals
Buddha	- the enlightened one, ninth avatar of Vishnu
Buddhi	- intelligence, reason
Chitta	- mind in the broadest sense of the term, mindstuff
Deva	- God
Devi	- Goddess

Dharana	- science of concentration
Dharma	- natural law, way of truth
Dhyana	- science of meditation
Guru	- teacher, spiritual guide
Havan or Homa	- Vedic fire offerings
Ishvara	- God as the Creator or cosmic lord
Ishvari	- God in the feminine as the Creator and cosmic ruler
Jainism	- religion based upon the teachings of Mahavira and other Jain Tirthankaras
Jnana	- spiritual or Self-knowledge
Jnani	- person of spiritual knowledge
Jyotish	- Vedic astrology
Kama	- desire or enjoyment as a goal of life
Karma	- the law of cause and effect
Krishna	- eighth avatar of Lord Vishnu
Kshatriya	- member of the noble, warrior or ruling class
Kundalini	- serpent power, energy of the higher mind
Lakshmi	- Goddess of beauty, love and prosperity, consort of Vishnu
Mahabharata	- great epic of the late Vedic age involving the story of Krishna and the Pandavas
Mahesh	- name of Shiva
Manas	- mind, particularly the outer or sense mind
Manava Dharma	- dharma of human beings
Mantra	- repetition of spiritual words or sounds
Moksha	- liberation as the supreme goal of life
Paramatman	- the Supreme or Absolute Self
Parvati	- Goddess of meditation and transformation, consort of Shiva
Patanjali	- sage who compiled the *Yoga Sutras*
Prakriti	- nature, primal matter
Pranayama	- yogic breathing practices

Puja	- Hindu rituals consisting of various offerings like flowers to the Divine in its various forms
Puranas	- Hindu scriptures after the Vedic era
Purusha	- the conscious being, inner Self or Atma
Radha	- consort of Lord Krishna
Rama	- seventh avatar of Lord Vishnu
Ramayana	- story of Rama and his wife Sita
Rigveda	- oldest Veda and repository of mantra
Sacchidananda	- Being-Consciousness-Bliss
Samaveda	- Veda of sound and chanting
Samadhi	- spiritual realization
Sanatana Dharma	- the universal or eternal tradition of truth
Samkhya	- Hindu system of philosophy founded by Kapila
Sarasvati	- Goddess of Wisdom
Satya	- truth or reality
Shaiva	- worshipping of the Divine in the form of Shiva
Shakta	- worshipper of the Divine in the form of the Goddess
Shankaracharya	- great Advaitic philosopher and sage of the early medieval period
Shanti	- peace
Shiva	- the Divine in its destructive or transformative function
Shudra	- member of the labour class
Tantra	- medieval Hindu texts of Goddess worship and yoga practice
Uma	- Divine Mother, form of Parvati
Unaryan	- a person lacking in spiritual and ethical values
Upanishads	- last level of Vedic scriptures relating specifically to Self-realization
Vaishnava	- worshipper of the Divine in the form of Vishnu

Vaishya	- member of the trading or farming classes
Vastu	- Vedic architecture and directional science
Vedas	- the Hindu scriptures or source teachings
Vedanta	- the science and philosophy of Self-realization
Vishnu	- the Divine in its protective and preserving function
Yajurveda	- Veda of ritual
Yoga	- spiritual practices leading to Self-realization
Yoga Sutras	- classical work on yogic spirituality

Index

About the Author

Dr David Frawley D.Litt. (Pandit Vamadeva Shastri), born in 1950, is an American Hindu and a Vedic teacher and Hindu acharya. He is the author of more than fifty books published in over twenty languages worldwide. His fields of expertise include Yoga, Ayurveda, Vedanta, Vedic astrology and ancient Vedic texts. He has also written on historical, social and cultural issues confronting Hinduism and India today.

Honoured with the Padma Bhushan Award, the third highest civilian award of the Government of India, in 2015 Dr Frawley has a D.Litt from S-VYASA (Swami Vivekananda Yoga Anusandhana Samsthana), Bengaluru, and another D.Litt from Dr Ram Manohar Lohia Avadh University, Uttar Pradesh. He is also the recipient of a National Eminence Award from the South Indian Educational Society (SIES), Mumbai.

Vamadeva, as he is popularly known, carries on the teachings of Kavyakantha Ganapati Muni, the chief disciple of Bhagavan Ramana Maharshi. He is a disciple of Sadguru Sivananda Murty of Andhra Pradesh and has been associated with many Hindu organizations including Swaminarayan BAPS, Chinmaya Mission, Arsha Vidya Gurukulam, Sri Ramanashram and the magazine Hinduism Today. He is the director of the American Institute of Vedic Studies (www.vedanet.com).